D1201845

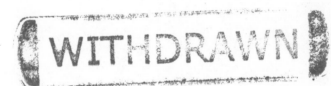

DICTIONARY

PÁPAGO & PIMA to ENGLISH
O'othham–Mil·gahn

ENGLISH to PAPAGO & PIMA
Mil·gahn–O'othham

Compiled by

DEAN and LUCILLE SAXTON

THE UNIVERSITY OF ARIZONA PRESS
TUCSON, ARIZONA

About the authors ...

Dean and Lucille Saxton, since the mid 1950's, have been helping the Papago Indian people of Arizona analyze their language and put it into writing. Together, they have developed this vocabulary over the span of their field work in villages of the Papago Indian Reservation at Sells, Arizona — a full-time assignment that began in 1953 under the direction of the Summer Institute of Linguistics. The project has been the result of the many years of "sensing the need" for a written language. Dean Saxton holds the D.V.M. from Michigan State University and is a member of the Linguistic Society of America. He has contributed scientific articles and papers to the International Journal of Linguistics, the American Anthropological Association, the Arizona Academy of Science, and has taught a special course in Papago linguistics at Sells since 1966. Lucille Saxton holds a degree in Semitics from Shelton College in New York and has taught linguistics for the State Department of Education in Arizona.

Second printing 1977

THE UNIVERSITY OF ARIZONA PRESS

S. B. N. 8165-0250-1
L. C. No. 77-77801

DEDICATED TO
JUAN DOLORES

University of California who began the work
of reducing Papago, his own language, to
writing and produced the basis for a dictionary in his books, Papago Verb Stems and
Papago Nominal Stems.

PROLOGUE

This vocabulary is of great importance for the contribution it makes to the Papago-Pima speaking peoples of the Southwestern United States and northern Sonora and to the many persons -- including teachers, doctors, missionaries, officials -- who have voiced a strong desire for scientifically sound, practical material which can be of use in acquiring an understanding of the Papago-Pima language.

Papago, and its mutually intelligible neighbor to the north, Pima, constitute one of the most important American Indian languages of the Southwest. Yet, by comparison with its importance, published accounts of it are meager indeed. J. Alden Mason's grammar, entitled The Language of the Papago of Arizona (1950), is of high quality, but it is brief. Articles and notes on Papago have been published by Juan Dolores, Albert Alvarez, Madeleine Mathiot, Dean Saxton, and myself. But, so far as I am aware, this is the first modern work which makes available to the public a substantial body of Papago-Pima data. Its scientific validity, accuracy, and practical usefulness make it of extreme value for linguists and laymen alike.

The Piman languages, of which Papago-Pima is the northermost, are of considerable interest for the fact that they constitute a close-knit, well defined subfamily within Uto-Aztecan. As such, they provide an especially good laboratory for the study of linguistic change. Despite the close relationships which the languages show to one another, the linguistic boundaries are surprisingly clear. The recent separate, though similar developments in the phonology and syntax of the Piman languages promise interesting and theoretically significant insights into the ways in which successive generations reinterpret grammatical systems --i.e., insights into the notion 'possible grammatical change.' It is precisely the kind of material contained in this volume that is needed to further this work.

I join the group of linguists and educators who can be truly grateful to Dean and Lucille Saxton for this latest contribution to linguistics and pedagogy.

Kenneth L. Hale
Professor of Linguistics
Massachusetts Institute of Technology

INTRODUCTION

The vocabulary recorded here was compiled during field work in villages of the Papago Indian Reservation under the direction of the Summer Institute of Linguistics from 1953 to the present.

Papago is the language of the Desert People (Tohono O'odham), 14,000 people living in scattered villages of southern Arizona and northern Sonora, Mexico. The majority of Papago speakers now occupy four reservations of Arizona: Sells, San Xavier, Gila Bend, Ak Chin, the latter being under Pima jurisdiction. Pima is the dialect of the River People (Akimel O'odham), mutually intelligible with Papago and consisting of several subdialects. Pima speakers occupy the Gila River and Salt River reservations. Since the dialects of Papago and Pima are mutually intelligible the language is referred to by its speakers as O'odham. Thus the whole complex of Papago and Pima dialects is referred to in this book as O'odham.

An endeavor is made to include the differences in the major Papago dialects: Totoguani, Kokololodi, Gigimai, Huhhu'ula, and Huhuwash. Where known to the authors, the differences peculiar to Pima are also included.

An acquaintance with the parts of this work will make it more useful to the reader. The most complete Papago entries are given in the Papago-English section. To locate a complex entry in this section, the basic form under which it is entered can be found in the English-Papago section. Further help in use of the vocabulary sections is given in the appendices. The alphabet and a guide to pronunciation is given in Appendix I. The format of entries and citations and features of word formation helpful in deducing basic entry forms is given in Appendix II. The basic features of grammatical structure are given in Appendix III. Selected word domains essential to understanding the culture are given in Appendix IV : sociological, medical, temporal, and geographical.

We have attempted to use pedagogically practical terms rather than anthropological and linguistic terminology in order to make this work the most useful tool for speakers of the language and closely associated personnel. However, adequately labeling highly complex grammatical structures exhausts the ingenuity, and we trust that both linguists and laymen will be patient with the results until specifically pedagogical and technical materials can be published. It should be added that a dictionary compiled by a non-native speaker of any language is subject to the possibility of many errors and distortions. The real work of dictionary writing must fall on the shoulders of someone who, like Juan Dolores, is willing to devote himself to an intense and fascinating study of his own language, perhaps in pursuit of a graduate degree in a university.

The work of a number of people has made this book possible. Without involving them in any inaccuracies in recording and compiling the information, we would like to express sincere appreciation to Irene Adams, Albert Alverez, Sam Angelo, Edith Antone, Juan Antone, Sam Cachora, Ramon Chavez, Suzie Enos, Joe Garcia, Lena Garcia, Ramon Garcia, Raymond Johnson, Cipriano Manuel, Lolita Manuel, Cruz Marks, Juan Mattias, Joe Thomas, Juan Thomas, Lupe Thompson, Thomas Segundo, Frank Stein, and others who have contributed information compiled here.

We would like to express sincere appreciation to Dr. Kenneth Hale, Professor in Linguistics at the Massachusetts Institute of Technology, for his help and encouragement in study of the language. Sincere appreciation is also due to the University of Illinois for providing the opportunity to do graduate studies in linguistics, and to the University of Arizona for cooperation in research projects.

Sincere appreciation is also due to The National Park Service, and the University of Arizona for the use of pictures from publications listed in the bibliography.

DEAN AND LUCILLE SAXTON

TABLE OF CONTENTS

Contents (*continued*)

PAPAGO & PIMA
-ENGLISH

O'odham–Mil·gahn

a'ag   horn, horns

a'an   wings, feathers

a'anchud   to feather

A'an Wopnamim   Plains Tribes-men, Oklahoma Indian

a'appem   to test, try

a'atapuD   buttocks

a'aDo   peacocks

abai (ab)   there, at, facing this way

abamk, s-   to cause to be lucky, fortunate

abamdag   luck, fortune

abchud   to accuse of, blame

abchuda   accusation, blame

abchudas   to be in an accused state

abchuddam   accuser

aDaw   buffalo gourd

agshp   downgrade, steep

agshpaDag, s-   to be downgrade

agwua, e-   to take revenge, get back at

ah!/aha!   Oh!

ah'ach   head lice

ah'ad   to send

ah'ada   one sent, messenger

ah'addam   one sending, dispatcher

ahchim (ach, at, t-)   we, us

ahd (ai)   to hang around neck

ahdch   to have hung around the neck

ahg, (a'aga)   to tell, say, sing, to talk about
ho'ok ahg   to tell legends

ahga, a'aga   message, saying, proclamation

ahgachug   to bear a message

ahgahim   to go bearing a message

ahgas   to be told, "it is told"

ahgdam   a story-teller, messenger

ahgeli   acre (Sp. acre)

ahgid   to tell someone, proclaim

ha'icha ahgidaDag   discipline, instruction, legend, maxim, tradition

ahgowi   crucifixion thorn

ahhimeD, ahhiop   to flee to

ahidag, a'ahidag   year

ahli, a'al   child

ahlichud   to act or treat like a child
a'alim, s-   childishly
a'alima, s-   to be childish, cry baby

ahlos   rice (Sp. arroz)

ahmo, a'amo   boss (Sp. amo) employer

ahn   desert willow

1

Ahngam Desert Willow Village and dialect

ahni (ani, ni-) I, me

ahpi (ap, m-) you

ahpim (am, em-) you (plural)

ahshos garlic (Sp. ajos)

aigo, a'ai across, opposite, other side, reverse

aigojeD, a'aijeD from across, other side, reverse

aihim (a'ahe, ah'i) to overtake, reach, cycle
  ahidch to cause to reach, or make up
  aichug to be abreast of, ahead
  ais to be reaching to, up to, sufficient

aj, a'aj narrow

ajij to be narrow

ajijkad (ajijkai) to make narrow, to make slender, reduce

ajijkada something narrowed, thinned, reduced in diameter

ajijkadas to be in a narrowed state

ajijkahim to become narrow

aki, a'aki arroyo

akimel, a'akimel river

Akimel O'odham River People, Pima

al, a'al little

al ba'ag small eagle

Al Chuk Shon Little Tucson Village

alhin; a'alhin threshing floor

Al Jeg Little Opening Village

alidag, a'alidag a man's child

alidt, a'alidt to beget a child

alijeg childhood

Al-mahno German (Sp. alémaŋ)

alshani sorrel (Sp. alazan)

al-whahndi elephant (Sp. elefante)

amai, (am) there, facing away

amjeD from

amjeDkam something from

amichud, s- to understand, know
  chu amichud, s- to be wise intelligent
  chu amichudam, s- wisely
  chu amichuddam, s- wise one

amichudaDag knowledge, understanding, wisdom, mind

amog to proclaim

amogid to proclaim to, address

anai (an) there, at eye level, facing across

a-nihl blueing (Sp. anil)

anilo ring (Sp. anillo)

apapa father term for apapagam sib of the coyote moiety

apapagam members of a sib of the coyote moiety

ap, s- right, well, good, normal

ap'e, a'ap'e to be right, well, good, normal

ap'echud to fix, correct

ap'echuda what is fixed

ap'echudachud to fix for

ap'echudamk, s- to want to fix

ap'echudas to be fixed

ap'echudch to have fixed

ap'edag good

apki   father term for apkigam
sib of the coyote moiety

apkog, s-   to be straight, easy

apkodag, s-   to be straight,
easy

apkojeD, s-   to the right of

apoladag   lining, ceiling

as   even
chum as   even though
ni as   not even

a-saidi   gasoline (Sp. aceite)
chuk a-saidi   oil

ash   to be laughing at
a'aschud   to cause to laugh at

asugal/a-suhga   sugar (Sp.
azucar)

asugalmad   to sugar

at   anus, center of basket

atpo   anal hair

atol   gravy (Sp. atole, Aztec
atulli)

atosha, a'atosha   loin cloth,
diaper

atoshaDad   to diaper

auppa   cottonwood

a'ut   century plant

B

ba'a (bah, bab'e, bah'i)   to
swallow

ba'ag   eagle

ba'amaD, bahbmaD   man's
daughter's child

ba'amaD ohg   man's son-in-law
or father-in-law

babad   frog

babawi o'odham   Papago, bean
people

baga, babga, s-   to be angry

bagachud   to anger

bagam, s-   angrily

bagatahim   to get angry

bagatalig   anger

Bah-   see hebai

bahb   mother's father and his
brothers

bahb oks   mother's father's
sister

bahba/bahbas   potatoes (Sp.
papa(s)

bahi, bahbhai   tail
bahigid   to switch the tail, to
wag

bahmud, i   to plead to

bahnimeD, bahniop   to crawl

bahsho, babsho   chest, in front
of

bahtkhim (bahtkhi)   to wilt

bahwui   wild beans, red, used
to gamble

bahijid   to cause to ripen, cook

bahidag   fruit, to be fruited

bahidaj   fruit of (Saguaro)

baihim (babhe)   to get ripe,
cooked

ba'ich, bab'aich   beyond, past,
ahead

ba'ichkam   a greater one,
further one

ba'ichu   front of neck

ba'ichud   to cause to swallow

ba'i-chuklim   small black bird
species

ba'iham   to put objects in a
container

ba'iham   contents

ba'itk   throat

baiuga   necklace, string of
beads

ba'iwech   to pass, exceed, out-
last

ba'iwechkim   further

balwani, babawani, s-   scarred

3

bamustk, s- to be unflinching, even tempered

ban, bahban coyote
Ban Dak Coyote Village

banmad to cheat

ban wuhiosha mattock

banimeD, baniop to wiggle, squirm against something

bashpo chest hair

bawi tapery bean

bebedk to rumble

bebedki thunder, rumbling

beihim, (bebhe, beh'i, bek) u'u (ui, uh'i, u'uk) to get
ta behima, s- obtainable
behedam, u'udam a picker, harvester
behi, u'i booty, gain, captive
behidka'i, u'idka'i to take and go
behijid, u'ijid to get for
behimk, u'imk, s- to want to get
beichug to bear
beikuD a handle
beka'i, u'uka'i to take and go
bekch, u'ukch to have in the grasp

bi'a (bia, bibia, bia'i) to serve food
biakch to have served
bih a serving, food in a container
bihchug to bear servings
bihdch to have a serving for someone
bi'i (bih, bibid, bihd) to serve someone

bid mud, clay, adobe

bidameD, bidop to go get adobe

bidhun to contaminate, to plaster

bidshp to plaster, fill with syrup, contaminate

bihag to surround, to wrap

bihagch to have wrapped

bihim to get constipated

bihims to be constipated

bihinoD to wrap

bihinoDch to have wrapped

bihsh to wrap, tie

bihshch to have wrapped, enveloped

biht feces

biht (bihb, bihbt) to defecate
bitwua to drop feces

bihtagi, bibtagi, s- to be dirty

bihtagichu, s- dirty one

bihtagim, s- dirtily

bihtameD, bihtop to go to defecate
bihtamk, s- to want to defecate

bihugig famine

bihugimchud to cause to get hungry

bihugimdag hunger

bihugimk, bihugk to get hungry
s-ta bihugimma to be famishing

bijim to go around

bijimhim to go along encircling

bijims to be around

bischk to sneeze

bischkchud to cause to sneeze

bitokoi stink bug

bohl ball (Eng)

C

ch and

chahgih check (Sp. cheque)

chahngo/gogs o'odham monkey (Sp. chango)

chahngo mo'o coconut

chapa-lihya chaps (Sp. chaparajos)

cheawogid to infect with disease

chechemaitakuD   griddle

che'ehid   to cover

che'ehidch   to have covered

che'ew   to pick

che'ewimeD, che'ewiop   to go
to pick small stuff

cheggia   to fight
s-chu cheggiaDkam   warrior

cheggiaDag   war

cheggiahim   to carry on battle

cheggiakuD   place or instru-
ment of battle

chegitog   to think
e chegitog   awake from faint
or death
chegitog, s-   to remember

chegitoi   thoughts

chegitoiDag   mind

chehani   to command

chehanig   law, command

chehchk, hab   to name, call
chehgig, hab   to be named

chehchk   to dream
chehchki   dreams

Chehcho   "The caves" Village

chehdagi, chehedagi   green,
blue, to be

chehdagi mashad   green month
(March)

chehegam   small bird

chehg (chechga, chehgi)   to
find, examine

chehgid (chechgid)   to show,
exhibit

chehgida   exhibit

chehgidaDag   exhibition

chehgidakuD   exhibition place

chehgidas   to be on exhibition

chehgidch   to have on exhibit

chehgim, chehgio   to visit

chehia, chechia   young girl

chehk (chechka, chehki), to'a
(toa, toaw)   to lay, put, store
away

chekch, to'akch   to have something laid, aside, stored

chehkul, chechekul   squirrel

chehm   to gather

chehm, chehchem   heel

chehmi   senita
cactus

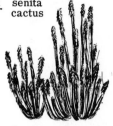

chehmo   to permeate, cover

cheho, chehcho   cave

chehpidakuD   grain mashing
stone

chehpo   natural hole in a rock

chehpsh   fleas

che'i (chei, cheche, cheh'i
che'iok) hab   to say

che'idag   sound, pronunciation

che'is, hab   to be said

che'isid   to mock, mimic,
repeat

cheka, i   reach a point
(usually time)

cheka (chechkaD)   to put on
shoes

chekaidag   sense of hearing

chekaidag, s-   to have sense of
hearing

chekaidchud   to restore sense
of hearing

chekaidkam   one who can hear

chekid   to vaccinate

chekopig   to undermine

chekoshda   ankle rattle

chekshani   line, district

chekshan (chekshaD)   to make a
line

chekwo, chechkwo   ankle

chelkon   to scratch off

chelshan (chelshaD)   to rub off

chelwin to rub

chemamagi, chechemamagi
 horned toad

cheoj, chechoj male
 si cheoj real man

cheojdag manliness
 s-chechojim to be brave

cheolim cane cholla cactus,
 edible buds

cheopi church

chepa mortar with hole for
 mashing grain

chepelk, che'echpelk to be
 blunt, even
 chepeD even
 chepeDk, s- to be even
 chepeDkad (chepeDkai), i to
  make even
 chepeDkahim to become even

cheposid to brand, mark

cheposida branding
cheposidakuD branding iron
cheposig brand

cheshaj (chechshaj), chehchsh
 to ride, climb

cheshajhim to go along
 climbing

cheshoni mountain sheep

cheto fireplace stone, stand
 for cooking

che-tonDag, chech-totonDag
 center beam

che'ul arroweed

Che'ul Sha'igk Willow Brush
 Village

chewagi cloud

chewagig, s- to be cloudy

chewaimeD drag

chew, che'echew long

chewaj, che'echewaj to be long

chewchu longer one

chewdahim to get longer

chewdajid to lengthen

chewelhim to get long

chia hail

chiadag, chichiadag Gila
 monsters

chichwih to play (with), compete (with), trifle (with)

chichwihdag play, competition,
 triviality

chichwihkuD toy, plaything,
 athletic field, recreation area

chichwihmk, s- to be playful

chihgadi/chihgida chewing gum
 (Sp. chicle)

chihil, chichil scissors
 (Sp. tijeras)

Chihno, Chichno Chinese
 (Sp. chino)

chihpia, (chichppiaD), i to move

chihpiadag travel

chihwia, (chichwia) to move or settle

chikpan work

chikpan, chichkpan to work
  chikpandam worker
  chikpanid to work for
  chikpnachud to give work to
  chikpnakuD tool
  chikpnameD, chikpanop to go to work

chi-lihhi, chich-lilihi police (Sp. charifo)

chimkko to nick

chi-mohn wagon tongue (Sp. timón), hitch

chinDad to press lips to, kiss

chini, chihchini mouth

chini elidag lip

chinig to move the lips

chinishch (chinishp) to hold in mouth
chiniwo mustache

chiniwua to hit the mouth

chinniak, to yawn

chipshun to lick, using fingers

cho-lihsa Spanish sausage (Sp. chorizo)

chiwi-chuhch killdeer

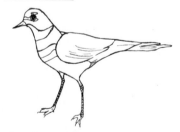

chuagia net bag

chuama, chuchama to roast in ashes
  chuama, chuchama a roast

chuawi ground squirrel

chu'aDkim to gallop

chu'aggan(chu'aggash) to puncture

chu'aggana puncture wound

chu'aggaD, s- bayonet

chu'alk to be slender and tall

chu'alkahim to become taller

chu'al daha to squat

chu'alkaid to stand on tiptoe

chu'amun to tamp, poke, prod

chu'awogi to be standing in a group

chuchkad nightly

chuchul chicken
  chuchul i'ispul/kuksho wuhplim larkspur

chuhch see kehk

chuhcha see kehsh

chuhchuD younger brother's or cousin's child

chuhchuD-je'e, chuhchuD-ha-je'e younger brother's or cousin's wife

chuhchwis organ pipe cactus

chuhdagi coals, charcoal
  chuhdt to make coals

chuhdp, chu'uchudp six, by sixes

chuhkug/chuhhug flesh, meat
  chuhkug s-gaki dried meat, jerky
  chuhkug shoniwia ground meat

chuhko way in, far back

chuhl, chuhchpul corner
  chuhchpulk, s- to be square cornered

chuhl, chuhchul hip bone

Chuhlk "Hipbone" Village

chuhug night, last night
  chuchakad nightly
  chuhugam; s- to be dark

chuhugid, s-e   to faint, forget

chuhsh (chui, chuchku),
   chuhchsh   to quench a flame
   or light

chuhugia   spring spinach greens

chuhwi   jackrabbit
   chuk chuhwi   black species
   toha chuhwi   white species

Chuhwi Ko'adam   Pima Bajo
   Tribesman

chuishpa   lunch

chu'i   flour, ground stuff

chu'i (chui)   to grind
   chu'idas   to be ground

chu'ichig   blame, offense

chu'ichigchud (chu'ichigch)   to
   blame

chu'ichk   to question, interro-
   gate

chu'idag   a part or piece

chu'ig, hab   to be thus, customary, necessary, legal

chu'ig, pihk   to err, make a
   mistake

chu'iko   out in the open, alone

chu'i wuadam   ceremonial
   bearers of pollen to sprinkle
   on families at homes and on
   participants in wihgida ceremony

chu'ijkam   doer

chuk, chuchk, s-   black, to be
   black

chukma   dark

chukmug   gnat

chukuD, chuhchkuD   owl

ChukuD Kuk   "Owl Hoots"
   Village and District

chukuD shosha   dates (owl nasal
   discharge)

chukugshuaD, chuchkugshuaD
   cricket

chuku-lahdi   cocoa (Sp. chocolate)

chum   trying, wanting

chum as   even though

chum as hems   even if

chum alo   almost

chum haschu   anything

chum hasko   anyway

chum hebai   anywhere

chum heDai   anyone

chum hekid   always, any time
   ash chum___   any___

chum, chu'uchum   small

chumaj, chu'uchumaj   to be
   small

chumchu, chu'uchumchu   small
   one

chuwidk   hill, to be mound-
   shaped

D

da'a (dah, dad'e, dah'i)   to fly,
   jump
   nehni (ne'e, nen'e, nehni)
   plural

dada (daiw)   see jiwia

dadge   to wrestle

dadpk washai   side oats

dag   caliche

dagkon/dagion   to wipe, drop

dagkonid   to wipe for

dagimun/dagshun   to massage

dagimuna   massage

dagiod   to support, care for

dagitokch   to have discarded

dagito (dadagitoD)   to discard,
   leave, omit

dagshch (dagshp) to press on

daha, daDha to be sitting, be present

dahd mother's older sister or cousin, Godmother

dahid to learn to sit

dahidag tuber, handle

dahidag, s- to be good at riding

dahiwua, daDhaiwua to sit down

dahiwuakuD outhouse

dahk, dahdk nose
dakpo nasal hair
dakwua to bump the nose

dahm, da'adam over, to be over

dahmjeD from over

dahm juhk noon, to be noon

dahm kahchim sky, heaven

dahpi interj. "who knows?"

dahpiun, dadapiun to smoothe, iron

dahpiunakuD drag iron

dahpk, s- to be smoothe, slippery, naked

dahsh (dai, dadsha, dah'i) to set an object

dahshch to have an object setting

dahum burlap

daikuD, dadaikuD chair

da'ichud, nehnchud to throw something

dapidwua to slip, slide

dapkon to slip

dashwua to pile

dashwuis to be piled

doa, doda to be living

doa, doda, s- to be healthy

doajid, dodajid to heal someone

doajida healing

doajig healing, health

doajk, dodajk, s- to be wild, timid

doajkam, s- wild, timid
s-ta doajkam north (Pima)

doakag, dodakag life, soul

doakdag, dodakdag lifetime

doakam, dodakam living creature

do'ag, dohda'ag mountain

dodolimk, s- to be under control, disciplined

dodolimatahim to become peaceful

dodolimdag peace, control

Doh- see heDai

dohm (dohd, dohdom) to copulate

dohwai ready!

do'i raw
do'ig to be raw

do'ibia to save, rescue

do'ibiakam savior, rescuer

do'ibiadag salvation

domig Sunday, week (Sp. domingo)

E

e himself, his own, themselves, their own, yourself, your own, yourselves

eDa, e'eDa in, within, interior
eda, s- in the middle
eDam, s-ta- disgracefully, ungraciously
eDama, s-ta to be ungracious

eDa/wenog still, yet

eDagid to possess, find

eDa hugkam half

eDastk, s- unruffled, not a cry baby

eDapig to remove insides

eDa wa'ug   backbone

eDhaidag, e'eDhaidag   blood vessels

eDho   red dye plant

e'es   plants, crops

ehb   to stop crying

ehbid (ehbini), s-   to be afraid of, to fear
  s-chu ehbid   to be fearful
  s-chu ehbiddam   coward
  s-ta ehbidam   dangerously
  s-ta ehbidma   dangerous

eh'eD   blood

eh'eDpa   to bleed

ehkeg/ehheg, s-   to be shaded

ehkahim   to become shady

ehkegko, s-   in the shade

ehkdag   shadow

ehktahim   to make shade

ehkchulidakuD   umbrella

ehp, ep   again

ehsid, e'esid   to steal from
  s-chu ehsk, s-chu e'esk   stealthy
  s-chu ehskam, s-chu e'eskam   thief

ehsto , e'esto   to hide a thing

elid (e'elid)
  has elid   to respect, revere
  hab elid   to plan, think
  pihk e elid   to concern one's self for
  s-e, si e elid   to be ashamed of self, timid
  s-paDog elid   to think evil of
  hab elida   plan, guess
  hab elidaDag   care, thought
  paDog elidaDag   evil thoughts
  pihk elidaDag   concern

elidag, e'elidag   skin, bark, husk, peel, to have skin

elkon, e'elkon   to skin, dehide

elkona, e'elkona   a hide, dehiding

elpig, e'elpig   to remove bark, peel

em-   you, your (plural).

eniga   to be in possession of

eniga, e'eniga   acquired possessions

enigaDad   to clothe

enigaDadch,e   to be wearing

epai   also, again

esh (ei, e'esha)   to plant
  esha   a planting
  eshabig   planting

esh, e'esh   chin

eshpo, e'eshpo   beard

etpa, e'etpa   woven door

G

ga'a (gai, gag'e, gah'i)   to roast

ga'abai (ga)   over there (facing this way)

ga'ajeD, ga'agajeD   from there

gagDa   to sell something to someone
  gagli   wares

Gagga   "The Clearing" Village

gaggat   to clear land

gahg   to look for

gahghim, gahghio   to go to look for

gahi, gahghai   across

gahiobin, gaghiobin   to cross

gahiobs   to be laying across

gahi wua, gahghai shulig   to turn over

gahsh hab/gahj hab   over there

gaht, gahgt   bow, gun

ga'iwsa   roasted crushed boiled corn

gaki, gagki, s-   to be dry, skinny

gakidag   dried stuff

gakijid   to dry something

gakimchul   praying mantis

gakoDk, ga'agkoDk   crooked,
  curved; to be crooked, curved

GakoDk   mountain north of Sells

gakoDkahim   to become crooked,
  curved

gakoDkajid   to make crooked

gaksim (gaksh)   to become dry

gal-nahyo   pomegranate (Sp.
  granado

ga-lohn   gallon (Sp. galón)

gamai, (gam)   over there
  facing away, further

ganai (gan)   over there facing
  across

ganiwua   to dig up, remove

gantan (gantaD)   to scatter

gaso-lihn   gasoline

gaswua   to brush or comb
  someone

gaswuikuD   comb

ga-tohdi, gag-totodi   marbles
  (Sp. catota)

gatwua   to shoot off something

gatwuid   to shoot something

gawos, gagwos   gun, rifle (Sp.
  arcabúz)
  ge'e gawos   cannon

gawul, ga'agwul,   different,
  separate
  gawulk, ga'agwulk to be
  different, separated

ge   unusual, big

Ge Aiji   Central Papago dialect,

Ge Kih   Big House (Sacaton)

Ge Komlik   Big Flat Village

ge kuhkunaj   male homosexual

Ge Oidag   Big Field Village

Ge Pihchkim   Hermosillo

ge shuhdagi   large body of
  water

Ge Wo'o   Big Pond Village

Ge Wo'o Chekshani   Big Pond
  District

ge'e, ge'egeD   big, elder, chief

ge'echu   the bigger, older

ge'edahim, ge'egehim   to get
  big

ge'edajid   to make big

ge'eho   long ago, long time

ge'ehog, s-   to be mature

ge'ehogam, s-   maturely

ge'ehogat   to mature

ge'ej, ge'egeDaj   to be big,
  adult

ge'ejig, ge'ege'ejig   leaders of,
  officers of

ge'elhim   to grow

ge'elid, ge'egelid   to raise
  young

gegkio, gegegkio   shoulders

gegok   (see kehk)

gegokiwua   (see kekiwua)

gegosid   to feed

gegosig   a meal

gehsh (gei, gegsha), shulig   to
  fall
  e gehsid   to get tired
  heki gehsh   to spend

gepi/miloni   watermelon
  (Sp. melónes)

gew (gehg, gehgew)   to beat,
  strike, ring
  gehgewi   victory, prize, spoil

gew   ice, snow

gewho, gegewho   wildcat, bobcat

Gegewho Kih   wildcat mountain and village (San Luis)

gewichkwua, gewichshulig   to
strike down

gewikon   to strike a glancing
blow

gewikuD   whip

gewitan   to whip

gewito   to defeat

gewitoi   winning

gewitoidag   victory

gewk, gewpk, s-   to be strong

gewkad (gewkai)   to strengthen

gewkahim   to get strong

gewkam, s-   strongly

gewkamhun   to encourage
  gewkamhuna   encouraging

gewkamhunaDag   encouragement

gewkchu, s-   the stronger one

gewkdag, s-   to have power

gewkdag, gewpkdag   strength,
powers, spirits

gewko, gewpko   to get tired
  s-ta gewkogima   to be weari-
some

gewkogig   fatigue

gewshch (gewshshap, gewshp)
  to lay against

gewshp   to snow on

gi'a (gia, gigia, gia'i)   to
grasp

gi'achug   to carry in the grasp

gi'aDad   to put on a handle

gi'aDag   hat string, handle

gigi'ik, gi'igi'igik   eight

Gigimai   Western Papago
dialect

gigimaichud, e   to boast

gigitwal   swallow

gigiwuk   to tremble

gigiwukchud   to make tremble

gigiwukdam   a trembler, jello

gihg, s-   to be fat
  gi'ichud   to fatten
  gi'ihim (gih, gigi)   to become
fat
  gi'ipig   to remove fat

gihgchu   fat one

gihgi   fat

gihki, gigki   wooden plow or
digger

gihkio/gihkoa   crown

gihnsi   fifteen (Sp. quince)
  gins   a gambling game
  ginskuD   sticks for playing
gins

Giho Do'ag   Carrying Basket
Mountain

gihsho, gigsho   cheese (Sp.
queso)

gihug, s-   to be in danger, be
worried

gi'iho   to lose weight, flesh

Gi'ihodag Mashad   lean month,
January

gi'ik, gi'igik   four

gikujid   to whistle

gimaihun, e/woikchud, e   to
show off, brag

gimaima, s-/woikima, s-   to
be boastful, showoff

giwho/giho   carrying basket

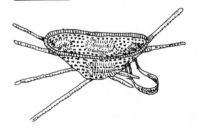

gishalwua   to become famished

gisoki   small purple cactus, edible

gitaihun   to go after the enemy

gital   guitar (Sp. guitarra)

gitaiokam   war party

gitaion   to go on war path

giushani (giushuD)   to strike a match
  giumuD (Pima)

giwuD   belt, band, strap

giwuDk   to be strapped, tied, constricted

giwulk   constriction, constricted place

gogs, gogogs   dog

s-gogsim neok   to use bad language

Gogs Mek   Burnt Dog village (Topawa)

gohhim (gogohim)   to limp

gohih   mulberry tree

gohimeli   a ceremonial dance

gohk, go'ogok   two

gohki   track, footprint

golwin   to rake or hoe out

go'ogam   gray, black, and white bird species

go'ol, go'ogol   other

go'olko, go'ogolko   elsewhere

go'olkojeD   from elsewhere

H

ha   them, their

ha   some, part of

ha'a, haha'a   olla, jar

ha'ab/ha'ag   the other way or side

ha'abjeD   from the other side

ha'adkaj (haha'adkaj)   to gape at, yawn

ha'ahama, haha'ama, s-   to be mean

ha'akia   that number

ha'akiachu   that number thing

ha'akiaj   that number of

ha'akid   last year
  D hema ha'akid   year before last
  D huh i hema ha'akid   three years ago

ha'akio   that many times

ha'as, haha'as   that size, that much

ha'asa   to quit

ha'asij   that size of, much of

ha'aschu, haha'aschu   that size thing

ha'asig, haha'asig   size

ha'asko, haha'asko   so far

hab   thus
  has/Shah. . .   how

hab   on one side

hab ahga   meaning

habaDk   to be flat

habalkahim   to become flat

habshuD   to deflate

hadsid   to sprinkle

haDam, s-   to be sticky

haDshaDkam   teddybear Cholla

haDshp   to glue, paste

haDwuag   to burp

hagito   to burn up, melt away

hah!   what?

hahaisha   squash chips

hahawa   afterward

hahawek   lungs, to pant

hahd   Papagolily

hahghim (hah, hahag)   to melt, thaw

hahgid   to cause to melt, thaw

ha hekaj   immediately

hahhag   leaves

hahk   to roast grain with coals in a basket
   hahki   roasted grain, pinoli

hahkwoD   mistletoe

hahl   squash, pumpkin

hahsa, hahasa   axe (Sp. hacha)

hahshani   Saguaro cactus

Hahshani Kehk   Saguaro Standing village (Sacaton Flats)

hahwul   to tie a knot

hahwulid   to tie a knot for someone

hahwul'ok   to untie

hain (hahaish)   to crack

haini   to be cracked

haiwani   cattle

haiwani, hahaiwani   cow

ha'i   some

ha'ichu, haha'ichu   thing, something, kind or class of
   ha'ichu bahidag   kind of fruit

ha'ichuchud   to honor, esteem

ha'ichudag   a part, piece

ha'ichug   to be present

hajuni   relatives, neighbors
   hajunidag   relationship
   hab juni   what relative

hakimaD, hahakimaD   older brother's or cousin's child, etc

hakima je'e, hahakimaD ha-je'e   older brother's or cousin's wife, etc.

hakit, hahakit   father's younger brother, etc.

hakko   looped carrying cushion

hako'oDad   to insert lariat loop

hakko'oDag   to have loop inserted

halibwua (Pima)   to gallop

hambdogim, s-   incanting manner

ha-mohn   bacon (Sp. jamón)

hanam   green cholla cactus, edible buds

hapot, hahapot   arrow

haschu, Shahchu...   what thing

haschu ahg   why

hashaba/shaba   but

hash/wash   just, only

hashDa, hahashDa   woven basket

hasig, s-   to be difficult

hasigam, s-   difficulty

hasko, hahasko   somewhere

haskojeD   from somewhere

hauk, s-   to be light, easy

haukahim   to become light

haukajid   to make light

haupal, hahupal red tailed hawk

ha'u, haha'u dipper

hawani, hahawani crow

hawol lima beans

hebai, heb where, somewhere

hebai i/Bah- where?

hebaijeD from where

heDai, heDam who

heDai i, heDam i/Doh- who?

he'eDkaj, (he'eDkai), e to grimace

he'ek, s- sour, to be sour

he'ekia i how many?

he'ekiaj i how many of

he'ekio i how many times?

he'eni, he'ewo!/he'enio take it! Here!

he'es i, hehe'es i what size? how much?

he'esij i what size of

he'esko i how far?

hegai/heg (o) that, he, she, it

hegam (o) they, them

hehem (hehhem) to laugh
 s-ta hehem laughably
 s-ta hehema to be laughable

hehewo eyebrows

hehg, heheg co-wife

hehgam, s- to be jealous
 s-chu hehgamk, to be jealous natured

hehgchulid to make happy

hehkig, s- to be happy

hehliwua to slide

Hehliwusk slide, place of a slide (Mexican place name)

hehliwuikuD playground slide

hehogi, s- to be cool

hehogidakuD cooler

hehogihhim to become cool

hehogijid to cool

hehpid, s- to be cold
 s-hehpich-eD in winter
 s-hehpich-eDkam winter

hehpihhim to become cold

hehpijid to make cold

hehwasjel large blue bird species

hejel, hehe'ejel self, alone

hejelko, hehe'ejelko alone, by itself

hek, hehek armpit
 hekpo hair of armpit

hekaj to use
 heg hekaj using that, for that reason
 id hekaj using this, for this reason

hekia whole, pure, completely

hekiakam an entity, whole

heki previous

hekid when

hekid i when?

heki huh already

hekihukam old thing

hekshch (hekshp) to hold under arm

helig (hehelig) to spread, to dry

heligch to have spread to dry

hema a, an, another

hemachud to mistake for another

hema chuhug night before last

hemajim, s- gently
hemajima, s- to be gentle

hemajimatalig favor, gentleness

hemajkam people

hemajkam, hehemajkam person, persons

hemajkamchud to act or treat like a human

hemako, hehemako one
hemakochud to unite

hemapad (hemapai) to gather

hemapadch to have gathered

hemapdas to be gathered

hemho once

hemhowa must

-hems maybe
hemsi, s- "how about the time"

hemu/hemuch now, soon

hemuchkam new thing

henihop to hiccup

heosid to decorate

heosidakuD decoration

heosig blossoms

heosig, s- to be flowery

heotahim to bloom

hetasp, hehetasp five

het/wegi red earth

hetmad to apply red earth

hetmag, s- to be red

heubagid (Pima) to rest

heumk, heukk to be chilled

heu'u interj. yes

hewachuD, hehewachud gray bird species

hewagid to scent, smell

hewajid to cool, alleviate pain

heweD to be windy

hewel air, wind

hewel e'es wind plants, pink flowered

heweto to stop blowing

hewgiameD to go scenting

hewkon to blow on

hewshan to follow the scent of

hi on one hand, on the other

hia maybe

hia sand dune

Hiach-eD O'odham Sand People

hiashp (hihashp) to bury

hiashch to have buried

Hiakim, Hihakim Yaqui tribesman

Maio hiakim Mayo tribesman

hialwui poison

hialwuimad to poison

hiani, hihani tarantula

hi'a (hia, hihia, hia'i) to urinate

hi'am, s- to want to urinate

hi'amchud, s- to cause desire to urinate

hi'ameD, hi'op to go to urinate
hi'i urine
s-chu hi'ama to be a frequent urinator
s-ta hi'ama to be diuretic

hidoD, hihidoD to cook

hidoDakuD, hihidoDakuD cooking vessel

hidolid, hihidolid to cook for

hig how about

hiha'ini/hihi'ani grave, graveyard

hihih guts, intestines

hihij guts of

hihim see him

hihk to clip, mow

hihka cuttings

hihkakuD   clipper, mower

hihlo   thread (Sp. hilo)

hihnk (hihin)   to yell, bark

hihnko'id   to yell at, bark at

hihoin (hihoini)   to bewitch

hihtpag (hihitpag)   to braid

hihtpaDag, hihitpaDag   braid

hihwai, hihiwai   sunflower, squash strips

hihwsid, hihiwsid   to cause sores
  hihwog, hihiwog   a sore
  hihwdag, hihiwdag   a sore, hives

hiji   scram! move! out of the way!

hik, hihik   navel

hikpo   navel hair

Hik Wo'o   round pond south of San Miguel

hikiwij, hihikiwij   hairy woodpecker

hikiwoni   to cut jaggedly

Hikiwoni   "Jagged Cut" Village

Hikiwoni Chekshani   "Jagged Cut" District

hikchk, hikumiak   to cut

hikchkakuD   cutter, saw

hikshan (hihshaD)   to trim

hikshani   something trimmed

hikshpi   to drizzle

hiktani   deep, narrow wash or gully

hikugdag   saguaro cactus button

Hila-wihn   Gila Bend

hilio, hihilio   blacksmith (Sp. herrero)

him (hih, hihhim, hihm)   walk
hihim (hihih, hihhim, hihim)   plural of above
ab___   to come
am___   to go
heb huh___   to get lost, go off

himchud, hihimchud   to cause to move

himid   to learn to walk

himim, hihimim, s-   to want to move

himimchud, hihimimchud, s-   to cause to want to move

himdag   way of life, culture, customs, tradition

himdag, s-   to be a good walker

himhim, hihimhim   to wander, amble

himlu   to go along (baby talk)

hims, hihims   to be on the way, as a road

himto (himttog)   to finish going

hinwal   grass mat

hiopch   body louse, termite

hiowichud   to soak underground

hipig   to spread open to dry
hipiga   food for drying

hipshun (hipshuD)   to spray, or sprinkle with the mouth

hitpoD   to operate on, cut open

hi'usha   bladder

hiw   to rub basket for music

hiwchu, hihiwchu   groin

hiwchulid to rub the rubbing stick

hiwchulida treating with a rubbing stick

hiwchulidakuD ceremonial rubbing stick

hiwchu-wegi, hihiwchu wepegi black widow spider

hiwig to depend on

hiwigid to allow to

hiwium (Pima) see hiwkon

hiwk, s- to be rough
s-hiwk wainomi file

hiwkahim to break out in bumps

hiwkalig measles

hiwkon to scrape smooth, shave

hiwshan to scrape smooth

hiwshana smooth arrow shaft

hoa, hoha sewed basket
hoata basketry

hoan to look for something by stirring, rummaging

hoanid to search for someone, rummaging for someone

hoas-ha'a, hohas-haha'a plate

hobinoD (hohobinoD) to wrap

hobinol wrapped

hodai, hohodai stone, gravel

Hodai Shon Wo'o Rock-base-pond Village

hodoDk dented

hoggaD, hohoggaD cactus wren

hogi leather

hogiDad to saddle

hohag to haul in something

hohagchug to bear along in something

hohhi/hohhoi mourning dove

hohhi e'es gold poppy

hohho'id, s- to like

hohho'idachud, s- to please
s-ta hoho'idam interestingly
s-ta hohho'idama to be interesting

hohnig, hohonig wife

hohnimeD to go for a wife

hohnchud to marry off

hohnt to take a wife, to approach marriage

hohokimal small yellow butterfly

hoho'onma rib

Hohpih Hopi tribesman

hohtgid, s-e to be hurried

hohtmagid, s- to hurry someone

hoinik to move, flutter, stir

ho'i thorn, sticker, cactus

ho'ipaD needle

ho'ipaDjeg eye of needle

ho'idag to be thorny

ho'idkam, hoho'idkam ironwood tree

ho'ige'id (ho'ige'el), s- to show mercy to

ho'ige'idaDag kindness, mercy, blessing

ho'ige'idahun, e   to pray

ho'ige'idahuna   prayer

ho'ige'idam, s-   kindly, mercifully

ho'iggan (ho'iggash)   to stick,
pierce

ho'ipig   to remove a thorn

ho'ishch   to stick

ho'iumi   (Pima) nail

holiwk, hoholiwk   snail shell

holiwkad (holiwkai)   to roll up,
fold up

homita   insides

hon, hohon   body

honchk   to lean against

honchkwua, honchshulig   to
push along with the body

hongew   to shake involuntarily

hongid   to shake self

honhain (honhaish)   to hit with
body

honshpaDag, hohonshpaDag
body

honwua   to walk beside, press
against

ho'ok, hoho'ok   witch, monster

ho'ok-wah'o   witch's tongs,
night blooming cereus

ho'oma   favorite

hotsh   (Pima) to send

howi   species of yucca

howij   banana, yucca banana

howichk   to breath in

howichkwua, howichshulig   to
suck in with breath

huashomi   buckskin bag, wallet

huawi/huai   mule deer

huchigam   small red and gray
bird

huchwua   to stumble

huDa   waist, midriff

huDawog/jegima   to pay attention to, to notice

huDuni (huhuDuk), huhuDuni
to descend

huDunig   sunset, west, evening

huDunihim, huhuDunihim   to go
along descending
huhuDukad   evenings, by even·
ing

huDwuakch, e   to get upset,
frightened

hug, huhug   to be the end of
huhugedam   temporary
pi ha huhugedam   everlasting

hugi   food

hugdag   edge, boundary, to be
bounded

hugid, huhugid   side

hugiog, huhugiog   to use up

hugiogam, s-   to want to use up

hugkam   until

huh   see ko'a

huh   remote in time or space
"ago", "away"

huhch   claws, nails, hooves

Huhhu'ula   dialect and people of
NW reservation, Gila Bend,
and Aki Chini reservation.

huhk, s-   to be warm
huhkahim   to become warm
huhkajid   to warm

huhm (huhuma)   to become
empty (liquid)

huhni   corn

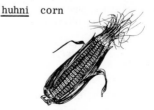

huhpsh   to pull out a thorn

huhugam   those who are gone

huhulga   menstruation

huhulgat   to menstruate

huhulga kih   menstrual house

huhuD   to grease

Huhumu   dialect of Papago south of Sells

huhu'udag   bumble bee

huiwis   Thursday (Sp. Jueves)

hu'id, huhu'id   to chase

hujuD, huhu'ujuD   lizzard, black lizzard

huk   pine, lumber

hukshan/hukshum   to scratch, rake

hukshaDkam   thorny hook bush

hukshch   to have hooked

hukshchim wainomi   chain

hulkad   to bud

humukt, huhumukt   nine

hu'u, huhu'u   star

hu'udagi, huhu'udagi   small black cane wasp

hu'ul   mother's mother or female sibling
hu'ul kehlih   mother's mother's male siblings

huwid   to keep, cling to

I

i   here, now (inceptive), at this point

ia   to gather cactus fruit
iameD, iop   to gather fruit cactus fruit

iagchulid   to propitiate, offer something to appease
iagchulida   propitiatory giving

iagta, i'agta   propitiatory gift, ceremonial articles for wihgida

iapta, i'apta   hammock

iajid   to infect, cause illness

iatogid   to lie, falsify

iatomk, s-   to be dishonest, prone to lie

iatomkam, s-   liar

iawua   to spill, pour

iawuis   to be poured out

i'ajeD   from here, from now on

idani   now, at this season

ih!   Disgusting! unbelievable

ihbamk, ihbkk   to get out of breath

ihbdag, i'ibdag   heart, spirit

ihbhai   prickly pear and fruit

ihbheni   to breathe
i'ibtog   to breathe convulsively

ihbheiwua   to take a breath
si i ihbheiwua   to sigh

ihda/id (o)   this, he, she, it

ihdam/idam (o)   these, they, them

ih'e   to drink
i'ichud   to water
i'imk, s-   to desire drink
i'imkam, s-   heavy drinker
i'ito   drink up

ihgid   to shake fruit off plant

ihkowi   plant with edible tuber

ihkol   medicinal plant

ihm   to greet, address or call by relationship
ihmigi   relationship terms (relationship terms see Appendix IV A)

Ihmiga   Ihmigi Village (Emika)

ihma (im)   here facing away

ihmki   soot

ihna (in)   here, facing across

ihnagi/nahgi   ancient skirt

ihnamk, ihnkk   to crave some food

ihswigi, i'iswigi hedgehog
 cactus

iht (i'ita) to scoop or put in

ihtaikuD scoop

ihug devil's claw

ihwagi edible greens

ihwajim, s- greenish

ihwid to make fire with a drill

iia (ia) here, to be here

i'ihog to cough

i'ihogig tuberculosis

i'ito (i'ittoD) to drink up

I'itoi/Hihitoi Protector of the
 O'odham

i'iwuki to sprout

iks, i'iks cloth, rag

iol to stir

iolagid to fry

ioligam a plant

Ioligam Kitt Peak

i'oma, s- to feel well (Pima)

i'oshan, e to clear the throat

i'owi, s- to be tasty

I'owi shuhdagi Sweet Water
 village

i'owichu sweet one

i'owihhim to get sweet

i'owijid to sweeten

i'owim, s- sweetly

ip/op until

ipuD, i'ipuD dress or skirt

is-pahyo, i'is-papaio sword,
 spear (Sp. espada)

ispul, i'ispul spur (Sp.
 espuela)

is-tahmpa stamp (Sp. estampa)

istliw, i'istliw stirrup (Sp.
 estribo)

is-tuhwha stove (Sp. estufa)

J

je'e, jehj mother, parents

je'es mother's older brother,
 cousin

jeg, jehjeg opening, to be
 open

jeg-eD outside

jegda race track

jegelid to allow, make room
 for

jegima, s-, huDawog to notice,
 pay attention to

jegko in the open

jegos storm

jehk (jejka, jehki) to taste

jehkaich, e- to suffer the consequences, be struck with
 calamity

jehkch to find tracks

jehg mesquite bean flour balls

jehni (jehj, jehjen) to smoke

jehnigid to lecture

jehnigida meeting

jehnigidakuD meeting place

jejewk s- spotted

jekiameD to go tracking

jew, s- to be rotten

jewahim to rot

Jewak Rotted Place Village

jewakag, jejewhakag king
 snake

jewalig rotten thing

jeweD, jejeweD earth, country,
 land, soil, floor

JeweD Mek "Dirt Burned"
 Village

jeweDo on the ground

jewho, jejewho gopher

jewikon   to scrape off hair on hide

jiawul, jijawul   devil, barrel cactus (Sp. Diablo)

Jiawul Dak   "Barrel Cactus Sitting" Village

jiosh, jijosh   god (Sp. dios)

jisk, jijsi   mother's younger sister or sibling

jiwhiadag   arrival

jiwhias   to be extended to

jiwia, (jijiwhia), dada (daiw) to arrive

juDumi, jujuDumi   bear

juDwua, jujuDwua   to bounce

juhagi, jujhagi, s-   to be resilient

juhk (jujju)   to be situated in the sky, i.e. the sun
ga huh i juhk, ia hab i juhk to be morning
dahm juhk   to be noon
gam huh i juhk, im hab i juhk to be afternoon

juhk (jujku)   to rain
juhkig, s-   to be rainy
jujgid   to cause rain
jujku, s-   to be rainy season
jukito   to stop raining
jukshp   to rain on

juhki   rain

juhk, jujuk, s-   to be deep

juhkahim   to become deep

juhkalig   depth

juhkam, jujkam   Mexican

juhpin   north

juhpin   to soak in, sink down

jui   prickly pear-like cactus fruit

jujul, juhu'ujul, s-   zig-zag, crooked

jujulim, s-   crookedly
jujulk, s-   to be zig-zag

julashan/nulash (Pima)   peach (Sp. durazno)

jumaDk/omlk   humpbacked

jumalk   to be low

jumalkad (jumalkai)   to lower

jumalkchu   the low one

juni   dried cactus fruit

junihim, hab   to continue doing

junid, hab   to do for

junis, hab   to be done

jupij, ju'ujpij, s-   quietly

jushaDk, ju'ujshaDk   to be loose

jushaDkad (jushaDkai)   to loosen

jushaDkahim   to become loose

jusukal   large black species of lizzard

K

k, kch, ch   and (see Appendix III 4.3)

ka'al   white oak

ka'amaD, kahkmaD   a woman's son's child

ka'ama-je'e   a woman's daughter-in-law or mother-in-law

kah   to hear

kahk, kahkak   father's mother and her siblings

kahch, wehch, we'ewech   to be lying (inanimate)

kahchk/ge shuhdagi   lake, sea

kahm, kahkam   cheek

kahma, kakama   quilt (Sp. cama)

kahmpo camp (Sp. campo)

kahnia/kahnu cane (Sp. caña)

kahon, kakhon box, fort (Sp. cajón)

kahw, kakaw badger

kahwul, kakawul sheep (Sp. cabra)

kahya street (Sp. calle)

kai, kakai seed
kaij seed of (saguaro)

kaichug to hear continually

kaidag, s- to be loud

kaidam, s- loudly

kaidag a sound

kaidaghim to go making noise

kaidagid to make noise

kaidagig audibility

kaiham to listen
kaiham, s-ta interesting sounding
kaihama, s-ta to be interesting

kaij (kaijim), hab to say

kaij atol saguaro seed gravy

kaijelid to say for

kaijelidam, s- to want to say for

kaijka prepared seed, seed for planting

kaijkat to prepare seed, for future planting

Kaij Mek "Seed Burnt" Village (Santa Rosa)

kaikia/kaikia shuhshk sandle

kaipig to harvest grain, scraping grain from ears

kais, kakais, s- rich, wealthy

kaischud to make rich

kaischuda riches

kaishagi, kakaishagi crotch

kaishch to hold in the crotch

kaistalig wealth

kakaichu quail

kaka-wahdi peanuts (Sp.Az. cacahuate)

kalioni, kakalioni stallion (Sp. garañon)

kalit, kaklit wagon (Sp. carrito)

kalshani, kakalshani shorts (Sp. calzónes)

kal-sihda, kakal-sisida socks (Sp. calcetín) stockings

kal-tuhji cartridge (Sp. cartuchi)

kalwash chickpeas (Sp. garbanzos)

kammialt to change (Sp. cambiar)

ka-miio/opochk ohkam camel (Sp. camello)

kamish, kakmish (Pima) shirt (Sp. camisa)

ka-mohdi yam, sweet potato (Sp. camote)

kam'on to debate

kampani, kakampani bell (Sp. campanilla)

kamshch (kamshp) to hold in mouth

kanaho, kakanaho boat (Sp. canôa)

ka-nohwa trough (Sp. canóa)

kanjel, kakanjel lights (Sp. candela)

kan-tihna bar, stand (Sp. cantina)

kapaDwua battle antic

kapijk, ka'akpijk to be gathered

kapon (kakpon) clap, gunshot

kapsid to make clapping noise

kaponahim to trot along noisily

kastigal to punish (Sp. castigar)

kawaD, kakawaD shield

kawhain (kawhaish) to quarrel with

ka-whih coffee (Sp. café)

kawk, kawpk, s- hard, callous

kawkad (kawkai) to make hard

kawkahim, kawpkahim to become hard

kawkchu, s- hard one

kawlik knoll, hill

Kawlik "The Knoll" Village

kawoDk to be grouped together

kawiyu, kakawiyu horse (Sp. caballo)

kch, ch, k and

keDwua/kechwua to ejaculate semen

keDwuadag semen

keDkolid to tickle

kehg, keheg, s- good, beautiful
  kegchud to fix, beautify

kehgahim to become beautiful

kehgaj, kehegaj, s- to be good, beautiful

kehgchu, s- good one, beautiful one

kehiwin/kehiwia to thresh by hoof

kehiwina threshings

keh'id (keh'el), s- to hate, scold

keh'idag hatred

kehk, chuhch, chu'uchuch to be standing (inanimate)

kehk, gegok to be standing (animate)

kehkhim, gegokhim to step aside

kehli, kekel old man, father's older brother or cousin

kehlibaD, kekelibaD the deceased

KehlibaD Wo'oga Dead-Man's Pond

kehlitakuD, okstakuD mushroom

kehsh (kei, keksha), chuhcha to stand something, appoint

kehshakuD candle (etc.) holder

kehshch to have standing

keichkwua, keichshulig to kick along

keiggan (keiggash) to kick repeatedly

keihin to folk-dance, kick

keihina folk-dance

keihinakuD folk-dance ground

keikon to stumble

keishch (kekeishch, keishp) to step on

keishpa yard, pace/ Pima: mile

ke'i (kei, keke, keh'i) to bite
  ke'ijid,e to get bitten

kekiwua, gegukiwua to stand up

keliw to shell corn

keshwua to cause to stand, stop

-ki evidently

kia still, yet, until

kia! Wait!

kih than (Sp. que)

kih, kihki house, wall

kih to be dwelling, living

kihdag, kihkdag home and property

kiheh, kikiheh spouse's siblings, in-laws

kihhim village

kihjeg, kihkjeg doorway

kihkam dweller
  wehm kihkam co-dwellers

kihsupi black and gray bird

kiht, kihkit to build

kihta, kihkita buildings

ki'ihin to bite off

ki'ikon to gnaw clean

ki'ishch to hold in teeth

ki'ishpakuD pliers, tweezers

ki'iwih/wihbam gum

ki'iwin to chew up

ki'iwina chewings

kiohoD, kikihoD rainbow

kiot to rustle stock

klahwo, klalwo nail (Sp. clavo)

koa, koka forehead, bank
  koapo hair of forehead

koachk to sight, peek

koawua to bump head

koawel bush with edible red
  berry

ko'a (huh, huhgi) to eat

ko'adani ought to eat

ko'adma to seem to eat

koDog to rumble in the bowels

kodogid to yell in victory, to
  shake

kohadk something dried and
  burned

Kohadk Kohadk village, dialect

Kohadkam people of Kohadk
  area

kohba, kokoba drinking glass
  (Sp. copa)

kohds pre-historic snake

kohji, kokji swine, pig, javalina, peccary (Sp. coche)

Kohji Pi Bak Avra Valley
  (Pork not done)

kohk, (kow) to dig

kohkoD goose, crane, heron

kohlo'ogam, koklo'ogam
  whippoorwill

kohm tree species
  Kohm Wawhia kohm tree well
  Kohm Wo'o kohm tree pond

kohmagi, kokomagi, s- gray,
  to be gray

kohmagim grayly

Kohmagi Mashad gray month
  (February)

kohmch to have in the arms

kohmk (kohkomk, kohmki) to
  embrace

kohsh (koi), kohksh (koksha) to
  sleep

kohsid, kohksid to put to sleep

kohtpul, kohktpul cicada

kohwih, kokowih (Pima)
  beaver

kohwli copper (Sp. cobre)

koi not yet

ko'i the dead

koiata dun mottled grey-brown

koiataDag, s- to be dun,
  mottled grey-brown

ko'idag corpses, remains of the
  dead

kokaw staghorn cactus, edible
  buds

kokda see mu'a

kok'o see mumku

kok'odam ha-kih hospital

kokoho burrowing owl, ground
  owl

kokoi ghosts, spirits of the
  dead

kokotki sea-shells

kokshpa mascot or youngest
  performer in wipinim, ends
  songs with "kuh"

koksikuD pajamas, sleeping
  quarters

kolhai, koklhai fence, corral,
  (Sp. corral)

kolighid   to jingle

Ko-lohdi, Koko-lolodi (ChukuD Kuk)   southern Papago dialect group (Sp. Az. tecolote)

kolwis   nonconformist
   kolwisig   to be nonconformist

komaD   creeping of plant

komaiwuag   fog

komal   griddle (Sp. comal)

komal   godmother of one's child (Sp. comadre)

komalim   flatly

komalk, ko'okomalk   flat, to be flat, low terrain

komalk mo'okam   bird species

Komalk   "The Flat" Village

komalkchu   flat one

komi, kohkomi   back, shell

komitp   crack

komkch'eD, kokomkch'eD turtle

Komkch'eD, e Wah'osidk   "Turtle Wedged" Village (Sells)

kommo'ol   thousand legged worm

kompal   godfather of one's child (Sp. compadre)

kompig   to de-shell

kompish   to confess (Sp. confesar)

komshaD   to nap

ko'o (koi, kok'o, koh'i)   see muhk

ko'ok, s-   pain, to pain

ko'okam, s-   painfully

ko'okmaDk   dark-trunked palo verde

Ko'okmaD Kehk   suburb of Kaij Mehk (Santa Rosa)

Ko'ok Mashad   painful month, (May)

ko'okol   chile

ko'okolmad   to put chile on

ko'omash   to play girl's game

ko'omasha   girl's game

ko'omashakuD   sticks for girl's game

ko'owi, kohko'owi   rattlesnake

kop, kokp   to explode

kopsid   to explode

kopod   swollen

kopodk   to be swollen

kopodkad   to make swollen, inflate

kopodkahim   to become swollen

kosh, koksh   nest

koshagi, kokshagi   afterbirth
   koshaj   afterbirth of

koshdag, kokshdag   cover, case holder, holster

koshoDk, ko'okshoDk   to be puffed up, ballooned

koshoDkad (koshoDkai)   to puff up

koshoDkdakuD   baking powder

koshwa, kokshwa   skull

kos-nihlo, koks-ninilo   cook (Sp. cocinero)

koson, kokson   woodrat

kostal, kokstal   bag (Sp. costal)

kotDobi   sacred datura, jimson

kotoni, koktoni   shirt (Sp. cotorina)

kots, kokots   cross (Sp. cruz)

kotwa, koktwa   shoulder

kowk, kowpk, s-   thick, to be thick, high terrain

kowkahim   to become thick

kownal, kokownal   governor (Sp. gobernador)

kownaltalig   domain, kingdom

kownid   to kick, rattle

kowog, kokowog, s- to be full

kowogchud, s- to make full

kowoD, kokowoD to become full

kowoDk hollow, expanded

ku- and

kuadagi dark red ant

kuadi, kukadi twin (Sp. cuate)

kuapa, kukapa Cocopa Indian

ku'ag to get firewood

ku'agameD, ku'agop to go get firewood

ku'agi firewood

ku'agid to get firewood for

kuchki firebrand, burning post

kuchul, ku'ukchul curved

kuDat cactus bird

kuDut· to trouble, worry

kuDutaDag trouble, worry

kugia erection

kuhagid, kukagid to cook meat on a stick

kuhbs dust, fog, smoke, vapor
kubjuwi, s- brown
kuhbsig, s- to be dusty, smoky

kuhg, kuhhug end

kuhigam black bird species

kuhijid to call an animal or bird

kuhkta hanging shelf

kuhkwul elf owl

kuhm (kuhk, kuhkum) to gnaw

kuhp (kukpa, kuhpi) to close, shut, dike

kuhpaDag, kuhkpaDag door, top, cover

kuhpahim to seal, go along closing

kuhpi closed, shut in, shut up

Kuhpik "The Dike" village

kuhpiok, kuhkpiok to open

kuhpiokas to be open

kuhpiokch to have open

kuhsh, kuhksh to burn and stick to the vessel

kuhshad to chase game

kuhsjim large white and orange bird species

kuhta/kuhtagi torch

kuhtagit to ignite a torch

kuhtpa (kuktpa) to treat with heat

kuhu to crow, call, neigh, play music

kuhudam band

kuhwid, kukuwid pronghorn antelope

kuhwo bucket and rope (Sp. cubo)

kui, kukui mesquite

kuichud to razz losers

kuikuD, kuhkuikuD whistle, horn

kuint to count

kuinta counting, accounting

kuintaDag an assigned number

kuintakuD ruler, measure

kuipaD, kukuipaD crossed stick, for Saguaro harvest, Big Dipper

kuishani (kuishaD) to whine

Kui Tatk Mesquite Root village (Sasabe)

kuiwa (Pima) west

ku'inhogid to annex

ku'isham to be hooked together

ku'iwonid to boil it

kuk chehdagi light green palo verde

kuksho wuhplim larkspur

kukkjeg mirage

kuku-luhji bonnet (Sp. cucurucho)

kulani medicine (Sp. curar)

kulanimad to medicate

kul-wichigam, kukul-wipichigam curved-bill thrasher

kulwani, kukulwani, s- curly, kinky

kumikuD cob

kun, kuhkun husband

kupal, kuhkpal overturned with back presented

kuppiaD, kukuppiaD shovel

kupsh, (kupshap, kupshp) to blink, close the eyes

kusal, kuksal silverware, trowel (Sp. cuchara)

kushadk, kuhkshadk to be dry, stiff, cramped

kusho, kuksho occiput, back of head

kusho dagshpa grasping the occiput when seeing a tarantula

kushul jam, jelly

kushulid to make jam

kushwiot to carry on back

kuswo, kukswo neck
kuswo oh'o cervical vertebrae

kushpo hair of neck

kutshani, s- to be foggy, dusty

L

la'ashp (lal'ashp) to trap (Sp. lazo)

lahbis, lalbis pen, pencil (Sp. lápiz)

lahmba, lalamba lamp (Sp. lámpara)

lahnis, lalnis spear, club (Sp. lanza)

lahnju, lalanju ranch (Sp. rancho)

lai, lahlai ruler, king (Sp. rey)

lanjeki lentil (Sp. lenteja)

lasion ration (Sp. ración)

lawit to drag (Sp. trabar)

lial money (Sp. real)
lial kih purse

liat, lihliat lariat (Sp. reata)

ligpig to deprive of, strip (Sp. rico)

lihbih, lilbih orphan, dogey (Sp. lepe)

lihma, lilma file (Sp. lima)

lihmhun to cleanse ceremonially (Sp. limpio)

lihmhuna cleansing rite

lihnda, lilinda rein (Sp. rienda)

lihso, lilso prisoner (Sp. preso)

lihsochud to take prisoner

lihwa, lilwa coat, jacket (Sp. abrigo)

li-juhwa lettuce (Sp. lechuga)

likintod, s- charcoal grey

li-mihda, lil-mimida glass, bottle (Sp. limeta)

li-mohn   lemon (Sp. limón)

limoshan   to dun for donation
(Sp. limosna)

limoshanamed, limoshanop   to
go for donation

lodait   to judge.

lodaidag/lodaisig   judgment

lohba   drygoods (Sp. ropa)

lohgo, lolgo   mental case (Sp.
loco)

lohna, lolna   canvas (Sp. lona)

lohmba, lolomba   Jew's harp
(Sp. birimbas)

lomaDad, lolmaDad   to saddle
(Sp. lomo)

lomaDag, lolmaDag   grass
saddle, to be saddled

luhlsi   candy (Sp. dulce)

luhnas   Monday (Sp. lunes)

luhnag   paired

luhya   grey horse (Sp. grulla)

luhyag, s-   to be sky blue

lu'ulu   coyote's word for atol

M

m-   you, your (singular)

machpoD, mamchpoD   toe (and
archaically, finger)

machwidag, mamchwidag
ritual feather

maD, mahmaD   female's
progeny, younger sister's
child

maD-ohg, mahmaD-ha-ohg
younger sister's husband

maDtahim   to give birth

maDpig   to pick fruit or
branches

magew   to swing the arm

maggat   to break through

magjid   to wave the hand

Ma-hahwih   Mohave tribesman

mahch, s-   to be knowing
s-chu mahch   to be wise
pi e mahchimch   to deny one's
knowledge of something

mahchimk, s-   to desire to
know

mahchig   knowledge

mahchulid   to cause to know

mahgina, mamgina   machine,
car (Sp. maquina)

mahhad   to raise the hand

mahk (mamka, mahki)   to give
to

mahkai, mamakai   medicine
man, medic

mahkch   to have given to

mahkig   gift, giving

mahkigdag   gift from

mahks   to be given

mahltis   Tuesday (Sp. martes)

mahm   father term of
mahmgam   sib

mahmgam   members of a sib of
buzzard moiety

mahmsh   tick, castor bean

mahniko   arthritic, stiff

mahs, mams, hab   to be like,
to be a color

mahs, s-   to be bright, visible,
light

mahschu, hab   a like thing

mahsho   to be tame, trained
(Sp. manso)

mahshochud   to train

mahsko   clearly

mahskogid   to clarify

mai (mamche)   to learn

mai, s-   to discover, find out

mai   food cooked in ground

maihogi   centepede

maikuD   earthen oven

maim, maik   to get indigestion

main woven straw

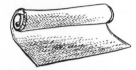

maintahim to weave

ma'i, mam'ai older sister's or cousin's child

ma'i ohg, mam'ai ha-ohg older sister's or cousin's husband

ma'iggan (ma'iggash) to pelt

ma'ihin (ma'ihish) to hit with a thrown object

ma'ikon (ma'ikosh) to graze with a thrown object

ma'ishch to have covered

ma'ishp to cover

ma'ishpa sweetheart

ma'ishpadag roof

ma'ishpakuD cover

makoDad, mamkoDad to couple, join

makoDadch, mamkoDadch to have hitched

makoDag coupling

maliom/malioni, mamaliom/mamalioni boss, watchman (Sp. majordomo)

ma-lohma, mam-loloma acrobat, circus (Sp. maroma)

mamakahim one of the four full chiefs

mamtoD scum, algae

mamhaDag branch

manaio herd of horses, unbroken horse (Sp. manada)

mandi-giia butter (Sp. mantequilla)

manjekih lard (Sp. manteca)

maniaDad to hobble an animal, apply brakes

maniaDag hobble, hobbled

mani-sahna apples (Sp. manzana)

mashad, mamashad moon, month, menstrual period

mashcham to teach

mashchama teaching

mashchamadag doctrine

mashchamakuD school

maskal, mamskal bandana, silk (Sp. mascara)

masma, hab as, like

matchuD, mamatchuD mortar, grindstone

matai ashes

matk palm of hand

matok to untangle, disassemble

mauppa coyote feet

mawid, maipid lion family, mountain lion

ma-yahdi green fruit beetle

mehi fire

mehi/meihim (mei, memhe) to burn

mehid (memheid) to burn something

mehiddag burnt part

mehk, me'emek far

mehkjeD from far

mehkod to remove far

mel, wo'i to arrive running

melchud, wohpo'ichud to cause to run

melchuda, wohpo'ichuda a race

melchudaDag, wohpo'ichudaDag, s- to be good at driving

meldag, wohpo'idag, s- to be good at running

melhog ocotilla

melidkam, s- a runner

melnam, wo'inam to meet on the way

melomin to disk

melopa, wo'iopa to come repeatedly

melto (melttog) to finish running

meD (meh, memDa, mehl) to run
wohpo (wopo, wohpo'i) plural

mia, mimia near

miabid, mimiabid to draw near

miabij, mimiabij near to

mialklos Wednesday (Sp. miércoles)

mihl thousand (Sp. mil)

mihsa/mihsh, mimsa/mimsh table (mesa)

mihsh, mimsh protestant (Sp. misa)

mihshmad, e to worship

mihstol/mihtol, mimstol cat

miia (Pima: keishpa) mile (Sp. milla)

miiu (Pima) nickel

mikigwuikuD stones for girls game

mi-lihda (see limihda)

milini/miloni muskmelon (Sp. melón)

mil-gahn Caucasian (Sp. Americano)

mihnas mine (Sp. minas)

"mi-nuhto" minute (Sp. minuto)

mischini wild (Sp. mesteño)

mischini siwol wild onion

mi-yohn million (Sp. millón)

moashan hump

moh to gather seed

mohg straw, sediment

mohndi to play cards (Sp. monte)

mohndikuD gambling cards

moho bear grass

mohon to thresh, pulverize

mohogid, s- to itch

mohogidchud, s- to cause to itch

mohogihhim to become itchy

mohoni, s- granular

mohs, mohms woman's daughter's child, sister's daughter's child

mohs-ohg a woman's son-in-law or man's mother-in-law

mohto (momtto) to carry on head or in vehicle

mohtoi burden

mohto'id to burden with, accuse of

moihun to soften, plow, cultivate

moihuna plowing, cultivation

moihunas to be plowed, cultivated

moik, momoik, s- to be soft

moikahim to become soft

moikam, s- softly

moikchu soft one

moikajid to make soft

momoisha to limber up, exercise

monjel, momonjel bandana (Sp. mantel)

mo'o, mohm head

mo'o hair

mo'obaD, mohmbaD   game head
mo'obDam, mohmbDam   hunter

mo'ochkuD   pillow
mo'ochkwua, mo'ochshulig   to push along with the head
mo'ochwig, mom'ochwig   toad
mo'ogew   to have tremors of the head
mo'oggan (mo'oggash)   to bunt, butt
mo'ogid   to shake the head
mo'ohain (mo'ohaish)   to smash with the head
mo'okwaD, mom'okwaD   tadpole
mo'otk   scalp
mo'otpig   to scalp
mo'owin   to clean antlers, horns
mo'owua   to hit the head
mostois   edible plant
mualig   to spin, dance
mu'a (mua, mum'a, mua'i), kokda   to kill
s-chu mu'aDag,   to be murderous
s-chu mu'aDkam,   a killer
muDadag   tassle of plant
muhaDag, mumhaDag, s-   to be brown
muhdag   wound
muhk/muhkhim (mumku, muh'i)   to die
ko'o (koi, kok'o, koh'i)   to die
muhki, ko'i   the dead
muhkig   death
muhkigdag, ko'idag   remains of the dead
muhks   to be numb, necrotic
muhla, mumula   mule (Sp. mula)

muhla tahtami   corn on the cob

muhla wanimeDdam   species of spider
muhni   beans
muhs   vagina
muspo   pubic hair of female
muhuDag, s-   to be greasy
muhwal, mumuwal   insect, fly
muhwij, s-   oblong, thin and long
mu'i   many
mu'ij   many of, to be many
mu'idahim   to become many
mu'idajid   to make many
mu'idajidas   to be multiplied
mu'ikpa   at many places
mu'iko   many times
mukchiwidam   long pointed fly
mukimakam, s-   desire for death
mulin, omin,   to break by bending
mulinig   something broken
mumkichud   to make sick
mumkidag   sickness
mumku, kok'o   to be sick, get sick
mumkudam, kok'odam   patient
muhsigo   musician, to make music (Sp. música)
mu'u (muh, mummu, muh'i)   to wound
mu'uk, mu'umuk, s-   to be pointed, a peak
mu'uhug, mu'umuhug, s-   to be sharp-edged
mu'ukdag   sharpness
mu'umuk, s-   to be bumpy
mu'umukad (mu'umukai)   to make bumpy
mu'umukahim   to become bumpy

N

na   simple question initiator
  Was...?, Is...?, Will...? etc.

na'a   dubitative initiator: maybe

na'a   (Pima) there

naggia, nahngia   to hang,
  hammock

naggiakch   to have hanging

nahagew   to shake the ears

nahagio, nanhagio   mouse

nahd (nai, nanda, nahj)   to
  make a fire

nahda   fire

nahdakuD   fireplace, oven

nahdch   to have a fire

nahk, nahnk   ear

nahkag   type of cactus

nahnko   various, different

nahnkogid/nahnko wua   to miss-
  use, ridicule

nahshp (nanhashp)   to fold

nahto (nattoD)   to finish

nahtokam   maker

nahtokch   to have finished

nahtois   to be finished

Nahwaho   Navajo

nakpig   to earmark

nakpidag   earmark

nakog   to endure, be able

nakosig, s-   to be noisy

nakosigam, s-   noisily

nakpo   hair of the ear

nakshch (nakshp)   to overhear

nakshel, nanakshel   scorpion

nakwua   to bump the ear

nalash   orange (Sp. naranja)

namk (nanmmek)   to meet

namki   meeting

namkid   to pay

namkida   pay, pay time

namkidaDag   price, wage

namkig, s-   to be expensive

namkigam, s-   expensively

nanakumal   bat

nanhagio   earrings

napaDk   to be sprawled

napaDwua   to sprawl

nasi-yohn   nation (Sp. nación)

naumk, naukk   to get intoxicated

naumki, naukkoi   drunkard

naw   leaf cactus

nawait   wine

nawait   to make wine

nawash, nanwash   pocket knife
  (Sp. navaja)

nawedju, nanawedju   master of
  wihgida ceremonies

Nawedju Hiashp   Ceremonial
  Leader's Burial

nawoj, naipiju, nan'aipiju
  friend, brother
  naupuj, nan'aupuj   (Pima)

nawojdag   friendship

nawojt/nawodt   to make friends

nea (nea'a!), nenea   to look

neahim   to wait for

neal   to visit someone for a
  meal

nealimeD, nealop   to go to visit
  someone for a meal

ne'e (nei, ne'e, neh'i)   to sing

nehbig   ancient beast

nehn (nenna)   to wake up

nehn/nehnahim (nea, nenea,
  nea'i)   to awake

nehnchud   see da'ichud

nehndag   ability to see

nehndag, s-   to be alert

nehni (ne'e nen'e)   see da'a

nehni   tongue

nehol   slave, servant

nehpoD, nenepoD   nighthawk

neid (nenneid)   to see, discover, experience, visualize
ab neid to look at

neidakuD, neneidakuD   mirror

neijig, s-   disaster, calamity, tragedy

ne'i, nen'ei   song

ne'ibim (ne'ibij)   to run around, pass

ne'ihim   to go along singing

ne'imeD, ne'iop   to go to sing

ne'ikuD   singing place

ne'ito   to finish singing
nem   liver

nena   in sight

nenashani, nenenashani   to be early waking

neniDa   to wait for

nen'eid, s-   to be careful

nenhoghim   to look around

neok (neoki), neneok (neneoki)   to talk

neokdam, neneokdam   speaker

neokim, s-   to desire to speak

neokchulid   to read

nepoDk, ne'enepoDk   to be loaf shaped

njuh!   oh yeh!

ni-   me, my

"ni"   neither, nor (Sp. ni)

"ni'is"   not even

noD, nohnoD   to turn, bend

noDa   to get dizzy

noDags   to be bent, turned

noDagid, nohnogid   to turn a thing

noDagam, nohnDagam   rabid animal

nohnhoig   to stir

noji-wihno   Christmas eve (Sp. nochebuena)

nolawt (nonolawt)   to buy from

nolawtakuD/tianna   store

nonha   egg

nowi, nohnhowi   hand, arm

nowidag, nohnhowidag   sleeve

nowiyu, nonowiyu   steer (Sp. novillo)

"nuhmlo, nunumlo"   number (Sp. número)

nu'a (nua, nua'i)   to rake together

nuippa   large black bird species

nu'ichk   to push on

nu'ichkwua, nu'ichshulig   to push along

nu'ihin   to push

nu'ihinahim   to go along pushing

nuhkud   to care for

nulash (Pima)   peach (Sp. durazno)

nuhwi, nunuwi   buzzard

O

o,   or (Sp. o)

o   he, she, it, they

oaga, o'aga   brain, nerve

oam, o'am, s-   brown, orange, yellow;

oamahim   to become brown

oamajid   to brown

oamajida (Pima)   popover

oamhun   to contaminate

oamhuna   contamination

oamhunas   to be contaminated

oamhunDag   contaminant

Oam Mashad   orange month, April

oan   to erase, wipe off

oana   erasure

oanas   to be erased

oanid   to erase for

obga   enemy

obgadag   enmity

oD   to gather fruit

ogol   father term of Ogolgam

ogolgam   those who call their father ogol

oh, o'o   back

Ohb   Apache, enemy

Ohbadi   Opata tribesman

ohbgam   small type of Palo Verde tree

ohche'ewi (o'oche'ewi)   to find by chance

ohg, o'og   father

ohgig, s-   left

ohgigjeD, s-   from the left

ohgigko, s-   on the left

ohhod, s-/tamhaig, s-   to reject, discard

ohhoda   reject, discard

oh'id   to forebode evil, grieve by mentioning the dead

ohla   gold (Sp. oro)

ohla   hour, time, timepiece (Sp. hora)

oh'o   bone, beak

oh'oD   sand

oh'og   tears

oh'okid   to cause illness by spiritual power

ohshaD   to stretch out on the back

ohshaD, o'oshaD   tiger, jaguar

ohso, o'oso   scythe, sickle (Sp. hoz)

ohwua   to bump the back

oi   soon, now (Sp. hoy)

oid (o'oid)   to follow, accompany

oidachud   to go after, think of

oidag, o'oidag   field, farm

oidahim   to consider, follow

oidam   during

oidk, o'oidk   through

oij, o'oij   following, after

oijkam   one following

oimeD, oiopo   to walk around

oimelig   travels, stamping grounds

oiopo   see oimeD

oi wa   yet, but, instead

okokoi, o'okokoi   white winged dove

oks, o'oki   adult woman, female

oksi, o'oksi   father's older sister, cousin

ola   double ball for game of toka

olas, o'olas   spherical

olas, o'olas, s-   to be spherical

olasim, o'olasim, s-   spherically

olatahim, o'olatahim   to roll up, bundle up

ol-giia   pitchfork(Sp. horquilla)

olhoni, o'olhoni   maverick (Sp. huerfano)

ol-niio, o'ol-nihnio/ol-nihha, o'ol-nihniha   oven (adobe) (Sp. hornillo)

olshch   to have hooked

olshp   to hook

olshpiok   to unhook

omin   see mulin

omlk   to be humpbacked

on   salt

onamed, onop   to go for salt

onk, s- to be salty

Onk Akimel Salt River

onk kui tamarack

onkahim to get salty

onkdag saltiness

onmad to salt

onpig to remove salt

O'obab Maricopa tribe

O'obmakam Sand Papago, Maricopa-like

o'odham tribesman, person, human

o'odhamchud to act or treat like a human

o'odhamdag human dignity or worth, personality

o'oD sand, crystals

o'oDgid to crystalize

o'ohadag picture

o'ohan to write, draw

o'ohana writing, drawing, book

o'ohanas to be written, drawn

o'ohia fine sand dune

o'owi, s- to be pretty, color-ful, striped

o'olopo kidney

o'ot to drip

o'osid to percolate

opochk humped, to be humped

opochk ohkam/ka-miio camel

opon leafy winter food plant

osal, o'osal bead (Sp. rosario)

oshkon to skin a sore place

owgam, o'owgam construction stick, bush

owij awl

o-wihspla, o'o-wipispla bishop (Sp. obispo)

ownag, o'ownag clavicle, collarbone

P

paD, pa'apaD bad, spoiled, wrecked

paDaj, pa'apDaj to be bad, spoiled

paDchud, pa'apDachud to take apart, wreck, spoil

paDchuda spoilage, wreckage

paDchudas to be in a spoiled or wrecked state

paDma, s- to be lazy

paDmaDag, s- laziness

paDt to spoil (food)

pahdo, papdo duck (Sp. pato)

pahl, papal religious leader (Sp. padre)
pahl wakon to baptize

pahla, papla shovel (Sp. palo)

pahn bread (Sp. pan)

pahntakuD oven

pako'ola ceremonial clown (Yaqui Sp. pascola)

pal-mihdo palomino (Sp. palomino)

pal-mihdog/pal-mihdodag, s- to be palamino colored

pa-nahl bee (Sp. panal)
pa-nahl sitol honey

pa-nihdo handkerchief (Sp. pañuelito)

pa-nohji unrefined sugar (Sp. panoche)

papa-lohdi windmill (Sp. papa-lote)

paplo pigeon (Sp. paloma)

pasam to see the town, look around (Sp. pasar)

pasamameD, pasamop to go to (see the) town

pas-tihl baked goods (Sp. pastel)

paw-lihna godfather (Sp. padrino)

pa-yahso, papa-yayaso clown (Sp. payaso)

pegih okay, well then

pehegi, s- to be easy

pehegia supposed to be

pehegim easily

pen trying to remember

pi not (substitutes for s-)

pia'a no

piach (Pima) see pi and ha'ichug

piast celebration, (Sp. fiesta) e piast to celebrate

piastameD, piastop to go to a celebration

pi'ajeD from nowhere

piha huhugedam never ending

pi has nothing

pihba, pipba pipe (Sp. pipa)

pihgo, pipgo pick (Sp. pico)

pihhun (pihhush) to get off work

pihk chu'ig to make a mistake

pihkchul, pipikchul/pigchul picture (Eng.)

pihkchulid to take a picture of

pihk elid to be concerned for

pihk elidaDag concern

pihlas pear (Sp. peras)

pihlosim, s- to be pear shaped

pihnia fine toothed comb (Sp. piña)

pihnto, pipinto spotted (Sp. pinto)

pihntog/pihntoDag, s- to be spotted

pihsh dollar (Sp. peso)

pi'ichud to dare, endure, undergo

pilin, piplin bridle, bit (Sp. freno)

pilkani wheat

pilsa, pipilsa blanket (Sp. frazada)

pion workman (Sp. peon)

Pi O'owik "Not Pretty" village

pisal linear measure

pisalt to weigh (Sp. pesar)

pisaltakuD scales

pisin species of animal

Pisin Mo'o Pisinemo Village

pis-tohl, pipis-totol pistol (Sp. pistola)

plahnja, plalanja to iron (Sp. plancha)

plahnjakuD iron

plahda silver (Sp. plata)

plohmo lead (Sp. plomo)

poDnim, s- with thumps

poDoni, popoDoni to thump

poshol, popsho'ol boiled food (Sp. Az. posole)

potol   bronc (Sp. potrillo)

pot-liia, pot-lilia   pasture
(Sp. potrero)

pualt, pupualt   door (Sp. puerta)

puhl   pool (Eng.)

puhlo   cigar (Sp. puro)

puhst (Pima)   saddle (Sp. fuste)

puindi, pupuindi   bridge (Sp.
puente)

puiwlo, pupuiwlo   city (Sp.
pueblo)

S

s-   prefix affirming a condition
or attribute

sahgo, sasago   blouse, sweater
(Sp. saco)

sahnto, sasanto   religious
picture, image (Sp. santo)

sahnto kih   Catholic Church

sahwano, sasawano   bedsheet
(Sp. sábana)

sahyo, sasayo   rival (Sp.
adversario)

sal-tihn   frying pan (Sp. sartén)

San Migil   San Miguel village

S-auppagk   Florence

S-chuchkk   "The Black" village

S-chuchuligk   "Many chickens"
village (Gunsight)

S-chuk Do'ag   Black Mountain
district

sha, sha'al   if, sort of, a bit

sha'aDk   forked, to be forked

sha'aDkad (sha'aDkai)   to make
forked

sha'aligi, shashaligi   forked
brace for carrying basket

sha'alk   ravine saddle between
mountain peaks

sha'awai   to buy from

shab   to splash

shag wepo   "seems like"

shags   injection, shots

Shah!   Get along dogey!

Shah-   see has

shahchu   see haschu

shahd (shai, shashda)   to herd,
drive herd

shahda   herd, drove

shahD   wild potato

shahgid, shahshagid,
sha'ashagid   between, among

shahgig, shahshgig   canyon,
ravine

shahk (shashku)   to palm

shahkch   to have in the palm

shahkim   halter (Sp. jáquima)

shahko/hasko   which side

shahmt   adobe brick

shahmud (shashamud)   to shoo,
shake off

shahmug   to shake

shahmuni   to make a sound,
rustle

shahmunim, s-   noisily

shahshagid   to mix,

shahshani   to groan

shahwaidag   fibers in plant stalk
used for ropemaking

shahwai   Saturday (Sp. sábado)

sha'i   grass, brush, waste

sha'i   a bit

sha'ichud, shasha'ichud   to
hang up

sha'ichuda   hanging things

shajkon   to scrape, to chip off

shajkona   object chipped

shakal, shashkal   side by side

shakalwua to stagger

shaliw, shashaliw trousers (Sp. jaripero)

shapij oblong

shapijk to be oblong, also a species of squash

Shapijk White Horse Pass

shapol, sha'ashpol aspherical

shapolk to be aspherical

shapolkad (shapolkai) to make aspherical

shashani blackbird

shashawk to echo

shashkad mirage

shaw to rattle

shawaD, sha'ashwaD thick around

shawaDk to be thick around

shawaDkahim to become thick

shawaDkam thickly

shawant to look for stock

shawantameD, shawantop to go for stock

shawikuD, shashawikuD rattle

shawoni, shashawoni soap (Sp. jabón)

shawonimad to soap

shegoi greasewood, creosote bush

shehpij, sheshepij younger brother, cousin

sheh'e, shesh'e wolf

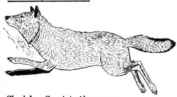

Shehl Seri tribesman

shehlwua to practice shooting

shehmachud to act boldly

shel permission, license, directly

sheliki, shesheliki prairie dog

shelikam noDa/wohokam noDa to panic, get frightened

shelin (shelsh), sheshelin (sheshelsh), i to straighten

shelina arrow shaft

shelini, shehshelini to be straight

shelinim, s- straight

shoak, shoani (shosha) to cry shoshakid to cause to cry

shobbiaD, shoshobaD doll

shohba, shoshoba joint, hip

shohbid (shoshbid) to hinder, forbid

shohm, shohshom to sew something

shohmjelid to sew something for someone

shohni to knock

shoh'o, shosho'o grasshopper

shohwua to blow the nose

shoiga, shoshoiga domestic animal, pet, to have an animal

sho'ig to be poor

sho'igchud to impoverish cause to suffer, humble

sho'igchuda cause of poverty

sho'igchudaDag ill fortune

sho'igdag suffering, poverty

sho'igkam the poor

shomaig (shoshomaig) to catch cold

shomaigchud to give a cold

shomaigig a cold

shomaigkam cold victim

shon, shohshon beginning, foundation, spring
  Al Shohshon Little Springs (Arizona)
  Shon Oidag Springfield (Sonoita)

shonchk, shoniak to chop down

shonchki war club, tomahawk

shonchkwua, shonchshulig to hit something away by hand

shonchud, shohshonchud to start it

shongam spring fed pond

shoniak see shonchk

shoniggan to box, punish

shonigiwul, shoshonigiwul racing ball

shonihin to hammer

shonihinakuD hammer

shonikon to strike with something, to beat

shoniwikuD pestle

shoniwin to pound

shoniwina pounded stuff

shontal soldier (Sp. soldado)

shontpag to pound, knock, rap

shonwua, shohshonwua to start, begin

shonwuichud, shohshonwuichud to cause to start

sho'owa bullsnake

shopolk, sho'oshpolk short, to be

shopolkad (shopolkai) to shorten

shopolkahim to become short

shopolkchu short one

shopolkdas to be shortened

shosha nasal discharge

shoshagi crying

shoshkdag nostril

shuhd, shuhshud to be full

shuhdad, shuhshud to fill

shuhdagi liquid, to be liquid

shuhg, shushug mocking bird

shuhshk, shushushk shoe

shuh'uwaD plant

shulig see gehsh

shuwijul, shushuwijul saddle blanket (Sp. sudadero)

S-huhu'ujuDk suburb of Santa Rosa, see hujuD

S-hukagk Prescott, place of pines, see huk

si very, really, real, true
si cheoj real man
si meD really running

siakam hero, one who has endured

siant hundred (Sp. ciento)

siawog danger (obscure)

si'al east, early
si'alidgio, si'al tahgio eastward

si'alig morning, dawn

si'alim tomorrow, early

S-i'owi Shuhdagi Sweet Water village

sidolim coiled

sigal, sisgal cigarette (Sp. cigarillo)

sihbani to drizzle, sprinkle

sihchkwua, sihchshulig to hook and toss

sihki white-tailed deer

sihkon/sihmun to hoe, mash

sihl, sisil saddle (Sp. silla)

sihl at back of saddle

Sihl Mek "Burnt Saddle" Village

sihl mo'o saddle horn

Sihl Naggiak "Saddle Hanging" Village

sihnju cinch (Sp. cincho)

sihngo five (Sp. cinco)

sihowin/sihon to stir, scrape, scratch, dig out

sihs older brother, sister, cousin

sihshp (sihsh, sihshshap) to nail, pin

40

sihsh, sisish elbow; to fasten, nail

sihskid to sift

sihskidakuD sifter

sihwoda topknot of bird

si'i (sih, sisi, sih'i) to suck, nurse

si'ichud to nurse the young

Si'ihe Older Brother, I'itoi

si'ikuD baby bottle

si'ishpakuD pin

sijkid to rattle something

sikol, si'iskol circle, to be circular

Sikol Himadk Whirlpool Village

sikolkad (sikolkai) to make circular

sikolkahim to become circular

sil-wihsa beer (Sp. cervesa)

simito, sismito bun

simuDkaj, si'ismuDkaj to grimace

sinot, sisinot eligible girl (Sp. senorita)

sin-tahwo cent (Sp. centavo)

sini'ulga internal pain

sini'ulwua to get an internal pain

sipshuD to cause to exude

sipuD, si'ispuD bent at the hips
  sipuDk si'ispuDk to be bent over at the hips
  sipuD daha to be squatting
  sipuD kehk to be stooping

sipuk cardinal

sipulk, si'ispulk to be piled

sipulkad (sipulkai) to pile

sipuni to break open and exude fluid

sisi'almad each morning

sishwua to bump the elbow

siskul (kohadk) mouse

siswua to spit

siswuaDag saliva

siswuamad to spit upon

sitol syrup

siw bitter; to be bitter

Siw Oidag Chekshani Bitter Field District

si-wahyo barley (Sp. cebada)

siwani chief

siwani mahkai chief medicine man

Siwani Wa'akih Casa Grande Ruin

siwat, siswat goat (Sp. chivato)

siwat huhch crowbar

siweg to simmer

siwol onion (Sp. cebolla)

siwulogi, si'isiwulogi/si'isiwulig dust-devil, twister

sohla pop (Sp. soda)

sohba soup (Sp. sopa)

stohta u'uhig white bird species

Stotonigk Many Ants Suburb of Santa Rosa, also Pima village

T

t- us, our

taD, tahtaD foot

taDai roadrunner

taDan (tahtaD, tahtDan) to spread

taDani, tatDani, s- to be wide

taDanihhim to become wide

taDanim, s- widely

TaD Memel 'Footrunner' Village

taDgew to have a twitch of the foot

taDgid to shake the foot

tahabidam species of bird

tahchulid to reach, cause to touch

tahgio, ta'atagio before, in the direction, in the way
juhpin/wi'inim tahgio north
wakoliw tahgio south
si'ali tahgio east
huDuni/kuiwa tahgio west

tahhadag, s- to be interesting
s-ap tahhadag to be enjoyable
pi ap tahhadag to be unenjoyable

tahhadam, s- enjoyably

tahhadkam emotion, one with emotions
s-ap tahhadkam happiness, happy one
pi ap tahhadkam sadness, sad one

tahni (tai) to ask something of someone

tahp to be split

tahpan (tapsha) to split something

tahsa, tatsa cup (Sp. taza)

tahtami tooth

tahtam (tattam) to touch, feel

tahtk to feel emotion
s-ap tahtk to feel happy
ab i e-tahtk to become wholesome

tahtko jaw

tahtshakuD / gaswuikuD comb, splitter

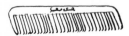

tahwlo, tatawlo border (Sp. tabla)

tai/giumudam match, fire

taiwig, tataiwig firefly

ta'i back, up, East

ta'ibim (ta'ibij) to pass around

ta'ihim to rise in and fill

Ta'ik/Sihl Mek 'Upper' Village (Gila Bend Village)

ta'iwush to come out

tako yesterday
D hema tako day before yesterday

takui yucca leaves

talwin to make rope

tamal tamale (Sp. tamal)

tamblo, tatamblo drum (Sp. tambor)

tamhaig, s- to reject

tamhain to have 'teeth set on edge' with bitter taste

tamiam (Pima) to wait for

tamko stick for gathering organ pipe cactus fruit

tamsh gums

tapaho, tatpaho blinder (Sp. tapaojo)

tapahoDad to put blinders on

tapial, tatpial paper (Sp. papel)

tash/ge'eho a long time

tash, tatsh sun, day, time, timepiece

tash mahhad four o'clock flower

tasho clear, clearly, to be clear

tashogid to clarify, explain

tashogida clarification, illustration

tashogidas to be clarified

tatai   tendon

tatal   mother's younger brother or cousin

tataniki   thunder and lightning

tatchua   to need or want
 si tatchui   to love

tatchui   the will, needed or loved things

tatchuidag   need, love, desire

tatk   roots

tatkpig   to remove roots

tatshagi   medicinal plant, bursage, burroweed

ta-wahgo/tawago   tobacco (Sp. tabaco)

tiampo   time (Sp. tiempo)

tianna, titianna/chiando   store (Sp. tienda)

tihna   tub

ti-kihla, nawait   wine (Sp. tequila)

Tiko-lohdi   "Owl" Village (Sp. Az. tecolote) ChukuD Kuk

ti-lahndi, titi-lalandi   suspenders (Sp. tirantes)

tlahmba, tlalamba   tramp

tlohgih, tlologih   truck (Sp. troque)

toa/wi-yohdi   oak

toahim   to thunder

to'a (toa, to'aw)   to pour

to'ahim   to pile along

to'akch   to have something piled

tobaw, totbaw   species of hawk

todkesh   to jerk with fright

todsid   to frighten

toDk, totoDk   to snore, growl

toha, tohta, s-   white, to be white, dime

Toha Bidk   "White Clay" Village

tohajid   to whiten

tohajidakuD   whitening, face powder

tohawes   "Brittlebush"

tohbi, totobi   rabbit, cottontail rabbit

tohlo, totolo   bull (Sp. toro)

tohmog/tohmug   milky way

tohn, tohton   knee

tohnk, to'otonk   dike, bank, dam

tohnkad (tohnkai)   to dike

tohnkdas   diked

tohnto, totonto   degenerate, perverted

tohntodag   to be degenerate, perverted

tohono   desert/Pima:south

Tohono O'odham   The Desert People (Papago)

tohwa, totowa   turkey (Sp. tova)

tohwush, totowush   handkerchief

to'id   to bet

toka   women's field hockey
 e toka   to play field hockey

tokaio, totkaio   namesake (Sp. tocayo)

tokih   cotton, string

tokihtuD, totkihtuD   spider or web

toliant, totoliant   to aggrevate

tondam, s-   brilliant

tonhain (tonhaish)   to crush with knee

toni, s-   heat, to be hot

toniabkam summer

tonihhim to become hot

toniko, s- in the heat

tonim, s- hotly

tonjig, s- fever

tonlid to shine on, light up

tonlig light

tonlig s- to be light

tonoD (tohonnoD) to shine, twinkle

tonomk, tonkk to get thirsty

tonomdag thirst

tonomchud to make thirsty
ta tonomma, s- to be thirst causing

tonwua, tohtonwua to kneel

to'olwadag cactus fruit dried on the plant

topdam race or hunt caller

topidk, to'otopidk, s- askew, to be askew

toskon to swell

tosi'igo (Pima) bacon (Sp. tocino)

Totoguani Eastern Papago dialect

totoni ant

totpk to boil

totpsid to boil something

totshagi foam

tuhlko, tutulko Jew (Sp. turco)

U

u'a to carry

u'apa (u'apaD) to bring

uDawhag cattail

ugijid to shake

uhDwis grape (Sp. uvas)

uhg, u'ug high, chief, to be high

uhgahim to go up

uhgchu, u'ugchu a higher up, highest, headman

uhimal "Cowkiller", a black bug that plays dead

uhksh, u'uksh calf of the leg

uhksha, u'uksha windbreak

uhli, u'uli rubber (Sp. hule)

uhmug species of yucca used for woven basketry

uhpaD, u'upaD catclaw

uhpam/uhhum back to a previous place, back home

uhs, u'us tree, bush, stick, crutch

Uhs Kehk/Chukma Shuhdagi Tree Standing/Blackwater

uhsh, u'ush insect stinger, arrow point

uhug/ukijid to notch an arrow or stick

uhw, s- to be odorous

uhwalig odor

Uhwalig Mashad odor month, February

uhwo to stop giving off odor

u'i see behi

u'ihim to go gathering

u'imeD, u'iop to go to get things

u'imk, s- to want to get things

ujigid, u'ujigid to rock or shake something

ulin (uh'ulin) to hold something thing out
ab ulini to be skilled

ulinch to hold

ulinid, uh'ulinid to hold something out for someone

uliñihogid (uh'ulinihogid) to give rest, take rest

ulinihogig rest

ulugid to toss a baby

um, u'um thigh

umwua to bump the thigh

usaga, u'usaga toka stick, gavel

usagakam, u'usagakam toka player, presiding officer, judge

ushabi pitch, resin

ushabiDag to have pitch, resin

uskon to scoop, fork, gore

uskonakuD scoop, fork

utko soapweed stalk

utko jehj soapweed

u'u (Pima) rifle shell, war arrow

u'u (see behe)

u'uwhig bird

u'ukch (see bekch)

u'umhaiDad to finish an arrow

uwi, u'uwi woman

uwiga, u'uwiga sister, cousin

uwikwuaD sissy

uwikwuaDag to be a sissy

uwio to pass gas

uwpio, u'uwpio skunk

uwpio, u'uwpio tree species

W

Wa'a-kih Pima village site

wabsh/wash/hash just

wabshaba but

wachiho wooden bowl (Sp. batihoja)

wachki charco, pond

wachumukdam small black water bird

wachumk, wachkk to drown, become submerged

wachwih, e to swim, bathe self

wadadk, wa'apdadk shiny, bald, to be

waDag, s- to be wet

waDagi juice

waDagid to wet

wag, wahpag hole

wagima, wapagima, s- to be industrious

wagimam, wapagimam, s- industriously

wahawua, wahshulig to remove remove, take off

wahg (wapga) to moisten

wahga cement, dough

wahk (wapke, wahki), wahpk (wapke, wahpki) to enter

Wahk San Xavier (where water sinks in)

wahkid to put in, bring in
  ab wahkid to clothe someone with something

wahkidalig (Pima) coat, jacket, sweater

wahks to be in

wahks, wahpaks rug, floor-mat

wahl rifle shell (Sp. bala)

wahldi, wapaldi bucket (Sp. balde)

wahlko, wapalko boat (Sp. barco)

wahm/wahn rather, the more so, further

wahmud, i to stir up, prod

wahmug mosquito

wahn ohg/wajelho whiptail lizzard

wah'o cactus rib tongs

wah'osid to get wedged

wahpai container for game of ginsi

wahpai saguaro cactus rib

wahpk bamboo, cane, reeds

wahso, wapso can (Sp. vaso)

wahuD, s- to sweat

wahuDdag sweat

wahuDdag, s- to be sweaty

wahulchud s- to cause to
sweat

wahw father term of wahwgam
sib

wahwgam members of a sib of
buzzard moiety

wahyog/wahyoDag, s- to be
yellow-brown

waid to call, invite

waida calling

waidaDag invitation

waik, wa'awaik three

waikka, wapaikka ditch

waila, e to dance (Sp. baile)

wailadag dance

wailakuD dance floor

wainomi metal, iron, knife
aj wainomi telephone
aj wainommad to telephone

Wainomi Wohg "Railroad"
Town (Casa Grande)

waiwel cockleburr

Waiw Wo'o "Cockleburr Pond"
village

wa'i only

wa'ig to get water, liquid

wa'igameD, wa'igop to go to
get liquid

wa'igi possessed liquid

wa'igid to get liquid for someone

wa'igkuD vessel for liquid

wajelho, wapjelho/wahn ohg
whiptail lizzard

wakaig, wapkia'ig mud hen

wakch to soak something in

wak'e to milk

wakial, wapkial cowboy (Sp.
vaquero)

wakimagi, s- to be worn

wakimagihhim to wear out

wako, wapko water gourd,
canteen

wakola flood debris

wakoliw south

wakon to wash
pahl wakon to baptize

wakoni baptized one, washed
thing

wakuichud to cause diarrhea

wakuidag diarrhea

walaho (Pima) to play cards
(Sp. barajo)

walin, waplin barrel (Sp.
barril)

walit digging bar (Sp. barrote)

wamaD, wahammaD snake
chuk wamaD Blue racer
wegi wamaD Red racer

wamig (wahammig), wahpamig
to rise

wamigid, wahpamigid to raise

Wamul Vamori Village

wanchk, wanikumiak to pull off

wanchkwua, wanchshulig to
pull along, draw in

wanimeD to lead, guide

wanimeDdam leader

wani'on to pull on

wanjel, wapanjel flag (Sp.
bandera)

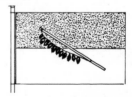

"wan-nihha"/wan-dihha　pan
　(Sp. bandeja)

wantsh　to rip

wapshuD　blister

was　to dip liquid

washa　covered basket, suit-
　case

washai　grass

Washai Gak/Gakidag Mashad
　dry grass month, September

washomi　large grain storage
　basket

wasib　a drink

wasibid　to give a drink

wasibwua　to mix by dipping
　and pouring

watksh　sand lizzard

watopi, waptopi　fish, worm

watopi hidoD　sardines,
　salmon

watto, waptto　arbor

wa'uch　to wet

wa'udag, s-　to be damp

wa'ug　straw, stalks, chaff

wa'usig, s-　to be damp

waw　rock, cliff

Waw Giwulk　Constricted Rock
　Mountain (Baboquivari)

Waw Giwulk chekshani　Con-
　stricted Rock District

wawini　to quench thirst

wawinig, s-　to be thirst
　quenching

wawli　trunk, valice (Sp. baúl)

wawnaDag　ridgepole, line,
　straight

wawnim　row, verse

wawhia/wahia, waipia　well

Wawhia Chini　"Well Mouth"
　Village

wawuk, wawpuk　racoon

wechij, wepchij　new, young

wechijhim　to become new

wechijid　to make new

wecho, wepcho/we'ewecho
　under

wechodag　underclothing

wechokam　underling

wegi, wepegi, s-　red, to be
　red

wegi/het　red clay

Wegi Akimel　Colorado River

wegihhim　to become red

wehgaj, we'ewegaj/wehbig
　around, behind

wehch　(see kahch)

wehch, s-　to be heavy

wehchihhim　to become heavy

wehchdag　weight

wehhejeD, we'ewejeD　on
　behalf of

wehhejeDkam　benefit, purpose,
　use

wehm, we'ewem　with

wehmaj　to be with

wehmt, i　to help

wehmtaDag, i　help

wehmkal　totemic helper,
　group emblem

wehmkam/wehmjim　companion

wehnad　with something, to be
　with, to put with

wehnag, wepnag　brother, sis-
　ter, cousin

wehnags　to be with

wehoh　(see wohoh)

wehpeg　first

wehpegkam　the first

wehs　all

wehschu, wepschu
　possessions

wehsig　mentally normal
　pi wehsig　feebleminded

wehsij　all of

wehsko　everywhere

wehskojeD from everywhere

wenog/eDa then, at that time

wepegih lightning, battery, flashlight, moving picture

e wepegid to go to moving picture

wepegih kanjel electric lights

wepo, we'eppo even with, equal to, same as, at the same time

i wepot to do the same as, imitate

wepodag, s- to be level

wepodagim, s- evenly

wepogid to level, compare

west-mahm ten

wewa'ak, wepwa'ak seven

weweg to whirr

wewegim loudly (whirring)

wewkuD sling, bullroarer

wha-mihlia family (Sp. familia)

wia to leave something

wia (wipia, wia'i), s- to ruin, wear out
wias, s- to be worn

wialos Friday (Sp. viernes)

wiapo pubic hair of male

wiapogel/wiapoi, wiapo'oge'el/wipiop boy

wiDut (wipiDut) to swing or wave something

wiha, wihpia penis

wihb milk

wihbam milkweed, gum of milkweed

wihdakuD/wihdagikuD upper grinding stone

wihgi pinfeathers and down of bird

wihgida a ceremony

wihkol, wipikol great grand-parent generation (wihshaD in ko-lohdi dialect)

wihnam, s- difficultly

wihnim, wipinim singer in wihgida ceremony

wihnk, s- difficult, to be difficult

wihni (wihp, wihpin) to suck, lick with tongue

wihnui whiskey (Sp. vino)

wihog bean pod

wihogdag to be podded

wihol peas

wihonagi, s- to be tangled, matted

wihot (wipiot) to vomit

wihos vomit

wihoschud to cause to vomit

wihpdo testicle

wihpdopig to castrate

wihshaD, wipishaD great grandchild generation (wihkol in ko-lohdi dialect)
wipshbaD ancestors

wi'i (wih, wipi, wih'i) to stay

wi'ichkwua, wi'ichshulig to be blown about

wi'idag, wihpi'idag leftovers

wi'ihin to erode

wi'ikam, wipikam remnant

wi'ikon to wash away, erode something
wi'inog water borne object

wi'in to carry away in a current

wi'indag flood

wi'inim, wipinim/juhpin north

wi'is to be remaining

wi'ishani, wipishani small wash

wijin to twist rope

wijin, s- to be wrinkled

wijina rope

wikla   to owe

wikladag   debt

wi-nahl   vinegar (Sp. vinaro)

wintani, wipintani   window
(Sp. ventana)

wio-lihn   violin (Sp. violín)

wipnhoD/wipnoi   Christmas
cholla, edible buds

wipia   a hunt, to hunt

wipiameD, wipiop   to go to
hunt

wipiamdam   hunter

wipih   nipple

wipismal   hummingbird

wipsh   species of wasp, hornet
hornets

wishag, wipshag/wisag   chicken hawk

wisilo, wipsilo   calf (Sp.
becerro)

wisit   to visit (Sp. visitar)

wi'ushawig   sand ripples

wiw   wild tobacco

wiwa (wiwaj)   pancreas

Wiwpul   "Wild Tobacco"
Village

wi-yohdi/toa   oak

wo/ho   will (future)

wogsha   quiver

wohd (woi, wopda)   to lay
something down, sign

wohda, wopda   boot (Sp. bota)

wohdch   to have something
laying

wohg, wopog   road, path

Wohg HuDunk   "Road Dip"
Village

wohgid   to instruct

wohgida   instructions

wohiw   to singe

wohk, wohpk   belly
wokshch (wokshp)   to hold on
the belly

wohlih   hornless or dehorned

wohlim, s-   to be close crop-
ped

wohni (wohp, wohpon)   to pluck,
to pick or harvest beans

wohoh/wehoh   to be true, truly

wohochud   to believe

wohochuda   belief

wohochudaDag   faith

wohochuddam   believer

wohokam   truth

wohokamchud   to testify,
prove true

wohpo   see meD

wohpo'ichud   see melchud

wohppo'id   to deprive of, take
away from

wohshag, wopshag   pocket
(Sp. bolsa)

woikchud, wopoikchud, e
to boast, show off

woikima, wopoikima, s-   to be
boastful, proud

woiwis, wopoiwis   ox (Sp.
bueyes)

wo'i   see mel

wo'ihim   to move in prone
position

wo'ikuD, wohpikuD   bed

wo'inam   see melnam

wo'iwua, wohpiwua   to lie
down, of water lying flat in
large area

wokijid   to shake self

wonami, wopnami   hat

wo'o   natural pond

wo'o, wohp, wo'owop   to be
lying

wo'olakhim/woshdakhim to trot

wo'oshani floodland

wo'otk valley

wopo body hair, fur

wopopig to remove hair or fur

wosho, wopsho rat

wosk, wopsi father's father, or his brother or cousin

wosk oks, wosk o'oks father's father's sister or cousin

wosmaD, wopsmaD a man's son's child

wosma je'e, wopsmaD ha-je'e a man's daughter-in-law, a woman's father-in-law

wosun to sweep

wosunakuD/woskuD broom, brush

wotalt to vote (Sp. votar)

wotonDad to button

wotoni, woptoni button (Sp. boton)

wowoit, woipit father's younger sister or cousin

wua (wuhpa, wua'i) to lay something down, throw away
heb huh wua to lose something

wua (juh, jujju, juhni, juhnk) hab to do, make
nahnko wua to ridicule

wuaga girl's adolescent ceremony

wuagameD, wuagop to go to a wuaga, to pass on

wuagdam young people of endurance chosen as performers for wihgida ceremony

wuagid to perform a wuaga

wuandi, wupandi glove (Sp. guante)

wuD to be

wuhan, wuhpan to awaken someone

wuhD (wupDa) to rope

wuhlid to rope for

wuhi, wuhpui eye

wuhiga, wuhpuiga glasses

wuhigew to have a twitch of the eye

wuhigid to blink, raise eyebrows

wuhiosha, wupiosha face, mask

wuhlu/wuhlo, wuplo donkey, bench (Sp. burro)

wuhlo ki'iwia oatmeal

wuhshad, wuhasid to bring out, deliver

wuhshani, wuwhag, (wushke) to exit

wuhshanig plant life

Wuhshkam emergent Piman ancestors

wui, wu'uwui to, toward

wuichud to cause to come to

wuichuda running ball game

wuichwig sty

wuijid, hab to do for

wuikam something coming to

wuikon to glance at

wuipo eye lashes

wulim, wuhplim bale, bundle

wulkuD, wuplkuD cradleboard

wulshch to have tied

wulshp to tie, trap, restrict, apply brakes

wulshpakuD trap, brake

wulshpi to be tied

wulwega grass target

wul'ok (wupl'ok) to untie

wupaj   yucca shoots

wupiostakuD   tall purple flowering plant producing eye allergy

wuschkwua   to blow away

wusot   to blow on, treat disease, cleanse

wusota   treatment, cleansing
 s-chu wusotadag   to be able to heal

Y

yahnda, yayanda   tire (Sp. llanta)

yahwi, yayawi   key, lock (Sp. llave)

yahwiDad   to lock

yahwiDag   to be locked

yehwa   yoke (Sp. yugo)

yehwaDad   to yoke

yehwaDag   to be yoked

Yuhmi   Yuma tribesman

yuhngih   anvil, rail splitter

yuhs   to use

ENGLISH-
PAPAGO & PIMA

Milgahn-O'odham

a, an, other <u>hema</u>

abandon, to <u>ohhod, s-</u>

abdomen <u>wohk, wohpk</u>

able, to be <u>nakog, e</u>

accept, to <u>hohho'id, s; beihim,</u>
<u>u'u</u>

accident, calamity <u>neijig, s-</u>

accompany, follow, to <u>oid</u>

accounting, counting <u>kuinta</u>

accuse of, to <u>abchud,</u>
<u>chu'ichigchud, mohto'id</u>
accusation <u>abchudaDag</u>
accused, to be <u>abchudas</u>

ache or hurt, to <u>ko'ok, s-</u>

acre <u>ahgeli</u> (Sp. acre)

acrid or bitter <u>siw</u>

acrobat <u>ma-lohma</u>(Sp.maroma)

across, <u>gahi, gahghai</u>
to be laying across <u>gahiobs</u>

across, opposite <u>aigo, a'ai</u>
from across <u>aigojeD, a'aijeD</u>

address, proclaim <u>amog</u>

adobe, mud, clay <u>bid</u>
to go to get adobe <u>bidameD,</u>
<u>bidop</u>

adult <u>ge'e, ge'egaD</u>

afraid, to be <u>ehbid, s-</u>

after, following <u>oij, o'oij</u>

afternoon <u>im hab i juhk, gam</u>
<u>huh i juhk</u>

again, also <u>ehp, ep, epai</u>

aggrevate, to <u>toliant</u>

ahead <u>ba'ich, bab'aich</u>
to go ahead <u>ba'iwech</u>

alcoholic <u>i'imkam, s-</u>
to be alcoholic <u>i'imk, s-</u>

alert, to be <u>neandag, s-</u>

algae, scum <u>mamtoD</u>

all, every <u>wehs</u>

allow, to <u>hiwigid</u>

allow, make room for, to
<u>jegelid</u>

almost <u>chum alo</u>

alone, self <u>hejel, hehe'ejel</u>

alone, by itself <u>hejelko; chu'iko</u>

already <u>heki huh</u>

also, again <u>ehp, ep, epai</u>

always, anytime <u>chum hekid</u>

ambulance <u>kok'odam ha kalit</u>

among, between <u>shahgid,</u>
<u>sha'ashagid</u>

amuse, to <u>tahhadchud, s-</u>

ancestors <u>kekelbaD; wipshbaD</u>

ancient <u>hekihukam</u>

and <u>kch, k, ch</u>

anger <u>bagatalig</u>
anger, to <u>bagachud</u>

angel <u>dahm kahchim o'odham</u>

anglo, non-Indian <u>mil-gahn</u>
(Sp. americano)

angry, to be <u>s-baga</u>

animal <u>ha'ichu doakam; shoiga;</u>
<u>doajkam</u>

annex <u>ku'inhogida</u>

annex, to <u>ku'inhogid</u>

ant   totoni; kuadagi; ku'ukchul u'umam

antelope (pronghorned)   kuhwid, kukuwid

antlers, horns   a'ag
  to clean antlers, horns   mo'owin

anus, bottom, back of saddle   at

anyone   chum heDai

anything   chum haschu

anytime, always   chum hekid

anyway, either way   chum ha'sko

anywhere   chum hasko; chum hebai

Apache   Ohb

appear, to   wuhshani; mahsihim

appear as, to   hab mahs

apple   mani-sahna (Sp. mansana)

appoint, cause to stand, to   kehsh, chuhcha

arbor   watto, waptto

arm or hand   nowi, nohnhowi

armpit   hek
  to hold under the arm   hekshch

around, to be   bijims

around, to go   bijim, bibijim

arrive, to   jiwia, dada

arrive running, to   mel, wo'i

arrival   jiwhiaDag

arrow   hapot, hahapot/u'u

arrowhead   uhsh, u'ush

arrowshaft   shelina; hihwshana

arrow, to make   hapott; ho'o-mat; u'umhaiDad; a'anchud

arrowweed   che'ul

arroyo   aki, a'aki

arthritic, stiff   mahniko

as, like   hab masma
  as far as   ha'asko
  as many as   ha'akia
  as many times as   ha'akio
  as much as   ha'as

ashamed or self-conscious, to be   elid, e

ashes   matai

ask something of someone, to   tahni

askew, to be askew   topidk, to'otopidk, s-

aspherical, to be aspherical   shapolk, sha'ashpolk
  to make aspherical   shapolkad

at, there   abai, ab

at this point, here, now   i

audible, to be, to be loud   kaidag, s-

aunt   oksi; wowoit; dahd; jisk

awake from faint or death, think   chegitog, chechegitog, e

awaken someone, to   wuhan

awl for basketry   owij

axe   hahsa, hahasa (Sp. hacha)

avenge   agwua , e

B

baby, child   ahli, a'al

baby bottle   si'ikuD
baby boy   sulij
bachelor, widow   hejel wi'ikam

back oh, o'o

back in, way in chuhko

back to its place uhpam/uhhum

back, shell komi, kohkomi

back, up, East ta'i

backbone eDa wa'ug

bacon tosi'igo (Pima, Sp. tocino)

bad, spoiled paD, pa'apaD
  to be bad, spoiled paDaj, pa'apDaj

badger kahw, kakaw

bag kostal, kokstal (Sp. costal)

bake, to pahnt

baked goods pas-tihl (Sp. pastel)

baking powder koshoDkdakuD

bald or shiny, to be wadadk, wa'apdadk

bale, bundle, team wulim, wuhplim

ball bohl (Eng.)

ballooned or puffed up, to be koshoDk
  to become ballooned koshoDkahim

bamboo wahpk

banana, yucca fruit howij

band kuhudam

bandana monjel, momonjel (Sp. mantel)

bank, dyke tohnk, to'otonk

bank, forehead koa, koka

baptize, to pahl wakon
  baptized one wakoni

bar, stand kan-tihna (Sp. cantina)

barbed wire wainomi kolhai

bark, skin, husk, peel eldag, e'eldag
  to remove bark, peel elpig

bark or yell, to hihnk
  to bark at or yell at hihnko'id

barley si-wahyo (Sp. cebada)

barrel walin, waplin (Sp. barril)

base, foundation shon, shohshon

basket giho; hashDa, hahashDa; hoa, hoha; washa; washomi

basketry plant wahs

bat nanakumal

bathe or swim, to e wachwih

battery, flashlight, lightning wepegih

battle, war, fight cheggiadag

battle, to cheggia checheggia

battle, to carry on cheggiahim

battle antic kapaDwua

battlefield or weapon cheggiakuD

battleship cheggiakuD wahlko

bayonet chu'aggaD, s-

be, to wuD

beach shuhdagi hugid

beads baiuga; osal, o'osal (Sp. rosario)

beak, bone oh'o

beam (center) che-tonDag

beans muhni
  red gambling beans bahwui
  tapery beans bawi
  lima beans hawol
  black-eyed beans huhuDa-wuhpkam; u'us-bawi (Pima)

bear juDumi, jujuDumi

bear, to beichug; hohagchug;
u'a

bear a child, to maDtahim

bear grass moho

beard eshpo

beast ha'ichu doakam

beat, to shonikon

beautiful, good kehg, keheg, s-
to be beautiful, good kehgaj,
kehegaj, s-
to beautify, fix, assemble
kegchud

beaver kohwih, kokowih
(Pima)

because, therefore heg hekaj;
n ____ pi

bed wo'ikuD, wohpikuD

bedsheet sahwano, sasawano
(Sp. sábana)

bee pa-nahl (Sp. panal)

beer sil-wihsa

before, beyond ba'ich,
bab'aich

before, in front of bahsho,
babsho

before, in the direction, in the
way tahgio, ta'atagio

beg, to neal
to go begging nealimeD,
nealop

beget, to alidt, a'alidt

begin, to i shonwua

beginning shon, shohshon

belch, to haDwuag

believe, to wohochud

belief wohochuda

believe in or obey, to wohog
elid, s-

believer wohochuddam

belittle pi ha'ichuchud

bell kampani, kakampani
(Sp. campanilla)

belly wohk, wohpk
to hold on the belly wokshch

belt, band, strap giwuD

bench, donkey wuhlo, wuplo

bend, to noDagid, nohnogid
to be bent, turned noDags

benefit wehhejeDkam

bent over sipuDk, si'ispuDk

berry ha'ichu bahidag

beside hugid-an

bet, to to'id, e

better ba'ich i s-kehgaj

between shahgid, shahshagid

bewitch, to hihoin

beyond, past, ahead ba'ich,
bab'aich

big, elder, chief ge'e,
ge'egeD

Big Dipper, crossed stick for
Saguaro harvest kuipaD,
kukuipaD

bill, debt wikladag

bind or trap, to wulshp

bird u'uwhig

birth mahsidag

bishop o-wihspla, o'o-wipispla
(Sp. obispo)

bit, bridle pilin, piplin
(Sp. freno)

bite, to ke'i (kei, kek'e, keh'i)

bitter, to be siw

black, to be chuk, s-

blacksmith hilio, hihilio
(Sp. herrero)

bladder hi'ushag

blame chu'ichig
to blame chu'ichigchud,
abchud

blanket pilsa pipilsa (Sp.
frazada)
saddle blanket shuwijul,
shushuwijul (Sp. sudadera)

bleed, to eh'eDpa

bless, to ho'ige'id (ho'ige'el)

blessing, kindness, mercy
ho'ige'idaDag

blind pi neadam, pi neneadam

blinder tapaho, tatpaho (Sp.
tapaojo)
to put blinders on tapahoDad

blink, to wuhigid; kupsh
(kupshap, kupshp)

blood eh'eD
blood vessels eDhaidag,
e'eDhaidag

bloom, to heotahim

blossoms heosig

blouse, sweater sahgo, sasago
(Sp. saco)

blow, to heweD
stop blowing heweto

blow about, to wi'ichkwua

blow away, to wuschkwua

blow nose, to shohwua

blow on, to hewkon

blue or green, to be
chehdagi, chehedagi, s-
to be sky-blue luhyag, s-
(Sp. grulla)

blueing a-nihl (Sp. anillo)

blunt, to be chepelk, che'echpelk

board huk

boast or show off, to woikchud/
gimaihun, e

boastful or proud, to be
woikima/gimaima, s-

boat kanaho/wahlko (Sp. canoa
barco)

bobcat, wildcat gewho,
gegewho

body hon, hohon
to hit with body honhain
to push with body honchkwua

boil kawk hihwdag

boil, to totpk

boil something, to totpsid

bone, beak oh'o

bonnet kuku-luhji

book o'ohana

boot wohda, wopda (Sp. bota)

booty, gain, something taken
captive behi, u'i

border tahwlo (Sp. tabla)

born, begotten, come to light,to
mahsihim

boss ahmo, a'amo (Sp. amo)

bottle, glass li-mihda,
lil-mimida (Sp. limeta)

bound together, paired, to be wul

boundary, edge hugid, huhugid

bow, gun gaht, gahgt

bowl ha'a, haha'a

bowel hihih (hihij)
to rumble in the bowel koDog

bowl, wooden wachiho (Sp.
batihoja)

box, fort kahon, kakhon
(Sp. cajón)

box, to shonihiggan (shonihig-
gash)

boy wiapoi, wihpiop
baby boy sulij

brace for carrying basket sha'aligi

brag, show off, to gimaihun, e

braid hihtpaDag, hihitpaDag
to braid hihtpag

brain, nerve oaga, o'aga

brake, trap wulshpakuD

branch mamhaDag

brand or mark, to cheposid, chechposid

brand cheposig, chechposig

branding cheposida

branding iron cheposidakuD

bread pahn (Sp. pan)

break a horse mahshochud

break by bending mulin, ohmin
broken thing mulinig

break out in bumps hiwkahim

break open a blister, to habshuD

break open and exude fluid, to sipuni

break through maggat

breast, chest bahsho, babsho

breath, get out of ihbamk, ihbkk

breathe, to ihbheni
to take a breath ihbheiwua, i
to breathe convulsively i'ibtog

brick shahmt, ga'i shahmt

bridge puindi, pupuindi (Sp. puente)

bright mahs, s-

bridle, bit pilin, piplin (Sp. freno)

brilliant tondam, s-

bring, to u·apa

bring out or deliver, to wuhshad, wuhasid

brittle bush tohawes

bronco potol (Sp. potrillo)

broom, brush wosunakuD, woskuD

brother, sister, cousin wehnag, wepnag; nawoj, naipiju

brow koa, koka

brown, to be brown, orange, or yellow oam, o'am, s-

brush, broom wosunakuD / woskuD

brush or comb, to gaswua

brush, trash, grass sha'i

buckskin, leather hogi

buckskin sack huashomi

bucket wahldi, wapaldi (Sp. balde) kuhwo (Sp. cubo)

bud, to hulkad

build, to kiht, kihkit

buildings kihta, kihkita

bull tohlo, totolo

bull snake sho'owa

bully, to shehmachud

bumble-bee huhu'udag

bumpy, to be mu'umuk, s-

bun simito, sismito

bundle, bale, team wulim, wuhplim

burden, to mohto'id

bunt or butt, to mo'oggan

burlap dahum

burn, to meihim
to burn something mehid
burnt part mehiddag

burn and stick to vessel, to kuhsh, kuhksh

burn up or melt away, to hagito (hahagitoD/hagittoD)

burning post, firebrand kuchki

burp, to haDwuag

bury, to hiashp
to have buried hiashch

bush sha'i

busy   si ha'ichu hab wua

but   wabshaba, oi wa

butt or bunt, to   mo'oggan

butter   mandi-gihya (Sp. mantequilla)

butterfly   hohokmal

buttocks   a'atapuD

button   wotoni, woptoni (Sp. botones)

button, to   wotonDad

buy something from, to   nolawt

buzzard   nuhwi, nunuwi

by, near   mia, mimia

C

cabbage   li-juhwa (Sp. lechuga)

cactus   ho'i

calamity, accident   s-neijig

cake   toha komikam

call or invite, to   waid

calling, invitation   waida

call, name, to   chehchk
  to call animal or bird   kuhijid

caller for race or hunt   topdam

calf   wisilo, wipsilo (Sp. becerro)

calf of leg   uhksh, u'uksh

camel   ka-miio (Sp. camillo)
opochk ohkam

camp   kahmpo

can   wahso, wapso (Sp. vaso)

candy   luhlsi (Sp. dulce)

cane, reeds   wahpk

canned goods   wapso hihidoD

cannon   ge gawos (Sp. arcabúz)

canoe, trough   ka-nohwa

canteen, water gourd   wako, wapko

canvas   lohna, lolna (Sp. lona)

canyon   shahgig

captive, prisoner   lihso, lilso (Sp. preso)

car, machine   mahgina, mamgina (Sp. máquina)

cards   mohndikuD / walahokuD
play cards, to   mohndi (Sp. monte)/ walaho (Sp. barajo)

care, thought, plan   hab elidaDag

care for or guard, to   nuhkud

care for or support, to   dagiod

careful, to be   nen'eid, s-

carry, to   hohag; kushwiot; mohto; u'a

carrying cushion for head   hakko

cartridge   kal-tuhji (Sp. caltucho)

case, cover   koshdag

castrate, to   wihpdopig

59

cat mihstol, mimstol

cat claw uhpaD, u'upaD

catch, get behe, u'u

cattail uDawhag

cattle haiwani

Caucasian mil-gahn (Sp. americano)

cave cheho, chehcho

caw or crow, to kahkag

cement, dough wahga

cemetary hiha'ini/hihi'ani

cent sin-tahwo (Sp. centavo)

centipede maihogi

center, interior eDa

center beam che-tonDag

century plant a'ut

cervical vertebrae kuswo oh'o

chain hukshchim wainomi

chair daikuD, dadaikuD

change, to kammialt (Sp. cambiar)

chaps chapa-lihya (Sp. chaparajos) hogi shaliw

chapter number, size number kuintaDag

charco, pond wachki

chase hu'id, huhu'id

cheat, to banmad

check chahgih (Sp. cheque)

cheek kahm, kahkam

cheese gihsho (Sp. queso)

chest, breast bahsho, babsho

chest hair bashpo

chew up, to ki'iwin

chewings ki'iwina

chicken pox chuchul ha hihiwdag

chief ge'e, ge'ejig, uhgchu

child ahli, a'al
  act or treat like a child ahlichud
  to raise children ge'ehogat

childhood alijeg

childish, to be a'alima, s-

childishly a'alim, s-

chili ko'okol
  put chili on, to ko'okolmad

chilled, to get heumk, heukk

chin esh, e'esh

Chinese chihno (Sp. chino)

chip off, to shajkon
  chipped object shajkona

choose gawulkad; kehsh, chuhcha

chop shonch, nench

Christmas Eve noji-wihno (noche buena)

church cheopi, mihsh kih, sahndo kih

cicada kohtpul, kohktpul/ kohntpul

cigar puhlo (Sp. puro)

.cigarette sigal (Sp. cigarillo)
  roll a cigarette owich/uwach

cinch sihnju (Sp. cincho)

circle, to be circular sikol, si'iskol
  to make circular sikolkad
  to become circular sikolkahim

circus, acrobat ma-lohma, mam-loloma (Sp. maroma)

city puiwlo, pupuiwlo (Sp. pueblo)

clam shell <u>kokoDki</u>

clap, gunshot <u>kapon</u>, <u>kakpon</u>

clarify, to <u>mahskogid</u>, <u>tashogid</u>

clarification <u>tashogida</u>

clarified, to be <u>tashogidas</u>

clavicle, collar bone <u>ownag</u>, <u>o'ownag</u>

claws, nails <u>huhch</u>

clay <u>bid</u>
  red clay <u>het, wegi bid</u>

cleanse or disinfect, to <u>kegch</u>ud

cleanse ritually from disease, to <u>wusot</u>
  cleansing rite <u>wusota</u>

cleanse ritually from warfare, to <u>lihmhun</u>
  cleansing rite <u>lihmhuna</u>

clear land, to <u>gaggat</u>

clear, clearly, to be clear <u>mahsko, tasho</u>

clear the throat, to <u>i'oshan</u>

climb, ride <u>chesh</u>aj
  to go a long climbing <u>cheshaj-him</u>

cling to, to <u>bekch, u'ukch</u>

clip or mow, to <u>hihk</u>

clippers, mower <u>hihkakuD</u>

close, shut in, or dike, to <u>kuhp</u>
  to go along closing, sealing <u>kuhpahim</u>

closed, shut in, shut up <u>kuhpi</u>
  to close the eyes <u>kuhpsh</u>
  (<u>kupshap</u>)

cloth <u>iks, i'iks</u>

clothe, to <u>enigaDad, ab</u>

cloud <u>chewagi</u>

cloudy, to be <u>chewagig, s-</u>

clown <u>pa-yahso, papa-yayaso</u>
  (Sp. payaso)

club, spear <u>lahnis, lalnis</u>
  (Sp. lanza)

coals, charcoal <u>chuhdagi</u>

coat <u>lihwa, liliwa</u> (Sp. abrigo);
  <u>wahkidalig</u> (Pima)

cob <u>kumikuD</u>

cockle burr <u>waiwel</u>

Cockleburr village <u>Waiw Wo'o</u>

cocoa <u>chuku-lahdi</u> (Sp. Az.
  chocolate)

coconut <u>chahngo mo'o</u>

Cocopa tribe <u>kuapa, kukapa</u>

coffee <u>ka-whih/ko-whih</u> (Sp.
  café)

coiled, to be <u>sidolig, sisdolig</u>

coiled manner <u>sidolim,
  sisdolim</u>

cold, to be <u>hehpid, s-</u>
  to become cold <u>hehpihhim</u>
  to make cold <u>hehpijid</u>

cold (illness) <u>shomaigig</u>
  to catch cold <u>shomaig</u>
  to give a cold <u>shomaigchud</u>
  cold victim <u>shomaigkam</u>

collar bone, clavicle <u>ownagi,
  o'ownagi</u>

color, to be <u>hab mahs</u>

comb <u>gaswuikuD, tahtshakuD</u>

comb, fine toothed <u>pihnia</u>
  (Sp. piña)

comb, to <u>gaswua</u>

come <u>ab him</u>

come out <u>ta'iwush</u>

come repeatedly <u>melopa,
  wo'iopa</u>

come to, to make <u>ab wuich</u>ud

companion <u>wehmkam,
  wehmajim</u>

compare or equalize, to wepogid

compensate, to namkid

compensation namkidaDag

compete with, to chichwih

competition, play chichwihdag

completely hekia

concern pihk elidaDag
to be concerned for pihk e elid

cone-shaped, to be chuwidk

confess, to kompish (Sp. confesar)

consider, to oidahim

constipated, to get bihim

constipated, to be bihims

constricted, to be giwuDk

constriction, constricted place giwulk

contaminate, to oamhun
contaminated, to be oamhunas
contamination oamhuna

contaminate or plaster, to bidshp, bidhun

contents ba'iham

control, peace dodolimdag

cook kos-nihlo, koks-ninilo (Sp. cocinero)

cook, to hidoD
to cook for hidolid
cooking vessel hidoDakuD
cooked food hidoD, hihidoD

cook or cause to ripen, to bahijid
to get cooked, ripe bahi

cool, to be cool hehog, s-

cool, to hehogijid, hewajid
to become cool hehogihhim

cooler hehogidakuD

corn huhni

corn on the cob muhla tahtami

roasted, crushed, boiled corn ga'iwsa
to shell corn keliw

corner chuhl, chuhchpul
to have corners chuhchpulk, s-

corpse, death muhkig, ko'idag

corral, fence kolhai (Sp. corral)

correct fix, to ap'echud; kegchud

cotton tokih

cottontail tohbi, totobi

cottonwood auppa

cough i'ihog

count, to kuint (Sp. cuenta)
counting, accounting kuinta

country, earth jeweD, jejeweD

couple, hitch gi'aDag

couple or hitch, to gi'a, gigia

couple, join, to makoDad, mamkoDad

coupling makoDag

cousin, brother, sister wehnag, wepnag

cover, case koshdag kokshdag

cover, door, top kuhpaDag, kuhkpaDag; ma'ishpaDag

cover, to ma'ishch; che'ehid
to have covered che'ehidch

cover, permeate chehmo

cow haiwani, hahaiwani

coward chu ehbiddam, s-

cowboy wakial, wapkial (Sp. vaquero)

co-wife hehg, heheg

coyote ban, bahban

crack <u>komitp</u>

crack, to <u>hain</u>
to be cracked <u>haini</u>

cramped, dry, or stiff, to be
<u>kushadk, kuhkshadk</u>

crave some food, to <u>ihnamk</u>,
<u>ihnkk</u>

crawl, to <u>bahnimeD</u>, <u>bahniop</u>

crazy <u>lohgo</u> (Sp. loco)

creator and protector of the
People <u>I'itoi/Hihidoi</u>

creep, to <u>bahnimeD</u>, <u>bahniop</u>

cricket <u>chukugshuaD</u>,
<u>chuchkugshuaD</u>

crooked <u>gakoDk, ga'agkoDk</u>

crooked, zigzag <u>s-jujul</u>,
<u>s-juhu'ujul</u>

crookedly <u>s-jujulim</u>

crooked, to become <u>gakoDka-
him</u>

crooked, to make <u>gakoDkajid</u>

cross <u>kots, kokots</u> (Sp. cruz)

cross, to <u>gahiobin, gaghiobin</u>

crotch <u>kaishagi</u>
to hold in the crotch <u>kaishch</u>

crow <u>hawani, hahawani</u>

crow or caw, to <u>kahkag</u>

crowbar <u>siwat huhch</u>

crown <u>gihkio/gihkoa</u>

crush, to <u>habaDkad</u>

crutch, tree, stick <u>uhs, u'us</u>

cry, to <u>shoak, shoani</u>
to cause to cry <u>shoshakid</u>
to cause to stop crying
<u>e'ebichud</u>

cry baby <u>a'alima, s-</u>

crying <u>shoshagi</u>

crystal, sand <u>o'oD/o'ohia</u>

crystalize, to <u>o'oDgih</u>

cultivate, plow, soften <u>moihun</u>

cultivated or plowed, to be
<u>moihunas</u>

cultivation, plowing <u>moihuna</u>

culture, customs, way of life
<u>himdag</u>

cup <u>tahsa, tatsa</u> (Sp. taza)

curly <u>kulwani, kukulwani, s-</u>

curved <u>kuchul, ku'ukchul</u>

customary, necessary, legal, to
be <u>hab chum chu'ig</u>

customs, culture, way of life
<u>himdag</u>

cut, to <u>hikchk</u>, <u>hikumiak</u>

cut off blunt, to <u>chepel</u>,
<u>che'echpel</u>

cut in strips, to <u>hikshaD</u>
to cut raggedly <u>hikiwoni</u>

cut down, to <u>shoniak</u>

cutter, saw <u>hikchkakuD</u>

cuttings <u>hihka</u>

D

dam, bank, dike <u>tohnk</u>,
<u>to'otonk</u>

damp, to be <u>wa'udag, wa'usig</u>,
<u>s-</u>

dance, to <u>e keihin; e waila</u>
(Sp. baila); <u>mualig; gohimel</u>

dance <u>keihina; wailadag</u>

dance-floor <u>keihinakuD;</u>
<u>wailakuD</u>

danger <u>ehbidamkam, s-ta</u>
<u>siawog</u>

danger, to be in <u>s-gihug</u>

dangerous <u>ehbidma, s-ta</u>

dangerously <u>ehbidam, s-ta</u>

dare to, to <u>pi'ichud</u>

dark, to be dark <u>chuhugam, s-</u>

dates chukuD shosha

daughter of woman maD, mahmaD
of man alidag, a'alidag

day, sun, time, timepiece tash, tatsh

dead, the muhki, ko'i

dead, numb, necrotic, to be muhks

deaf, to be pi chekaidag

death muhkig

debate, to ne'owin

debt wikladag

deceased person kehlibaD, kekelibaD

decide hab e ahg

decorate, to heosid

decoration heosidakuD

deep, to be deep juhk, jujuk, s-

deer
mule huawi
whitetail sihki

defeat, to gewito

defecate, to biht (bihb, bihbt),
to go to defecate bihtameD, bihtop

deflate, to habshuD

deformed, to be pi ap'e

degenerate, perverted tohnto, totonto
to be degenerate tohntodag

dehide, to elkon

dehorn, to a'agpig

deliver, bring out wuhshad, wuhasid

demand, command, to chehani

deny, to pi mai

dented hodoDk

depend on, trust, to hiwig

deprive of, to wohppo'id;
ligpig (Sp. rico)

depth juhkalig

descend, to huDuni

desert, south tohono

deshell, to kompig

dethorn, to ho'ipig

devil, barrel cactus jiawul, jijawul (Sp. diablo)

diabetes asugal mumkidag

diaper, loincloth atosha

diaper, to atoshaDad

diarrhea, to cause wakuichud

die, to muhk, ko'o

different gawul; nahnko

different, to be gawulk

difficult, to be hasig; wihnk, s-
difficultly hasigam/wihnam, s-

dig kohk
to dig up, to remove ganiwua
dig a hole, to wagt

digging bar walit

dike, bank tohnk, to'otonk

dike, to tohnkad

diked tohnkdas

dip wohg huDunk

dipper ha'u, haha'u

direct, straight shel

directly shelinim

direction tahgio

dirt jeweD, jejeweD

dirtily bihtagim, s-

dirty, to be dirty bihtagi, bibtagi, s-

dirty one bihtagichu, s-

disassemble, to matok, paDchuD

disaster, calamity, tragedy neijig, s-

discard, leave or omit, to dagito

discard or reject, to   ohhod, s-
to have discarded   dagitokch;
ohhodch, s-
discard, reject   ohhoda

discipline   ha'ichu ahgidaDag

disciplined, under control, to be
dodolimk

discover, find out, to   mai, s-

discover, visualize, see, to
neid

disease, to infect with
cheawogid

disgracefully   eDam, s-ta

disgusting! unbelievable   ih!

disk, to   melomin

dispatcher   ah'addam

district, line   chekshani

ditch   waikka, wapaikka

diuretic, to be   hi'ama, s-ta

divide   gawulkad

dizzy   noDa

do, to   wua, hab

doctrine   mashchamadag

dog   gogs, gogogs

dogie, orphan   lihbih, lilbih
(Sp. lepe)

doll   shobbiaD, shoshobaD

dollar   pihsh (Sp. peso)

domain, kingdom   kownaltalig

donation, to dun for   limoshan
(Sp. limosna)
to go for donation
limoshanameD

donkey   wuhlu/wuhlo, wuplo
(Sp. burro)

door   etpa, e'etpa; kuhpaDag,
kuhkpaDag; pualt, pupualt
(Sp. puerta)

doorway   kihjeg, kihkjeg

doubt   pi wohochudaDag

dough, cement   wahga

dove   hohhi/hohhoi

down, fine feathers   wihgi

downgrade   agshp
to be downgrade   s-agshpaDag

drag, to   lawit (Sp. trabar);
chewaimeD

drag iron   dahpiunakuD

draw or write, to   o'ohon
drawing, writing   o'ohona
to be drawn, written
o'ohonas

draw a line, to   chekshan

draw near, to   miabid

dream   chehchki
dream, to   chehchk

dress, skirt   ipuD, i'ipuD

dress, to   e enigaDad

dried stuff   gakidag

drift   e wi'in

drill   wagt

drink   wasib
to give a drink   wasibid

drink, to   ih'e

drink up, to   i'ito

drip, to   o'ot

drive, to   melchud, wohpo'i-
chud

drive herd, to   shahd

driving, to be good at
melchudaDag, s-

drizzle, to   hikshpi, sihbani

drop, wipe off   dagkon

drove, herd   shahda

drowned, to   wachumk, wachkk

drum   tamblo (Sp. tambor)

drunkard   naumki, naukkoi

dry, skinny, to be   gaki, gagki s-

dry, stiff, or cramped, to be   kushadk, kuhkshadk

dry something, to   kushadkad
  to become dry   gaksim
  to spread to dry   helig
  to have spread to dry   heligch

dry goods   lohba (Sp. ropa)

duck   pahdo, papdo (Sp. pato)

due, reward   ab wuikam

dull, to be   pi mu'uhug

dumb, to be   pi chu amichud

dump, to   iawua

dun, gray and brown   koiata

dun, to be   koiataDag, s-

during   oidam

dust, smoke, fog   kuhbs
  to be dusty, smoky   kuhbsig, s-
  to be dusty, foggy   kutshani, s-

dwelling   kihdag

dwelling, to be   kih
  dweller   kihkam
  co-dwellers   wehm kihkam

dye, paint   mahsidakuD

E

each   hehemako

eagle   ba'ag

ear   nahk   nahnk
  to shake the ears   nahagew

earmark   nakpidag

earmark, to   nakpig

earn   namkid, e

earring   nanhagio

earth, land, country   jeweD, jejeweD
  the earth   jeweD kahchim
  red earth   het/wegi
  to apply red earth   hetmad

east   si'al

east, back, up   ta'i

eastward   si'al tahgio/ si'alidgio

easily   pehegim, s-

easy, to be   pehegi, s-

easy or straight, to be   s-apkog, s-apkodag

easy or light, to be   hauk, s-

eat, to   hug/ko'a
  to seem to eat   ko'adma
  ought to eat   ko'adani

echo, to   shashawk

edge, boundary, to be bounded   hugid, huhugid

effeminate, to be   u'uwimk, s-

egg   nonha

eight   gigi'ik, gi'igi'igik

elbow   sihsh, sisish

elder, big, chief   ge'e, ge'egeD

electricity, battery   wepegih

electric lights   wepegi kanjel

elephant   al-whahndi

elsewhere   go'olko, go'ogolko
  from elsewhere   go'olkojeD

embarrass, to   elidchud

emerge, to   wuhshani, wuwhag

emotion   tahhadkam
  happiness   s-ap tahhadkam
  sadness   pi ap tahhadkam

employer ahmo, a'amo (Sp. amo)

empty, to become (of liquid) huhm

encourage, to gewkamhun

encouragement gewkamhunaDag

encouraging gewkamhuna

end kuhg, kuhhug

end, to hug

endure or be able, to nakog

endure, dare, undergo, to pi'ichud

enemy (Apache) obga, ohb
to go after enemy gidaihun

engine mahgina, mamgina

enjoy hohho'id, s-

enmity obgadag

enter wahk, wahpk

entity, whole hekiakam

envious, to be hehgam, s-

envy hehgamdag

equal to, even with wepo, we'eppo
to make equal, level i wepot

erase or wipe off, to oan
erasure oana
to be erased oanas
to erase for oanid

erection kugia

erode something, to wi'ihin

erode, wash away, to wi'ikon

escape e do'ibia; i wuhsh, i wuha

esteem or honor, to ha'ichuchud

European Al-mahno

even with, equal to, same as wepo, we'eppo
to be even chepelk, che'echpelk

even, not ni'is

even if chum as hems

even tempered bamustk, s-

even though chum as

evening huDunk, huhuDukad

everlasting pi ha huhugedam

everywhere wehsko
from everywhere wehskojeD

evidently ‑ki

examine or find, to chehg

exceed, pass, to ba'iwech

excite, to kuDut; has tahhadag

exercise or limber up, to momoisha

exhibit, to chehgid

exhibit chehgida

exhibited, to be chehgidas

exhibition chehgidaDag

exhibition place chehgidakuD
to have on exhibit chehgidch

exit, to wuhshani, wuhag

expensive, to be namkig, s-

expensively namkigam, s-

experience or see, to neid

explain or clarify, to tashogid

explode, to kop, kokp; kopsid

extended to, to be jiwhias

eye wuhi, wuhpui
at eye level, there anai, an
to have a twitch of the eye wuhigew
to close the eyes kuhpsh (kupshap)

eyelashes wuipo

eyebrows hehewo
to raise eyebrows, blink wuhigid

F

face, mask wuhiosha, wuhpiosha

face down habal

faint or forget, to s-e chuhugid

fair, pretty o'owi, s-

faith wohochudaDag

fall, to gehsh, shulig

falsify or lie, to iatogid

family wha-mihlia (Sp. familia)

famine bihugig

famished, to become gishalwua

famishing ta bihugimma, s-

67

far mehk, me'emek
  from far mehkjeD
  so far ha'asko, haha'asko
  how far? he'esko i
  to remove far mehkod

farm, field oidag, o'oidag

farm laborer oidagch-eD
  chikpandam

fat, to be gihg, s-
  to fatten gi'ichud
  to become fat gi'ihim
  to remove fat gi'ipig
  fat one gihgchu
  fat gihgi

fatigue gewkogig

father ohg; apapa; apki; mahm;
  wahw

favor, gentleness
  hemajimatalig

favorite ho'oma

fear, to ehbid, ehbini, s-
  to be fearful chu ehbid, s-

feathers, wings a'an

  to feather a'anchud
  fine feathers, down wihgi

feather (for curing) machwidag
  mamchwidag

feather tassel sihwoda

feces biht

feed gegosid

feel or touch, to tahtam
  to feel emotion tahtk
  to feel well i'oma, s-

female uwi, u'uwi

female adult oks, o'oki

fence, corral kolhai

fever stonjig

few al ha'akia, pi mu'i

field, farm oidag, o'oidag

fiesta piast (Sp. fiesta)
  to carry on a fiesta piast
  to go to a fiesta piastameD

fifteen gihnsi (Sp. quince)

fig suhna (Mex. tuna, Yaqui
  chuúna)

fight cheggiaDag

fighter, warrior chu
  cheggiaDkam, s-
  to fight cheggi'a

file, to chelkon/chelshan/
  chelwin

file lihma, lilma (Sp. lima)

fill, to shuhdad, shuhshud
  to be full shuhd, shuhshud
  to rise and fill ta'ihim

find by chance, to oche'ewi
  find or examine, to chehg

finger (archaic), toe machpoD,
  mamchpoD

fingernails see nails

finish, to nahto (nattoD)
  to have finished nahtokch
  to be finished nahtois
  verb suffix 'to finish' ito(ittoD)

fire nahj, tai
  to make fire nahd, ihwid
  firedrill ihwidakuD
  fireplace nahdakuD

firebrand, burning post kuchki

firefly taiwig, tataiwig

firestone cheto

firewood ku'agi
  to get firewood ku'ag
  to get firewood for ku'agid
  to go to get firewood
    ku'agameD

first wehpeg
  the first wehpegkam

fish, worm watopi, waptopi

five hetasp, hehetasp; sihngo
  (Sp. cinco)

fix, beautify, to kegchud

fix, correct, to ap'echud
 what is fixed ap'echuda
 to have fixed ap'echudch
 to fix for ap'echudachud
 to be fixed ap'echudas

flag wanjel, wapanjel

flashlight, lightning, battery,
 movie wepegih

flat, to be flat habaDk

flat, to become flat habalkahim

flat, thin, low altitude, to be
 komalk, ko'okomalk

flatly, thinly komalim

flee to, to ahhim,ahhio

flesh, meat chuhkug/chuhhug

floodland wo'oshani

floor huk wahks, uhs wahks

floor mat, rug wahks, wahpaks

flour, ground stuff chu'i
 mesquite bean flour jehki

flower heosig
 to be flowery heosig, s-

fly muhwal, mumuwal
 long pointed species
 mukchwidam

fly or jump, to da'a, nehni

foam totshagi

fog kuhbs, komaiwuag
 to be foggy, dusty kuhbsig, s-
 kutshani, s-

folk dance keihina
 to folk dance e keihin
 folk-dance ground keihinakuD

fold, to nahshp

follow, to oid, oidahim
 following oij
 following one oijkam

food ha'ichu hugi
 prepared bih
 cooked in ground mai

foot taD, tahtaD
 to have a twitch of the foot
 taDgew
 to shake the foot taDgid

footprint gohki

for, on behalf of wehhejeD

for that reason, because heg
 hekaj, id hekaj

forbid or hinder, to shohbid

forehead, bank koa, koka

forget or faint, to chuhugid, s-

fork or scoop, to uskon

fork, pitchfork uskonakuD

forked, to be sha'aDk,
 sha'ashaDk

fortunate or lucky, to be
 abam, s-
 fortune, luck abamdag

foundation, shon, shohshon
 to found shonwua, shohshonwua

four gi'ik
 by fours gi'igik

Friday wialos (Sp. viernos)

friend, brother nawoj, naipiju
 to make friends nawojt/
 nawodt

friendship nawojdag

frighten, to todsid, totodsid
 to jerk with fright todkesh

frog babad

from amjeD, -jeD

from here, from now on i'ajeD

from nowhere pi'ajeD

front, in front bahsho, babsho

front of neck ba'ichu

fruit (ha'ichu) bahidag
 of saguaro bahidaj

to shake off   ihgid
to gather   oD
to pick   maDpig

full, to be   kowog, kokowog, s-
to become   kowoD, s-kokowoD, s-
full of liquid, to be   shuhd, shuhshud

further   ba'iwechkim

further one, greater one   ba'ichkam

G

gallon   ga-lohn (Sp. galón)

gallop, to   halibwua (Pima)

gamble   e to'id

game-ball, wooden   shonigiwul

gape at or yawn, to   ha'adkaj

garlic   ahshos (Sp. ajos)

gas, to pass   uwio

gasoline   a-saihdi, gaso-lihn

garden   oidag, o'oidag

gather   chehm, hemapad
to have gathered   hemapadch
to be gathered   hemapdas
to gather seed   moh

gavel, toka stick   usaga, u'usaga

gently   hemajim, s-
to be gentle   hemajima, s-

get, to   beihim, u'u
to go to   behimeD, u'imeD
to want to   s-behimk, s-u'imk

ghost   kokoi

gift   mahkigdag

Gila monster   chiadag, chichiadag

girl   chehia, chechia
eligible girl   sinot, sisinot (Sp, señorita)

give something to, to   mahk

to have something given to   mahkch
to be given   mahks
giving   mahkig

glance at, to   wuikon

glasses, glass eye   wuhiga, wuhpuiga

glove   wuandi, wupandi (Sp. guante)

glue, to   haDshp

gnat   chukmug

gnaw   kuhm
gnaw clean, to   ki'ikon

go, move, walk, to   him, hihim

go around or past, to   bijim

goat   siwat, sisiwat

god   jiosh, jijosh (Sp. dios)

godfather   paw-lihna (Sp. padrino)

godfather of one's child   kompal (Sp. compadre)

godmother   dahd

godmother of one's child   komal (Sp. comadre)

gold   ohla (Sp. ora)

good   ap'edag; kehg

good, beautiful, to be   kehgaj, kehegaj, s-

good, well, right, normal   ap, s-

good one, beautiful one   kehgchu, s-

goose, crane, heron   kohkoD

gopher   jewho, jejewho

gore or fork, to uskon

gourd (buffalo) aDaw

gourmet, to be hugidag, s-

governor kownal, kokownal
  (Sp. gobernador)

grain, to roast hahk
  roasted grain hahki
  to harvest grain kaipig
  large grain storage basket
  washomi

grandchild wosmaD; ba'amaD;
  ka'amaD; mohs

grandfather wosk; bahb

grandmother kahk; hu'ul

granular mohoni, s-

grape uhDwis

grasp, to have in the bekch,
u'ukch

grasp, to gi'a
  to carry in the grasp
  gi'achug

grass washai

grass, brush sha'i

grass mat hinwal

grasshopper shoh'o, shosho'o

grave, graveyard hiha'ini/
hihi'ani

gravel, stone hodai, hohodai

gravy atol (Sp. atole, Aztec
atulli)

gray, to be gray kohmagi,
kokomagi, s-
  grayly kohmagim, s-
  charcoal gray likintod, s-

graze gegusid, e

grease, to huhuD
  to be greasy muhuDag, s-

greasewood shegoi

greater, further, a ba'ichkam

great-grandparent wihkol;
  child wihshaD

great-great-grandparent
  shehpij/sikul
  child sihs/sikul

green or blue, to be chehdagi,
chehedag, s-
  greenish ihwajim, s-

greens (edible) ihwagi

greet or call by relationship
ihm

griddle chechemaitakuD;
  komal (Sp. comale)

grief, sorrow pi ap tahhadkam

grimace, to he'eDkaj,
hehe'eDkaj; simuDkaj; si'ismuDkaj

grind, to chu'i
  ground stuff, flour chu'i
  to be ground chu'idas

grindstone, mortar matchut,
mamtchut

groan or breathe heavily, to
shahshani

groin hiwchu, hihiwchu

ground mat wahks, wahpaks

grouped together, to be kawoDk

grow, to ge'elhim

growl, snore toDk

guess, think, plan hab elid

guide, lead, to wanimeD

guitar gidali, gigdal

gully, deep narrow wash
hiktani

gum ki'iwi/wihbam

gun, bow gaht, gahgt

gunshot, clap kapon, kakpon

guts hihih
　guts of hihij

H

habit himdag

hail chia

hair mo'o, wopo

half eDa hugkam

halter shahkim (Sp. jáquima)

hammer shonihinakuD

hammock iapta; neggia; kuhna

hand, arm nowi, nohnhowi
　on the other hand -hi
　to wave the hand magjid
　to raise the hand mahhad

handkerchief pa-nihdo (Sp.
　panuelito), tohwush, totowush

handle beikuD; gi'aDag; dahidag

handle, to put on a gi'aDad

hang, to naggia , nahngia

hang something, to naggia /
　sha'ichud
　to have hanging naggiakch/
　sha'ichudch

hang around neck, to ahd (ai)
　to have hung around neck
　ahdch

happy, to be hehkig, s-
　to make happy hehkchulid

hard kawk, kawpk, s-
　to become hard kawkahim
　to make hard kawkad
　hard one kawkchu

hat wonami, wopnami

harvest grain, to kaipig

harvesting stick for saguaro,
　Big Dipper kuipaD, kukuipaD

hate, scold, to keh'id (keh'el), s-

hatred keh'idag

haul, to hohag,

have, to eniga

hawk, wishag, wipshag/wisag,
　haupal

hay washai, sha'i

he, she, it o

head, hair mo'o, mohm
　to have tremors of the head
　mo'ogew
　to shake the head mo'ogid
　to smash with the head
　mo'ohain
　to hit the head mo'owua
　decapitated head mo'obaD,
　mohmbaD

healthy, to be doa, doda, s-
healing, health doajig
healing doajida

hear, to kah
　one who can hear chekaidkam
　sense of hearing chekaidag
　to have sense of hearing
　chekaidag, s-
　to restore sense of hearing
　chekaidchud
　to hear continually kaichug

heart, spirit ihbdag, i'ibdag

heat toni, s-
　in the heat toniko, s-

heavens, sky dahm kahchim

heavy, to be wehch, s-
　to become heavy wehchihim

heel chehm, chehchem

help i wehmtaDag

help, to i wehmt

henceforth i'ajeD

herd, to shahd
　herd, drove shahda

here, to be here iia, ia
　from here i'ajeD

here, now 1
here, facing away ihma, im
Here! Take it! he'eni, he'ewo
hero, one who has endured
 siakam
hiccup, to henihop
hide, skin eldag, e'eldag
hide somthing, to ehsto,
 (e'estoD)
high, chief, to be high uhg,
 u'ug
 highest, a higher up, headman
 uhgchu, u'ugchu
hill, knoll kawlk
 big hill kawoDk
hinder or forbid, to shohbid
hip, joint shohba, shoshoba
hipbone chuhl, chuhchul
hire or employ, to chikpana-
 chud
hit, to ma'ihin; ma'ikon;
 shonihin; shonchk
hitch, to be hitched makoDag,
 mamkoDag
hitch, to makoDad, mamkoDad
hitched, to have makoDadch,
 mamkoDadch
hive (bees') pa-nahl kih
hives, sore hiwdag, hihiwdag
hobble an animal, to maniaDad
 hobble, to be hobbled
 maniaDag
hoe or mash, to sihkon/
 sihmun
hold something out, to ulin
 for someone ulinid
 to have something held out
 ulinch
holder, hoster koshdag,
 kokshdag
holder, stand kehshakuD,
 kekshakuD
hole wag, wahpag
hollow kowoDk
holster, holder koshdag,
 kokshdag
home, back uhpam/uhhum
hominy poshol, popsho'ol

homosexual (male) ge kuhkunaj
honest, to be pi iatomk
honey pa-nahl sitol/muhwal
 sitol
honor or esteem, to ha'ichuchud
hoof, claw, nail huhch, huhuch
hook, to olshp
 to have hooked olshch
 to unhook olshpiog
 to be hooked together, have
 hooked with claws hugshch,
 ku'isham
hop chu'ulk dad'e
hope huh wo i
Hopi tribesman Hohpih
horn a'ag
horn, whistle kuikuD, kuhkuikuD
horn toad chemamagi,
 chechemamagi
hornets, wasps wipsh
horse kawiyu, kakawiyu (Sp.
 caballo)

 grey horse luhya (Sp. grulla)
 horses (unbroken) manaio
hospital kok'odam ha kih
hot toni, s-
 to be hot, heat toni, s-
 hotly tonim, s-
 to become hot tonihhim
hour, time ohla
house kih, kihki
how has masma? hab masma
 how about hig
 how far he'esko i? ha'asko
 how many he'ekia i? ha'akia
 how many times he'ekio i?
 ha'akio
 how much he'es i? ha'as

humming bird   wipismal

humble, poor   sho'ig

humility   sho'igchuda

humped, to be   mohshan; opochk; omlk

hump-backed   jumaDk/omlk
to be hump-backed   omlk

hundred   siant

hunger   bihugig

hungry, to be   bihugimk, bihugk

hungry one   bihugimkam, bihugkoi

hunt, to   wipia
to go hunting   wipiameD, wipiop

hunter   mo'obDam, mohmbDam

hurried, to be   hohtgid, s-
to hurry someone   hohtmagid, s-

hurt, to   ko'ok, s-

husband   kun, kuhkun

husk, bark, skin, peel   eldag, e'eldag

I

I, me   ahni

ice   gew

if, sort of, a bit   sha, sha'al

ignite brand for carrying, to   kuhtagit

ignore, to   pi chegima

illness   mumkidag

illness, to cause; to infect   iajid

illness, to cause   mumkihchud

image   sahnto, sasanto (Sp. santo)

imagination   chegitoidag

imitate, to   i wepot

immediately   ha hekaj

important   si ha'ichu

impoverish, cause to suffer, humble, to   sho'igchud

impoverishment, suffering, humility   sho'igchuda

in, within, interior, to be in   eDa, e'eDa

incanting manner   hambdogim, s-

include, to   i wahkid

indigestion, to get   maim, maik

industrious, to be   wagima, s-

industriously   wagimam, wapagimam, s-

infect or cause illness, to   cheawogid; iajid

inflated, to be   kopodk

inflated, to become   kopodkahim

injection   shags (Eng.)

injure, to   jehkaich; s-ko'okam has wua

innocent   pi ha'ichu chu'ichig

insect, fly   muhwal, mumuwal

insect stinger, arrow point   uhsh, u'ush

insides   homita

insides, to remove   eDapig, hitpot

instruct, to   wohgid

instructions   wohgida; ha'ichu ahgidaDag

instrumental suffix   -kuD

intelligent, to be   chu amichud, s-

interesting, to be   ta hohho'idama, s-; ta kakaima, s-; ta neidama, s-

interestingly   ta hohho'idam, s-

interfere, to   shohbid

interior, in, within, to be in   eDa, e'eDa

intestines, guts   hihih

into   eDa, e'eDa

intoxicated, to get   naumk, naukk

invitation   waidaDag

invite or call, to   waid

iron, metal, knife   wainomi

iron plahnjakuD

iron, to plahnja, plalanja
 (Sp. plancha)

iron or smoothe, to dahpiun,
 dadapiun

ironwood tree ho'idkam,
 hoho'idkam

irregular, species of squash
 shapij

irregular, to be shapijk

irritate, to kuDut

it, he, she, they o

itch, to mohogid, s-
 to cause to itch mohogidchud,
 s-
 to become itchy mohogihhim

ivy hejelko, hehe'ejelko

J

jacket, coat lihwa, lilwa;
 wahkidalig (Pima)

jackrabbit chuhwi; chuk
 chuhwi; toha chuhwi

jam, jelly kushul

jam, to make kushulid

jar, olla ha'a, haha'a

jaw tahtko

jealous hehgam, s-

jealous natured, to be chu
 hehgamk, s-

jello, trembler gigiwukdam

jelly, jam kushul

jerk, to todken

jerk something, to wanchkwua

jerky chuhkug s-gaki

Jew tuhlko, tutulko (Sp. Turco)

Jew's harp lohmba, lolomba
 (Sp. birimbas)

jingle, to kolighid

join makoDad, mamkoDad

joint, hip shohba, shoshoba

joy hehkig, s-

judge, toka player, presiding
 officer usagakam, u'usagakam

judge, to lodait (Sp. rodear)

judged lodais

judging lodaidag

judgment lodaisig

juice waDagi

jump, to fly da'a, nehni

just wabsh

K

key yahwi, yayawi (Sp. llave)

keep, to bekch, u'ukch;
 chekch, to'akch

kick something, to keiggan

kick along, to keichkwua,
 keichshulig

kick or dance, to keihin

kickball, wooden shonigiwul,
 shoshonigiwul

kidney o'olopo

kill, to mu'a, kokda

killer, a ha mu'adkam

kind, merciful, to be
 ta ho'ige'idma, s-

kindly, mercifully ho'ige'idam,
 s-

kindness, mercy, blessing
 ho'ige'idaDag

king snake jewakag,
 jejewhakag

king, ruler lai, lahlai (Sp.
 rei)

kingdom, domain kownaltalig

killdeer chiwi-chuhch

Kitt Peak Ioligam

knee tohn, tohton

kneel, to tonwua, tohtonwua

knife, pocket nawash, nanwash
  (Sp. navaja)

knife, metal, iron wainomi

knock, pound, to shontpag

knoll, hill kawulk

know, to understand amichud,
  s-
knowing, to be mahch, s-

know, to desire to mahchimk,
  s-
know, to cause to mahchulid

knowledge mahchig;
  amichudaDag

kohadk village, dialect Kohadk

L

lace s-jehjeg iks

lake, sea kahchk/ge shuhdagi

lamp lahmba, lalamba
  (Sp. lámpara)

land, dirt, floor, earth,
  country jeweD, jejeweD

land, to clear gaggat

lard manjuki (Sp. manteca)

large, important ge'e,
  ge'egeD
large, to be ge'ej, ge'egeDaj

large one ge'echu, ge'egeDchu

lariat liat, lihliat (Sp. reata)

larkspur chuchul i'ispul

lashes of eye wuipo

last si oijkam

last night, night chuhug

last year ha'akid

late pi oi

laugh hehem (hehhem)
  to be laughing at ash
  to cause to laugh at a'aschud
  to be laughable hehema, s-ta
  laughably hehem, s-ta

law, command chehanig

lay, to kahch, wehch, we'ewech
  to lay, put, pour chehk
    (chechka, chehki) to'a (toa,
    toaw, toa'i)
  to lay against gewshch
    (gewshp)
  to lay something down wua
    (wuhpa, wua'i)
  to lay something down, sign
    wohd (woi, wopda)
  to be laying across gahiobs
  to have something laying
    wohdch

laziness paDamaDag, s-
  to be lazy paDma, s-

lead plohmo (Sp. plomo)

lead, to wanimeD

leader wanimeDdam

leader, religious pahl, papal
  (Sp. padre)

leaf cactus naw, ihbhai

leafy winter food plant opon

leak, to o'ot

lean against, to honchk

lean month, January Gi'ihodag
  Mashad

learn, to mai
  to learn to run melid
  to learn to sit dahid
  to learn to walk himid

leather hogi

leave something, to wia

leaves hahhag

lecture, to jehnigid

left ohgig, s-
  from the ohgigjeD
  on the s-ohgigko

leg, calf of uhksh, u'uksh

legal, customary, necessary,
  to be hab chu'ig

legend ho'ok ahga; ha'ichu
  ahgidaDag

legends, to tell ho'ok ahg

lemon li-mohn (Sp. limón)

lengthen, to chewdajid

lentil lanji/lanjeki (Sp. lenteja)

let, to hiwigid

letter o'ohana, cheposig

lettuce li-juhwa (Sp. lechuga)

level or compare, to wepogid
to be level wepodag, s-

liar iatomkam, s-

license, permission shel

lick or suck, to wihni

lick with the fingers, to chipshun

lid ma'ishpakuD

lie to, to iatogid

lie down, to wo'iwua,wohpiwua

lie, to be prone to iatomk, s-

life, soul doakag, dodakag

lifetime doakdag, dodakdag

lift uhg i beihim

light tonlig

light, bright, visible, to be mahs, s-

light or easy, to be hauk, s-

light, to become haukahim

light, to make haukajid

lightning, battery, flashlight, moving picture wepegih

lightning and thunder tataniki

like, as hab masma

like, to hohho'id, s-

like, to be hab mahs

lima beans hawol

limber up or exercise, to momoisha

limp, to gohhim, gogohim

line, ridgepole, straight wawnaDag

line, district chekshani

line, to draw a chekshani

lining, ceiling apoladag

lion, mountain lion mawid, maipid

lip chini elidag

liquid, to be shuhdagi

liquid possessed, to be wa'igi
to get liquid wa'ig
to get liquid for someone wa'igid
to go to get liquid for someone wa'igidameD, wa'igidop
vessel for liquid wa'igkuD
to dip liquid was
to become empty of liquid huhm

listen, to kaiham

little al, a'al; chum, chu'uchum

little bit sha'i

little, to be chumaj, chu'uchumaj

liver nem

living creature doakam, dodakam

living, to be doa, doda

living, dwelling, to be kih

lizzard hujuD, huhu'ujuD

black lizzard hujuD, huhu'ujuD
sand lizzard watksh
whiptail lizzard wajelho, wapjelho/wan ohg

loaf shaped, to be nepoDk ne'enepoDk

lock, key yahwi, yayawi (Sp. llave)

lock, to yahwiDad

locked, to be yahwiDag

loin cloth, diaper atosha

long chew, che'echew
to be long chewaj, che'echewaj
long and thin, oblong muhwij, s-
to get long chewelhim, chewdahim

long ago heki huh; tash; ge'eho (Pima)

long one chewchu

Look! nea!, nea'a!

look around, go about town pasam , e

look at, to ab neid

look for, to gahg
  to go to look for gahghim

loop hakko

loop, to hakkoDad

loose jushaDk, ju'ujshaDk
  to become loose jushaDkahim
  to loosen jushaDkad
  (jushaDkai)

lose weight, to gi'iho

loud, to be kaidag, s-

loudly kaidam, s-

louse, body hiopch
  head ah'ach

love pihk elidaDag; si
tatchuadag

love, to pihk e elid; si tatchua

low, to be jumalk

low one jumalkchu

lower, to jumalkad

lowland, swamp wo'oshani

luck, fortune abamdag

lucky, fortunate, to be abamk,
s-

lumber, pine huk

lunch chuishpa

lungs hahawek

lying, to be wo'o, wohp,
wo'owop

lying (inanimate), to be kahch,
wehch, we'ewech

M

mad, to be baga, s-
mad, to get bagatahim
machine, car mahgina,
mamgina (Sp. maquina)
make or do, to wua (juh), hab
male cheoj, chechoj
male adult kehli, kekel
manliness cheojdag
mannerly, disciplined dodolim,
s-
many mu'i
  many of, to be many mu'ij
  to become many mu'idahim
  to make many mu'idajid

many times mu'iko
many places mu'ikpa
so many ha'akia
how many he'ekia i
so many times ha'akio
how many times he'ekio i

marbles ga-tohdih, gag-totodi
(Sp. catota)

Maricopa tribe O'obab

mark, to brand cheposid

marry off, to hohnchud

mash or hoe, to sihkon/sihmun

mask, face wuhiosha, wupiosha

massage, to dagimun

master of wihgida ceremonies
nawedju, nanawedju

mat hinwal, wahks

match, fire tai/giumudam
(Pima)

match, to strike a giushani/
giumuD (Pima)

material for basketry uDawag

matted, to be wihnagi, s-

mattock ban wuhiosha

mature, to ge'ehogat

mature, to be ge'ehog, s-

maturely ge'ehogam, s-

maverick olhoni, o'olhoni

maxim ha'ichu ahgidaDag

maybe hems, hia

Mayo tribesman Mahyo
Hiakim

me, I ahni

meal, a gegosig
  to visit someone for a meal
neal
  to go to visit someone for a
meal nealimeD, nealop

mean, to be ha'ahama, s-;
ke'idama, sta-

meaning hab ahga

measles hiwkalig

measure, ruler kuintakuD

measure, to weigh, linear
pisalt (Sp. pesar)

meat, flesh chuhkug/chuhhug

meat, dried chuhkug gaki, s-

meat, ground chuhkug shoniwia

medicate, to kulanimad

medicine kulani (Sp. curar)

medicine man, medic, doctor mahkai, mamakai

medicine man, chief siwani mahkai

meet, to namk

meeting hemapda; jehnigida; namki

meeting place jehnigidakuD

meet on the way, to melnam, wo'inam

melt or thaw, to hahghim

melt away or burn up, to hagito

melt or thaw, to cause to hahgid

menstrual house huhulga kih

menstruate, to huhulgat

menstruation huhulga

mental case lohgo, lolgo (Sp. loco)

mentally deficient pi wehsig

mercy ho'ige'ida, ho'ige'idaDag

mercy to, to show ho'ige'id (ho'ige'el), s-

mercifully, kindly ho'ige'idam, s-

mesquite kui, kukui

mesquite beans wihog

mesquite bean flour balls jehg

message, saying, proclamation ahga, a'aga

message, to bear ahgachug, ahgahim

metal, iron, knife wainomi

Mexican juhkam, jujkam

middle, in the eDa, e'eDa

mile miia (Sp. milla)

milk wihb

milk, to wak'e

milkweed, gum of milkweed wihbam

milky way tohmog

mimic or mock, to che'isid

mind chegitoiDag; amichudaDag

mine mihnas (Sp. minas)

minute "mi-nuhto" (Sp. minuto)

mirage kukkjeg, shashkad

mirror neidakuD, neneidakuD

mistake, to make a pihk chu'ig

mistletoe hahkwoD

mix, to shahshagid

mix, by dipping and pouring to wasibwua

mock or mimic, to che'isid

mocking bird shuhg, shushug

Mohave tribesman Ma-hahwih; NakshaD

moisten, to wahg

Monday luhnas (Sp. lunes)

money lial (Sp. real)

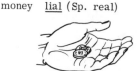

monkey chahngo (Sp. chango)

monster, witch ho'ok, hoho'ok

month, moon mashad, mamashad

moon, month mashad, mamashad

more so, further, rather <u>wahm</u>

morning <u>si'alig, sisi'almad</u>

mortar, grindstone <u>matchuD, mamatchuD</u>

mortar with hole for mashing grain <u>chepa, chechpa</u>

mosquito <u>wahmug</u>

mother, parents <u>je'e, jehj</u>

mottled, speckled, dun <u>koiato</u>

mountain <u>do'ag, dohda'ag</u>

mountain lion, lion <u>mawid, maipid</u>

mourning dove <u>hohhi/hohhoi</u>

mouse <u>nahagio, nanhagio</u>

mouth <u>chini, chihchini</u>

mouth, to hit the <u>chiniwua</u>

mouth, to hold in <u>chinishch</u>

move! scram! out of the way! <u>hiji</u>

move or flutter, to <u>hoini</u>

move or walk, to <u>him, hihim</u>

move, to <u>chihpia (chichppiaD)</u>

move, to cause to <u>himchud, hihimchud</u>

move, to settle <u>i chihwia</u>

move, to want to <u>himimk, hihimimk, s-</u>

move, to cause to want to <u>himimchud, hihimimchud, s-</u>

moving picture, lightning, battery <u>wepegih</u>

moving picture, to go to a <u>e wepegid</u>

mow, to clip <u>hihk</u>

mower, clipper <u>hihkakuD</u>

much <u>ge'e</u>
  so much <u>ha'as, haha'as</u>
  how much <u>he'es i, hehe'es</u>

much of, that size of, that <u>ha'asij</u>

mucky, sticky, to be <u>haDam, s-</u>

mud, clay, adobe <u>bid</u>

mud hen <u>wakaig, wapkia'ig</u>

mulberry <u>gohih</u>

mule <u>muhla, mumula</u> (Sp. mula)

mule deer <u>huawi/whai</u>

multiplied <u>mu'idajidas</u>

murderous <u>chu mu'adag, s-</u>

mushroom <u>kehlitakuD; okstakuD</u>

muskmelon <u>milani/miloni</u> (Sp. melón)

must <u>hemhowa</u>

mustache <u>chiniwo</u>

N

nail <u>sihsh, sisish/klahwo, klalwo/ho'iumi</u>

nail or pin, to <u>sihshp</u>

nails, claws, hoofs <u>huhch</u>

naked, smoothe, slippery, to be <u>dahpk, s-</u>

name <u>chehgig</u>

name, call, to <u>chehchk</u>

named <u>hab chehgig</u>

namesake <u>tokaio, totkaio</u> (Sp. tocayo)

nap, to <u>komshaD</u>

narrow <u>aj, a'aj</u>

narrow, to be <u>ajij, a'ajij</u>

narrow, to make <u>ajijkad</u>

narrowed thing reduced in diameter <u>ajijkada</u>

narrowed, to be <u>ajijkadas</u>

narrow, to become <u>ajijkahim</u>

nasal discharge <u>shosha</u>

nasal hair <u>dakpo</u>

nation <u>nasi-yohn</u> (Sp. nación)

Navajo <u>Nahwaho</u>

navel <u>hik, hihik</u>

navel hair <u>hikpo</u>

near   mia, mimia

near, to draw   miabid

necessary, legal, customary, to be   hab chu'ig

neck   kuswo, kukswo

neck hair   kushpo

neck, to hang around the   ahd (ai)

neck, to have hung around the   ahdch

necklace, string of beads   baiuga

necrotic, dead, numb, to be   muhks

need, want   tatchuidag

need or want, to   tatchua

needle   ho'ipaD

needle, eye of   ho'ipaDjeg

negro, blacker   chukchu, chuchkchu, s-

neither, nor   "ni" (Sp. ni)

nerve brain   oaga, o'aga

nest   kosh, koksh

net, net bag   chuagia

new, young   wechij, wepchij

new, to make   wechijid

new, to become   wechijhim

new thing   hemuchkam

next to   hugid am

nick, to   chimkko

nickel   sihngo/miiu (Sp. cinco)

night, last night   chuhug

night before last   hema chuhug

night blooming cereus   ho'ok-wah'o

nighthawk   nehpoD, nenepoD

nightly   chuchkad

nine   humukt, huhumukt

nipple   wipih

no   pia'a

noise, to make   kaidagid

noise, to go making   kaidaghim

noisy, to be   nakosig, s-

nonconformist   kolwis

nonconformist, to be   kolwisig

noon   dahm juhk

nor, neither   "ni" (Sp. ni)

normal   s-ap

normal, to be   s-ap'e

normal, mentally   wehsig

north   juhpin/wipnim/s-ta doajkam

nose   dahk, dahdk

nose, to blow the   shohwua

nose, to bump the   dakwua

nostril   shoshkdag

not   pi (pi substitutes for s- to form negative)

not yet   pi koi

notch, an arrow or stick to   uhug/ukijid

nothing   pi has

notice, to   huDawog/chegima

now, here   i

now, soon   oi (Sp. hoy)

now, today   hemu/hemuch

now, at this season   idani

necrotic, to be dead, numb   muhks

number   "nuhmlo, nunumlo" (Sp. numero)

number, lot, chapter   kuintaDag

number of   ha'akiaj

number of that thing   ha'akia-chu

nurse or suck, to   si'i

nurse or give suck, to   si'ichud

nursing bottle si'ikuD

O

oak toa/wi-yohdi (Sp. bellota)

oatmeal wuhlo ki'iwia

obey or believe in, to wohog eliD, s-

oblong, to be shapijk, sha'ashpijk

obtainable t a behima, s-

occiput, back of head kusho, kuksho

ocotilla melhog

odor uhwalig

odor, to stop giving off uhwo

odorous, to be uhw, s-

off work, to get pihhun

offense chu'ichig

offer something i n propitiation, to iagchulid

officers of, leaders of ge'ejig ge'ege'ejig

Oh! ah!/ aha!

oil chuk a-saidi

okay, well pegih

old thing hekihukam

older one, bigger one ge'echu, ge'egeDchu

Older Brother I'itoi, Si'ihe

olla, jar ha'a, haha'a

on one hand, on the other hand hi

once hemho

one hemako, hehemako

onion siwol (Sp. cebolla)

only wa'i

Opata tribe Ohbadi

open, to kuhpi'ok, kuhkpi'ok

open, to be jeg, jehjeg; kuhpiogas

open, to have kuhpi'okch

opening jeg, jehjeg
to leave open for jegelid, jehjegelid
in the open jegko, jehjegko; chu'iko

operate`on, cut open, to hitpoD

opposite, across, other side, reverse aigo, a'ai

orange nalash (Sp. naranja)

orange, yellow, brown oam, o'am, s-

organ pipe cactus chuhchwis

orphan, dogey lihbi, lilbi (Sp. lepe)

out of breath, to get ihbamk, ihbekk

out, away chu'iko

out of the way! scram! move! hiji

outhouse dahiwuakuD

outside jeg eD

oven pahntakuD

oven (adobe) ol-niio/ol-nihha (Sp. hornillo)

oven, earthen maikuD; olhin

over, to be over, above dahm, da'adam

over there ga huh; gan huh; gam huh

overhear, to nakshch, (nakshp)

overtake, reach, cycle, to ajhim (a'ahe, ah'i)
to have reaching ahidch
to overtake one in motion aichug

overturned, with backpresented kupal, kuhkpal

owe, to wikla

owl <u>chukuD, chuhchkuD</u>
  burrowing owl, ground owl
  <u>kokoho</u>

own, to <u>eDagid</u>

ox <u>woiwis, wopoiwis</u>
  (Sp. bueyes)

P

pace, yard <u>keishpa</u>

pain, to pain <u>ko'ok, s-</u>

painfully <u>ko'okam, s-</u>

pairs <u>go'ogok</u>

pajamas, sleeping quarters
  <u>koksikuD</u>

palm, to <u>shahk (shashku)</u>

palm of hand <u>matk</u>

palm, to have in the <u>shahkch</u>

palomino colored, to be
  <u>palmihdog, s-</u> (Sp. palomino)

palo verde <u>ahgo, ko'okmaDk;</u>
  <u>kuk chehedagi; ohbgam</u>

pan "wan-nihha"/"wan-dihha"
  (Sp. bendeja)

pan, frying <u>sal-tihn</u> (Sp.
  sartén)

pancreas <u>wiwa</u>

panic, to <u>shelikam noDa/</u>
  <u>wohokam noDa</u>

paper <u>tapial, tatpial</u> (Sp. papel)

parents, mothers <u>jehj</u>

part, piece, a <u>chu'idag;</u>
  <u>ha'ichudag</u>

part of, some <u>ha</u>

pass, exceed, to <u>ba'iwech</u>

pass around, to <u>ne'ibim;</u>
  <u>ta'ibim</u>

pass gas, to <u>uwio</u>

past, beyond, ahead <u>ba'ich</u>

paste, to <u>haDshp</u>

pasture <u>pot-liia, popt-lilia</u>
  (Sp. pradera)

path, road <u>wohg, wopog</u>

path, to go on war <u>gitaion</u>

pay <u>namkidaDag</u>

pay, to <u>namkid</u>

pay time <u>namkida</u>

pay attention to, to <u>huDawog/</u>
  <u>jegima</u>

peace, control <u>dodolimdag</u>

peach <u>julashan/nulash</u> (Sp.
  durazno)

peacocks <u>ahDho, a'aDho</u>

peak, to be pointed, <u>mu'uk,</u>
  <u>mu'umuk, s-</u>

peanuts <u>kaka-wahdi</u> (Sp. Az.
  cacahuate)

pear <u>pihlas</u> (Sp. peras)

pear shaped, to be <u>pihlosim,</u>
  <u>s-</u>

peas <u>wihol</u>
  chick peas <u>kalwash</u> (Sp.
  garbanzos

peal, skin, bark, husk <u>eldag,</u>
  <u>e'eldag</u>

peel, to <u>elpig, e'elpig</u>

peek, sight, to <u>koachk</u>

pelt, to <u>ma'iggan</u>

pen, <u>kolhai kokolhai</u>

pen, pencil <u>o'ohonakuD; lahbis,</u>
  <u>lalbis</u> (Sp. lapiz)

penis <u>wiha, wihpia</u>

people <u>hemajkam</u>

percolate, to <u>o'osid</u>

permission, license <u>shel</u>

permeate, cover, to <u>chehmo</u>

person <u>hemajkam,</u>
  <u>hehemajkam; o'odham</u>

personality <u>o'odhamdag</u>

perverted, degenerate <u>tohnto,</u>

totonto, ge kohlwis
to be perverted tohntodag,
ge kohlwesig

pestle shoniwikuD

pestle for mashing grain in a
mortar wihdakuD/
wihdagikuD

pet, domestic animal shoiga,
shoshoiga

pick pihgo, pipgo (Sp. pico)

pick fruit or branches, to
maDpig

pick small stuff che'ewi

picker behedam, u'udam

picture o'ohadag

picture of, to take a
pihkchulid (Eng.)

piece, a part chu'idag;
ha'ichudag

pierce, stick, to ho'iggan

pig, swine kohji, kokji
(Sp. coche)

pigeon paplo (Sp. paloma)

pile, to dashwua; to'a;
i sipulkad

piled, to be dashwuis; sipulk,
si'ispulk

piled, to have something
to'akch

pillow mo'ochkuD

Pima Akimel O'odham, Pihma

pin si'ishpakuD

pin, nail, to sihshp, sisishp

pinfeathers, down wihgi

pine, lumber huk

pinoli, roasted grain hahki

pipe pihba, pipba (Sp. pipa)

Pisinemo Village pisin mo'o

pistol pis-tohl, pipis-totol
(Sp. pistola)

pitch, resin ushabi

pitchfork ol-giia (Sp.
horquilla)

pity, to ho'ige'id, s-

proper or remote place chuhko

place, to chehk, to'a

Plains Indian A'an Wopnamim

plan, guess hab elida

plan, think, to hab elid

plant, to esh

planting, crop esha, e'esha

plants, crops e'es

plant, tassle of muDadag

plant life ha'ichu wuhshanig

plaster, fill with syrup,
contaminate to bidshp

plate hoas-ha'a, hohas-haha'a

play, compete, trifle, to
chichwih
play, competition, triviality
chichwihdag
to be playful chichwihmk, s-
toy, athletic field, recreation
area chichwihkuD

play cards, to mohndi/walaho
(Sp. monte, barajo)

plead, to bahmud, i

please, to hohho'idachud

plow, cultivate, to soften
moihun
plowing, cultivation moihuna
to be plowed, cultivated
moihunas

pliers, tweezers ki'ishpakuD

pluck, to wohni

pocket wohshag, wopshag
(Sp. bolsa)

pocket knife nawash, nanwash
(Sp. navaja)

poised, unruffled, to be
eDastk, s-

poison hialwui

poison, to hialwuimad

police chi-lihhi, chich-lilihi (Sp. charifo)

pomegranate gal-nahyo (Sp. granado)

pond, charco wachki; wo'o

pond, spring fed shongam

pop sohla (Sp. soda)

popover oamajida (Pima)

pool puhl (Eng.)

poor, to be poor sho'ig

possess, to eDagid, eniga

possession eniga, e'eniga

post uhs, u'us

potatoes, cultivated bahbas (Sp. papas)
wild potatoes shahD

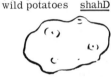

pound, knock, to shontpag

pour, to to'a

pour, spill, to iawua

poured out, to be iawuis

poverty, suffering, humility sho'igdag
from some cause sho'igchudaDag

powder, baking koshoDkdakuD

power, to have gewkdag, s-

powers, strength, spirits gewkdag, gewpkdag

prairie dog sheliki, shesheliki

pray, to ho'ige'idahun

prayer ho'ige'idahuna

praying mantis, walking stick gakimchul

prepare seed, to kaijkat

pretty, to be kehgaj, kehegaj, s-

pretty one, good one kehgchu, s-

present, to be ha'ichug

presiding officer, judge, toka player usagakam, u'usaga-kam

press against or walk beside, to honwua

press on, to dagshch

press the lips to, kiss, to chinDad

previous heki huh

prey behi, u'i

price, wage namkidaDad

prisoner lihso, lilso (Sp. preso)

prisoner, to take lihsochud

prize, spoil, victory gehgewi

proclaim, to amog

proclaim to, to amogid; ahgid

proclamation ahga, a'aga

prod, stir up, to i wahmud

pronghorned antelope kuhwid, kukuwid

pronounciation, sound che'idag

property, to be in possession of eniga

property, home and kihdag

propitiate or appease with a gift, to iagchulid

propitiatory gift iagta

propitiatory giving iagchulida

protestant mihsh, mimsh (Sp. misa)

proud or boastful, to be woikima, s-; gimaima, s-

prove true, to testify woho'kamchud

puff up, to i koshoDkad

puffed up, ballooned, to be koshoDk, ko'okshoDk

pull along, to wanchkwua, wanchshulig

pull on, to wanchk; wani'on

pull out a thorn, to huhpsh

pulverize, to shoniwin

pumpkin, squash hahl

puncture, to chu'aggan
(chu'aggash)

puncture wound chu'aggana

punish, to kastigal (Sp.
castigar)

punish, to box shoniggash

pure, completely whole hekia

purse lial kih

push on, to nu'ichk

push along, to nu'ichkwua,
nu'ichshulig

push along with the body, to
honchkwua, honchshulig

push along with the head, to
mo'ochkwua, mo'ochshulig

push, to nu'ihin

pushing, to go along nu'ihinahim

put or lay, to chehk; wohd

put in, to wahkid

put objects in a container, to
ba'iham

put on a hitch, to gi'aDad

put on shoes, to cheka
(chechkaD)

put with, to wehnad

Q

quail kakaichu

quarrel with, to kawhain

quench fire or light, to chuhsh
(chui, chuhchsh)

quench thirst, to wawini

quenching, to be thirst
wawinig, s-

question, to chu'ichk

quietly jupij, s-

quilt kahma, kakama (Sp. cama)

quit, to ha'asa

quiver, one's child wogsha

R

rabbit tohbi, totobi

rabid animal noDagam

raccoon wawuk, wawpuk

race melchuda

race caller topdam

rag, cloth iks, i'iks

rain juhki

rain, to juhk, (jujku)

rain on, to jukshp

raining, to stop jukito

rainy, to be juhkig, s-

rainy season, to be jujku, s-

rain, to cause jujkid

rainbow kiohoD, kikihoD

raise young, to ge'elid,
ge'egelid

rake or hoe out, to golwin

rake hukshomakuD

rake or scratch, to hukshan

rake together, to nu'a

ranch lahnju, lalanju
(Sp. rancho)

ramada, shelter watto, waptto

rap or knock, to shontpag

rat wosho, wopsho

rather, the more so, further
wahm

rattles, ankle chekoshda,
chechkoshda

rattle shawikuD,
sha'ashawikuD

rattle, to sijk

rattlesnake ko'owi, kohko'owi

ravine shahgig, shahshgig

raw do'i

raw, to be do'ig

reach, to aihim

reach a point, to i cheka

reaching, to be ais

read neokchulid

ready! dohwai!

really, very, real, superlative
si

receive, to beihim

recognize or know, to
amichud, s-

reddened, to be hetmag, s-

red wegi, wepegi, s-

red, to become wegihhim

red pottery paint het

reduce, make slender, make
narrow ajijkad

rein lihnda, lilinda (Sp.
rienda)

reject, discard, to
s-ohhod/s-tamhaig

relationship ihmigi; hajundag;
hajuntalig

relationship, to call by ihm

relative hajuni, hahajuni

relative, what has juni

religious leader pahl, papal
(Sp. padre)

remain ahead, to aichug

remaining, to be wi'is

remember (trying to) pen

remnant wi'ikam, wihpkam

remote huh

remove by scraping, to
hiwium

remove, to wahawua,
wahshulig

remove something from, to
-pig see Appendix III

repeat, mock, mimic, to
che'isid

rescue do'ibiadag
rescue, to do'ibiad

reservoir, pond wo'o; wachki

reside, to kih

residence, stay chihpiadag

resident kihkam

resin, pitch ushabi

rest ulinihogig/heubagig

revenge, to take, get back at
agwua, e

reverse, other side, across
opposite aigo, a'ai

rib hoho'onma

rice ahlos (Sp. aros)

rich, wealthy kais, kakais, s-

ride cheshaj

rider, to be a good dahidag, s-

ridge pole wawnaDag

rifle shells, bullets wahl/u'u

right apkojeD, s-

ring anilo (Sp. anil)

ring or strike, to gew

rip, to wantsh/wantp

ripen, to baihim

rise and fill a vessel, to
ta'ihim

rival sahyo, sasayo (Sp.
adversario)

river, running arroyo <u>akimel</u>,
  <u>a'akimel</u>

road <u>wohg, wopog</u>

roast, to <u>ga'a</u> (gai, <u>gag'e</u>,
  <u>gah'i</u>)

roast in a firepit, to <u>chuama</u>,
  <u>chuchama</u>

roast in a charcoal basket, to
  <u>hahk</u>

roasted grain <u>hahki</u>

rock or shake, to <u>ujigid</u>,
  <u>u'ujigid</u>

rock, cliff <u>waw</u>

roll up, fold up, to <u>olatahim</u>,
  <u>o'olatahim, holiwkaid</u>

root <u>tatk</u>

rope <u>wijina</u>

rope, to <u>wuhD</u>

rope for, to <u>wuhlid</u>

rope, to make <u>talwin, wijinat</u>

rope maker <u>talwindam</u>;
  <u>talwinakuD</u>

rotten, to be <u>jew</u>
  rotten, to get <u>jewahim</u>
  rotten thing <u>jewalig</u>

rounded <u>wohlim, s-</u>

row, line <u>wawnim</u>

rub basket for music, to <u>hiw</u>

rub the music stick, to
  <u>hiwchulid</u>

rubber <u>uhli, u'uli</u> (Sp. hule)

rude, to be <u>pi chu</u>
  <u>hemachudma</u>

rudely <u>pi chu hemachudam</u>

rug, floor mat <u>wahks</u>,
  <u>wahpaks</u>

ruin, wear out, to <u>wi'a</u> (<u>wipia</u>,
  <u>wia'i</u>), <u>s-</u>

ruler, measure <u>kuintakuD</u>

ruler, king <u>kownal, kokownal</u>/
  <u>lai, lahlai</u> (Sp. gobernador,
  rei)

rumble in bowel, to <u>koDog</u>

rumbling, thunder <u>bebedki</u>

rummage for, to <u>hoan</u>

rummage for someone, to
  <u>hoanid</u>

run, to <u>meD, wohpo</u>

S

sad, to be <u>pi hehkig</u>; <u>pi ap e</u>
  <u>tahtk</u>

sad one <u>pi ap e tahhadkam</u>

saddle <u>lomiaDag, lolmiaDag</u>/
  <u>sihl, sisil</u>/<u>puhst</u> (Sp. lomo,
  silla, fuste)

saddle back <u>sihl at</u>

saddle blanket <u>shuwijul</u>,
  <u>shushuwijul</u> (Sp. sudadero)

saddle horn <u>sihl mo'o</u>

saddle to <u>hogiDad</u>; <u>lomiaDad</u>

saddled, to be <u>hogiDag</u>;
  <u>lomiaDag</u>

saddle of mountain ravine
  <u>sha'alk</u>

sage, burro weed,
  <u>tatshagi</u>

saguaro cactus <u>hahshani</u>

saguaro harvest pole, Big Dipper kuipaD, kukuipaD

said, to be hab che'is

saliva siswuaDag

salmon, sardines watopi hidoD

salt on

salvation do'ibiadag

same as, even with, equal to wepo, we'eppo

same as, to make i wepot

sand, crystal o'oD; o'ohia

sand dune hia

sand ripples wi'ushawig

sandle kaikia shuhshk

sardines, salmon watopi hidoD

Saturday shahwai (Sp, sabado)

sausage, Spanish cho-lihsa (Sp. chorizo)

saw, cutter hikchkakuD

say ahg (a'aga)

saying, maxim ha'ichu ahgidaDag

saying, message, proclamation ahga, a'aga

scales pisaltakuD

scalp mo'otk

scalp, to mo'otpig

scarred balwani, babalwani, s-

scatter, to gantan

scatter or remove, to ganiwua

scent or smell, to hewagid

scent of, to go hunting the hewgiameD

scent of, to follow the hewshan

school mashchamakuD

scissors chihil, chichil

scold or hate, to keh'id (keh'el), s-

scoop or put in, to iht (i'ita)
scoop ihtaikuD

scorpion nakshel, nanakshel

scram! move! out of the way! hiji

scrape, to shajkon, sihowin

scrape, file, scratch, to chelkon/chelwin/chelshan

scrape smooth, to hiwshan

scrape smooth, shave, to hiwkon

scratch, to chelkon

scratch, rake, to hukshan/hukshum

scratch, stir, scrape, dig out, to sihowin; sihon

screen s-jehjeg wainomi

scum, algae mamtoD

sea, lake ge kakchki; ge shuhdagi

sea-shells kokotki

seal, to kuhp(kukpa, kuhpi)
go along sealing, to kuhpahim

search for, to gahg; hoan

season, to be rainy jujku, s-

sediment, straw mohg

see, discover, experience, to neid (nenneid)

see the town, to go to pasamameD, pasamop (Sp. pasar)

seed kai, kakai
prepared seed kaijka
to prepare seed kaijkat

seed, to gather moh

"seems like" shag wepo

self, alone hejel, hehe'ejel

sell something to someone, to gagDa

semen keDwuadag
to ejaculate semen keDwua/kechwua

89

send, to ah'ad/hotsh (Pima)

sender ah'addam

sent one ah'ada

separate hejel, hehe'ejel

separate, to gawulkad, ga'agwulkad

separated or different, to be gawulk, ga'agwulk

separately hemako, hehemako; hejelko, hehe'ejelko

Seri tribesmen Shehl

servant, slave nehol, nenehol

serve food, to bi'a (bia, bibia, bia'i)

set an object, to dahsh (dai, dadsha, dah'i)

settle or move, to chihpia

setting, to have dahshch

seven wewa'ak

sew something, to shohm, shohshom

sew something for someone, to shohmjelid

shaded, to be ehkeg/ehheg, s- in the shade ehkegko, s-

shadow ehkdag

shady, to become ehkahim

shake, to shahmug shake, to mix shahshagid

shake the belly, to wokijid

shake involuntarily, to hongew

shake off or shoo away, to shahmud (shashamud)

shake self, to hongid

shake the foot, to taDgid

shake the head, to mo'ogid

shake or rock something, to ujigid, u'ujigid

shake or swing the arm, to magew

shameful or ungracious, to be ta eDama, s-

shamefully, ungraciously ta eDam, s-

shave, to hiwkon

shavings shajkona

sheep, mountain cheshoni domestic kahwul, kakawul (Sp. cabra)

shelf, hanging kuhkta

shell, back komi, kohkomi to deshell kompig

shell, clam hohlwig, hoholwig

shell, rifle wahl/u'u (Pima)

shell corn, to keliw

shield kawaD, kakawaD

shine, twinkle, to tonot (tohonnot)

shine for or light up, to tonlid

shiny, bald, to be bald wadadk, wa'apdadk

shirt kotoni, koktoni/(Pima) kamish, kakmish (Sp. camisa)

shoe shuhshk, shushushk

shoo, shake off, to shahmud (shashamud)

shoot off, to gatwua

shoot something, to gatwuid

shoots, yucca wupaj

short, to be shopolk, sho'oshpolk

short, to become shopolkahim

short one shopolkchu

shorten, to shopolkad (shopolkai)

shortened, to be shopolkdas

shorts kalshani, kakalshani (Sp. calzones)

shoulder kotwa, koktwa

shovel kuppiaD, kukuppiaD/ pahla, papla (Sp. palo)

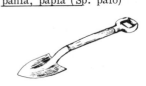

show or exhibit, to chehgid

show off, boast, to woikchud/ (Pima) gimaihun

shut, close or dike, to kuhp (kukpa, kuhpi)

shut in, shut up, closed kuhpi

sick, to get or be mumku, kok'o

sick, to make mumkichud, kok'ochud

sickness mumkidag

sickle, scythe ohso, o'oso (Sp. hoz)

side hugid, huhugid
one side, that side hab
the other side hab ha'ab

side by side shakal, shashkal

side oats, gamma grass dadpk washai

sift, to sihskid

sigh, to si i ihbheiwua

sight nena

sight or peak, to koachk

sign or lay something down, to wohd (woi, wopda)

silk, bandana maskal, mamskal (Sp. mascara)

silver plahda (Sp. plata)

silverware spoon, trowel kusal, kuksal (Sp. cuchara)

simmer, to siweg

sing, to ne'e (nei, nen'e neh'i/ahg (a'aga)

sing, to go to ne'imeD, ne'iop

sing for, to ne'ichud

singing, to go along ne'ihim

singing, to have finished ne'itoghim, s-

singe hair off, to jewikon

singe, to wohiw

sink down, to soak in, to juhpin

sissy uwikwuaD

sister uwiga, u'uwiga

sit down, to dahiwua, daDhaiwua

sitting, to be daha, daDha

six chuhdp, chu'uchudp

size ha'asig, haha'asig
that size, that much ha'as, haha'as
that size of, much of ha'asij
that size thing ha'aschu, haha'aschu
what size? how much? he'es i, hehe'es i
what size of he'esij i

size number kuintaDag

skilled, to be ab ulini

skin, bark, husk, peel eldag, e'eldag

skin, dehide, to elkon

skin a sore place, to oshkon

skinny, dry, to be gaki, gagki, s-

skirt or dress ipuD, i'ipuD

sky, heaven dahm kahchim

sky, to be situated in the juhk (jujju)

sky blue, to be luhyag, s-

skull koshwa, kokshwa

skunk uhwpio, u'uwpio

slave nehol

sleep, to kohsh, kohksh (koksha)

sleep, to put to kohsid, kohksid (koksid)

sleeping quarters, pajamas koksidakuD

sleeve nowidag, nohnhowidag

slender and tall, to be chu'alk

slender, to make ajijkad (ajijkai)

slide, to hehlwua
playground slide hehlwuikuD

slide or slip, to dapidwua

sling, bullroarer wewkuD

slip, to dapkon

slip or slide, to dapidwua

slippery, smooth, naked, to be dahpk, dadpk, s-

small chum, chu'uchum

small one chumchu, chu'uchumchu

small one of chumaj, chu'uchumaj

small, to be chumaj, chu'uchumaj

smash with the head, to mo'ohain (mo'ohaish)

smell or scent, to hewagid

smoke, to jehni (jehj, jehjen)

smoke, dust, fog kuhbs

smoky, to be kuhbsig, s-

smoothe, iron, to dahpiun, dadapiun

smooth, slippery, naked, to be dahpk, dadpk, s-

snake wamaD, wahammaD

sneeze, to bischk

sneeze, to cause to bischkchud

snore, growl, to toDk, totoDk

snow, ice gew

snow on, to gewshp

so hab masma
so far ha'asko, haha'asko
so many ha'akia
so many times ha'akio
so much ha'as

soak in, sink down, to juhpin

soak something in, to wakch

soak underground, to hiowichud

soap shawoni, shashawoni (Sp. jabón)

soap, to shawonimad

soapweed utko jehj
soapweed stalk utko

socks, stockings kal-sihda, kakal-sisida (Sp. calcetín)

soft, to be moik, momoik, s-
soft one moikchu
make soft, to moikajid
become soft, to moikahim
soften, plow, cultivate, to moihun
softly moikam, s-

soil, land, earth, country,

floor jeweD, jejeweD

soldier shontal (Sp. soldado)

some ha'i

some, part of ha

something, thing ha'ichu, haha'ichu

something from amjeDkam

somewhere hasko, hahasko
from somewhere haskojeD

sommersault, stoop, to sipuD kekiwua

song ne'i, nen'ei

soon, now hemu/hemuch

soon, now oi (Sp. hoy)

soot ihmki

sore hihwog, hihiwog

sore, small pox hihwdag, hihiwdag
to cause a sore hihwsiD, hihiwsiD

sorrel alshani (Sp. alazán)

sort of, a bit sha'i, sha'al

soul, life doakag, dodakag

sound, pronounciation hab che'idag, hab kaidag

sound or rustle, to shahmuni

soup sohba (Sp. sopa)

sour, to be sour he'ek, s-

south wakoliw/ (Pima) tohono

speaker neokdam, neneokdam

speak, to desire to neokim, s-

spear, club lahnis, lalnis (Sp. lanza)

spear, sword is-pahyo, i'is-papayo (Sp. espada)

spend, to heki gehsh

spherical olas, o'olas

spherically o'olasim, s-

spider tokihtuD, totkihtuD

spill, pour, to iawua

spin in dance, to mualig

spinach, greens chuhugia, ihwagi

spirit, heart ihbdag, i'ibdag

spirits, strength, powers gewkdag, gewpkdag

spirits of the dead kokoi

spit, to siswua

spit upon, to siswuamad

splash, to shab

split something, to tahpan (tapsha)

split, to be tahp

splitter, comb tahtshakuD
  rail-splitter yuhngih

spoil, victory, prize gehgewi

spoil, to cause to paDchud, pa'apDachud
  bad, spoiled paD, pa'apaD
  to be bad, spoiled paDaj, pa'apDaj
  to be in a spoiled state paDchudas
  spoilage paDchuda

spotted pihnto, pipinto (Sp. pinto)
  to be spotted pihntog, s-

sprawl, to napaDwua

sprawled, to be napaDk

spray with the mouth, to hipshun (hipshuD)

spread, to taDan (tahtaD, tahtDan)

spread to dry, to helig (hehelig)
  to have spread to dry heligch

spread open to dry, to hipig

sprinkle, to sihbani

sprinkle something, to hadsid

sprout, to i'iwuki

spur ispul, i'ispul (Sp. espuela)

square, to be chuhchpulk, s-

squash, pumpkin hahl
  oblong squash shapijk

squash chips hahaisha

squash strips hihiwai

squat, to chu'al daha, sipuD daha

squirm or wiggle, to banimeD baniop

squirrel chehkul, chechekul

stagger, to shakalwua

stalks, straw, chaff wa'ug

stallion kalioni, kakalioni (Sp. garañon)

stamp is-tahmpa (Sp. estampa)

standing in a clump, to be chu'awog

stand, bar kan-tihna (Sp. cantina)

stand for cooking, fireplace stone cheto

stand up or stop, to kekiwua, gegokiwua

stand on tiptoe, to chu'alkaid

standing (animate), to be kehk, gegok

standing(inanimate) , to be kehk, chuhch

standing in a group, to be chu'awogi

stand something, appoint, to kehsh, chuhcha

stand or stop, to cause to keshwua

standing, to have kehshch

star hu'u, huhu'u

start, begin, to shonwua, shohshonwua

start, to cause to shonchud, shohshonchud

stay, residence chihpiadag

stay, to wi'i (wih, wipi, wih'i)

steal from, to ehsid (e'esid)

stealthy <u>schu-ehsk,</u>
<u>schu-e'esk</u>

steep, to be downgrade
<u>agshpaDag, s-</u>

steep, to be downgrade
<u>agshpaDag, s-</u>

steer <u>nowiyu, nonowiyu</u>

step on, to <u>keishch</u>
(<u>kekeishch</u>)

stick, to <u>ho'ishch</u>

stick or pierce, to <u>ho'iggan</u>
(<u>ho'iggash</u>)

stick to vessel, to burn and
<u>kuhsh, kuhksh</u>

stick, crutch, tree <u>uhs, u'us</u>

sticky, to be <u>haDam, s-</u>

sticker, cactus, thorn <u>ho'i</u>

stiff, arthritic <u>mahniko</u>

stiff, cramped, dry, to be
<u>kushadk, kuhkshadk</u>

still, yet <u>kia</u>

stinger, arrow point, insect
<u>uhsh, u'ush</u>

stink bug <u>bitokoi</u>

stir, to <u>nohnhoig</u>

stir, to <u>iol</u>
stir, to stir up, prod <u>i</u>
<u>wahmud</u>

stir fire, to <u>sihon</u>

stirring, to look for something
by <u>hoan</u>

stirrup <u>istliw, i'istliw</u> (Sp.
estribo)

stock, to go for <u>shawantam</u>ed,
<u>shawantop</u>

stock, to rustle <u>kiot</u>

stockings, socks (Sp. calcetín)
<u>kal-sihda, kakal-sisida</u>

stone, gravel <u>hodai, hohodai</u>

stone for cooking, fireplace
<u>cheto</u>

stone for mashing grain
<u>chehpidakuD</u>

stone for grinding grain
<u>wihdakuD</u>
<u>matchuD</u>

stoop or somersault, to <u>sipuD</u>
<u>kekiwua</u>

stop or stand, to <u>kekiwua,</u>
<u>gegukiwua</u>

stop or stand, to cause to
<u>keshwua</u>

store, trading post <u>nolawtakuD</u>
<u>tianna, titianna</u> (Sp. tienda)

store away, put, to lay <u>chehk</u>
(<u>chechka, chehki</u>) <u>to'a</u> (<u>toaw</u>)

stored, to have something
<u>chekch, to'akch</u>

storm <u>jegos</u>

story, message <u>ha'ichu ahga</u>

stove <u>is-tuhwha</u> (Sp. estufa)

straight <u>shelinim</u>

straight, to be <u>shelini,</u>
<u>shehshelini</u>

straight or even, to be
<u>apkodag, s-</u>

straighten, to <u>i shelin</u>, <u>i</u>
<u>sheshelin</u>

strap, belt, band <u>giwuD</u>

strapped, tied, to be <u>giwuDk</u>

straw, sediment <u>mohg</u>

straw, woven <u>main</u>

street <u>kahya</u> (Sp. calle)

strength, powers, spirits
<u>gewkdag, gewpkdag</u>

strengthen, to <u>gewkad</u> (gewkai)

stretch out on the back, to
<u>ohshaD</u>

strike, ring, beat, to <u>gew</u>
(gehg, <u>gehgew</u>)

strike a glancing blow, to
gewikon

strike a match, to giushani
(giushuD)

strike down, to gewichkwua,
gewichshulig

strike with something, to
shonikon

string, cotton tokih

string of beads baiuga

strip or deprive of, to ligpig
(Sp. rico)

striped, to be o'owi, s-

strong, to be gewk, gewpk, s-
to get strong gewkahim
the stronger gewkchu, s-
strongly gewkam, s-

struck with calamity, to suffer
the consequences, to e
jehkaich

student e mashchamdam

stumble, to huchwua, keikon

sty wuichwig

submerge, to wachumk, wachkk

subsequently, then hahawa

suck, nurse, to si'i (sih, sisi,
sih'i)

suck in the mouth, to wihni
(wihp, wihpin)

suck in with breath, to
howichkwua, howichshulig

suffer, to cause to sho'igchud
cause of suffering
sho'igchudaDag

sufferer sho'igkam

suffering, poor, humble
sho'ig

suffering, poverty sho'igdag

sugar asugal, a-suhga
(Sp. azucar)
to sugar asugalmad

summer toniabkam

sun, day, time, timepiece
tash, tatsh

Sunday, week domig (Sp.
domingo)

sunflower hihwai, hihiwai

sunset, west huDunig

supposed to pehegia

support or care for, to dagiod

surround or wrap, to bihag

suspenders ti-lahndi,
titi-lalandi (Sp. tirantes)

swallow gigitwal

swallow, to ba'a (bah, bab'e,
bah'i)

swallow, to cause to ba'ichud

swamp, lowland wo'oshani

sweat wahuDdag

sweat, to wahuD, s-

sweater, blouse sahgo,
sasago (Sp. saco)/ wahkidalig

seep, to wosun

sweet, to be i'owih, s-
to get sweet i'owihhim
to sweeten i'owijid
sweetly i'owim, s-
sweet one i'owichu

sweet potato, yam ka-mohdi
(Sp. camote)

sweetheart ma'ishpa

swell, to toskon

swim or bathe, to e wachwih

swine, pig kohji, kokji
(Mex. Sp. coche)

swing or wave something, to
wiDut (wipiDut)

swing or shake the arm, to
magew

switch the tail, to bahigid

swollen kopod

sword, spear is-pahyo,
i'is-papayo (Sp. espada)

syrup <u>sitol</u>

T

table <u>mihsa, mimsa/mihsh, mimsh</u> (Sp. mesa)

tadpole <u>mo'okwaD</u>

tail <u>bahi, bahbhai</u>
  to switch tail, to wag <u>bahigid</u>

take <u>beihim, u'u</u>

take and go <u>bekai, u'ukai</u>

to take away from, to deprive <u>wohppo'id</u>

take it! <u>he'eni!, he'ewo</u>

tale <u>ha'ichu ahga</u>

talk, to <u>neok, neneok</u>

tall, to become <u>chu'alkahim</u>

tallow <u>gihgi</u>
  remove tallow <u>gi'ipig</u>

tamale <u>tamal</u> (Sp. tamal)

tamarack <u>onk kui</u>

tame, trained <u>mahsho</u>
  (Sp. manso) /<u>hemajima, s-</u>

tamp, to <u>chu'amun</u>

tangled or wrinkled, to be <u>wihonagi, s-/e eDa wahks</u>

tarantula <u>hiani, hihani</u>

target of grass <u>wulwega</u>

target practice <u>shelwua</u>

tassel of grain <u>muDadag</u>

taste, to <u>jehk</u>

tasty, to be <u>i'owi, s-</u>

teach, to <u>mashcham</u>

teachings <u>mashchama, mashchamadag</u>

team, bale, bundle <u>wulim, wuplim</u>

tear <u>oh'og</u>
  to drop tears <u>oh'ogwua</u>

tease <u>tahhadchud</u>

telephone <u>aj wainomi</u>
  telephone, to <u>aj wainomimad</u>

tell something <u>ahg</u>
  tell legends <u>ho'ok ahg</u>

ten <u>west-mahm</u>

tendon <u>tatai</u>

tent <u>iks kih</u>

termite <u>hiopch</u>

test <u>a'apem</u>

testicle <u>wihpdo</u>

testify <u>wohokamchud</u>

than <u>kih</u> (Sp. que)

that, he, she, it <u>hegai/heg</u>

thaw, to <u>hahg</u>

thaw something, to <u>hahgid</u>

them, their <u>ha</u>

them, those <u>hegam</u>

then, subsequently <u>hahawa</u>

then, at that time <u>wenog/eDa</u>

there, near
  away, below <u>amai, am</u>
  toward, above <u>abai, ab</u>
  transverse, on level <u>anai, an</u>

there, far
  away, below <u>gamai, gam</u>
  toward, above <u>ga'abai, ga</u>
  transverse, on level <u>ganai, gan</u>

these <u>ihdam</u>

thick, to be thick, to be high in elevation <u>kowk, kowpk, s-</u>
  to become <u>kowkahim</u>

thick around, to be <u>shawaD</u>

thief <u>chu ehskam, s-</u>

thigh <u>um, u'um</u>

thin and flat or low in elevation, to be <u>komalk, ko'okmalk</u>

thin <u>muhwij</u>; <u>gaki, s-</u>; <u>komalk</u>

thing, something <u>ha'ichu</u>
what thing <u>shahchu/haschu</u>

think <u>chegito</u>; <u>hab eliD</u>; <u>oidahim</u>; <u>oidachud</u>

thirst <u>tonomdag</u>

thirsty, to get <u>tonom</u>k, <u>tonkk</u>

this <u>ihda</u>

thorn, sticker, cactus <u>ho'i</u>
to remove thorn <u>ho'ipig</u>

thoughts <u>chegitoi</u>

thousand <u>mihl</u> (Sp. mil)

thread <u>hihlo</u> (Sp. hilo)

thread, to <u>hihloDad</u>

three <u>waik, wa'awaik</u>
thrice <u>waiko</u>

thresh <u>mohon</u>

thresh, to <u>kehiwin/kehiwia</u>
threshing <u>kehiwina</u>

threshing floor <u>alhin, a'alhin</u>

throat <u>ba'itk</u>
to clear throat <u>i'oshan, e-</u>

through, in <u>oidk</u>

thump, to <u>poDoni, popoDoni</u>
thump violently, to <u>poDnim, s-</u>

thunder <u>bebedki</u>
to thunder <u>toahim</u>

Thursday <u>huiwis</u> (Sp. jueves)

thus <u>hab, hab masma</u>

tick <u>mahmsh</u>

tickle, to <u>keDkolid</u>

tie knot, to <u>hahwul</u>

tie knot for someone, to <u>hahwul</u>id

tie or trap, to <u>wulshp</u>, bihsh

tight <u>wihnk, s-</u>

time <u>tiampo</u> (Sp. tiempo)

timid <u>e elid, s-</u>

tire <u>yahnda, yayanda</u>
(Sp. llanta)

tired, to get <u>gewko, gewpko</u>/ <u>e gehsid</u>

to, toward <u>wui</u>
to make come to <u>wuichud</u>
something coming to <u>wuikam</u>

toad <u>mo'ochwig</u>

tobacco <u>wiw, ta-wahko</u>
(Sp. tabaco)

toe <u>machpoD, mamachpoD</u>

toka stick <u>usaga</u>
toka player <u>usagakam</u>

tomahawk <u>shonchki</u>

tomorrow <u>si'alim</u>

tongs of cactus rib <u>wah'o</u>

tongue <u>nehni</u>

tongue of wagon <u>chi-mohn</u>

tools, implements <u>chikpnakuD</u>

tooth <u>tahtami</u>

top, cover <u>kuhpaDag</u>

toss a baby, to <u>ulugid</u>

torch <u>kuhta, kuhtagi</u>

totem <u>wehmkal</u>

touch <u>tahtam</u>
cause to touch, to <u>tahchul</u>id

tough, hard <u>kawk, kawpk, s-</u>

toy, athletic field <u>chichwihkuD</u>

track, to <u>jehgi, jehgchud</u>

trading post <u>tianna/chiando</u>
(Sp. tienda)

tramp <u>tlahmba</u> (Sp. trampa)

tradition, way of life, culture <u>himdag</u>

tragedy, calamity, disaster
neijig, s-

trap, brake   wulshpakuD

trap, to   wulshp, la'ashp
(Sp. lazo)

trash, waste, grass, brush
sha'i

treatment with rubbing stick
hiwchulida

treatment with heat   kuhtpa

treatment for cleansing   wusota

tree, stick   uhs, u'us

tremble, to   gigiwuk

tribesman   o'odham (see
Appendix IV B)

trick of cheat, to   banmad

trifle or play or compete, to
chichwih

trim, to   hikshaD

triviality, game   chichwihdag

trot noisily, to   kaponahim

trot   woshdakhim

trouble   kuDutaDag

trouble, to   kuDut

trough for watering stock
ka-nohwa (Sp. canoa)

trousers   shaliw, shashaliw
(Sp. jaripero)

truck   tlohgih

trunk   wawlih (Sp. baul)
tree trunk   shon

true, to be   wohoh

trust   wohochud

truth, true person   wohokam

try, to   a'appem

trying   chum

tub   tihna (Sp. tina)

tuber   dahidag

tuberculosis   i'ihogig

Tucson   Chuk Shon

Tuesday   mahltis (Sp. martes)

turkey   tohwa, totowa

turn something over, to   gahi
wua

turn or bend, to   noD, nohnoD

turn something, to   noDagid,
nohnogid

turtle   komkch'eD,
kokomkch'eD

Turtle Wedged village (Sells)
Komkch'eD e Wah'osidk

tweezers, pliers   ki'ishpakuD

twin   kuadi, kukadi (Sp. cuate)

twinkle   tonot

twist (rope), to   wijin

twister, whirlwind   siwloki/
siwlig

twitch in the eye, to   wuhigew
two   gohk, go'ogok
twice   goko

U

udder, nipple   wipih
ugly   paD, pa'apaD
to be ugly   paDaj, pa'apDaj

umbilical   hik

umbrella   ehkchulidakuD

unable, to be   pi e nakog

uncle   kehli, hakit, je'es,
tatal

under   wecho, wepcho

understand   amichud, s-

understanding, wisdom,
knowledge, mind   amichuda-
Dag

underwear   wecho eniga

unflinching, to be   bamustk, s-

unite   hemakochud

untangle   matok

until   am hugkam, wo ip

upset, turn over, to   aigo wua,
  gahi wua

upside down   aigo

upward, backward   ta'i

urge   bahmut

urine   hi'i

us, our   ahchim (t-)

use, to   hekaj

use up   hugiog

V

vaccinate   chekid

vagina   muhs

valley   wo'otk

value   namkidaDag

vapor, dust, fog, smoke   kuhbs

various   nahnko

vegetable   ihwagi

vein   eDhaidag, e'eDhaiDag

vengeance   agwuaDag

vengeance, to take   agwua, e

vertebrae, backbone, vertebral
  column   eDa wa'ug

victory   gewitoidag

village   kihhim

vinegar   wi-nahli

violin   wio-lihn (Sp. violín)

visible   mahs, s-

vise   ki'ishpakuD

visit   chehgim, chehgio
  to visit someone for a meal
    neal
  to go to visit someone for a
    meal   nealimeD, nealop

visitor   chehgimdam

visualize   neid

voice   che'idag

vomit   wihos

vomit, to   wihot

vomit, to cause to   wihoschud

vote   wotalt (Sp. votar)

vulture, buzzard   nuhwi,
  nunuwi

W

wag or switch the tail, to
  bahigid

wage   namkidaDag

wagon   kalit, kakalit

waist, midriff   huDa

wait   neniDa/tamiam

wait!   kia!

walk or move, to   him, hihim

walking stick   gakimchul

wallet, buckskin bag   huashomi

wall, house   kih, kihki

want or need, to   tatchua

want, desire, love   tatchuidag

war   cheggiaDag

war-club, tomahawk   shonchki

wares   gagli

warm, to be   huhk, s-

war party   gitaiokam
  to go on war path   gitaion

warrior   s-chu cheggiaDkam

wash, to   wakon, wapkon

wash, gully   hiktani

wash basin   wakonakuD

watchband, wrist guard
  shohba, shohshoba

water or liquid   shuhdagi

water or liquid, possessed
  wa'igi
  to get water   wa'ig
  to go to get water   wa'igameD
  to get water for someone
    wa'igid
  water vessel   wa'igkuD

water borne object   wi'inog

water carrier <u>wa'igamdam</u>
<u>wahpa'igopkam</u>

watermelon <u>gepi/miloni</u>

water gourd, canteen <u>wako</u>,
<u>wapko</u>

wasp, hornet <u>wipsh</u>

waste, trash, grass, brush
<u>sha'i</u>

wave <u>tohnk, to'otonk</u>

wave the hand, to <u>magjid</u>

ways, customs, tradition
<u>himdag</u>
one way <u>ha'ab</u>

we <u>ahchim, ach</u>

weak, to be <u>pi gewk</u>

weakness <u>pi gewkdag</u>

wealthy, rich <u>kais, kakais, s-</u>

weapon <u>cheggi'akuD</u>

wearing, to be <u>e enigaDadch</u>

weave, to <u>maintahim</u>

web, or spider <u>tokihtuD</u>,
<u>totkihtuD</u>

wedge, to <u>wah'osid</u>

Wednesday <u>mialklos</u> (Sp.
miércoles)

week <u>domig</u>

weigh or measure, to <u>pisalt</u>

well, good <u>s-ap</u>

well, water hole <u>wawhia/</u>
<u>wahia, waipia</u>

west <u>kuiwa</u> (Pima)

west, sunset <u>huDunig</u>

what? <u>hah?</u>

wheat <u>pilkani</u>

when <u>hekid</u>

when? <u>hekid i</u>

where <u>hebai</u>

where? <u>Bah/hebai i</u>

whine, to <u>kuishani</u>

whip <u>gewikuD</u>
to whip <u>gewitan</u>

whippoorwill <u>kohlo'ogam</u>

whistle, to <u>gikujid</u>

white, to be white <u>toha, tohta,</u>
<u>s-</u>

whitish <u>tohama, s-</u>

who <u>heDai, heDam</u>

who? <u>heDai i, heDam i</u>

"who knows" <u>dahpi</u>!

whole <u>hekia</u>

why <u>haschu ahg</u>

widow <u>hejel wi'ikam</u>

wide <u>taDani, tatDani, s-</u>

wife <u>hohnig</u>
to go for <u>hohnimeD</u>
marry off <u>hohnchud</u>
take a <u>hohntahim</u>

wild <u>mischini</u> (Sp. mesteño)

wild, untamed <u>doajkam, s-</u>

wild animal <u>doajkam</u>

will, desired thing <u>tatchui</u>

will (future) <u>wo/ho</u>

willow, desert <u>ahn</u>
Desert Willow Village
<u>Ahngam</u>

wilt <u>bahtkim</u>

win <u>gewito</u>

winch <u>siwihnia</u>

wind <u>hewel</u>

wind plants <u>hewel e'es</u>

windbreak <u>uhgsha, u'ugsha</u>

windmill <u>papa-lohdi</u> (Sp.
papalote)

wine (saguaro) <u>nawait</u>

whiskey <u>wihnui</u>

window <u>wintani</u> (Sp. ventana)

wing <u>a'an</u>

winter <u>hehpich'eDkam, s-</u>

wipe   dagkon

wisdom, understanding,
   knowledge, mind   amichuda-
   Dag

wise, to be   chu amichud, s-

wisely   chu amichudam, s-

wise man, shaman   chu mahch,
   s-

with   wehm, we'ewem

within   eDa

wolf   sheh'e, shesh'e

womb   koshagi, kokshagi

woman   uwi, u'uwi
   adult woman   oks, o'oki

wood, firewood   ku'agi

woodrat   koson

wooden bowl   wachiho (Sp.
   batihoja)

woodpecker, grey and white
   chehekam

woodpecker, black and white
   hikiuwig, hihikiuwig

word   ne'oki

work   chikpan/chipkan

work, to   chikpan/chipkan

workman   chikpandam; pion
   (Sp. peon)

worm, fish   watopi, waptopi
   thousand legged worm
      kommo'ol

worn, to be   wakimagi, s-

worry, trouble   kuDutaDag

worry or trouble, to   kuDut

wound   muhDag

wrap something, to   hobinoD
   (hohobinoD)

wrestle, to   dadge

wrist guard, watchband
   shohba, shohshoba

write or draw, to   o'ohan

writing   o'ohana

Y

Yaqui   Hiakim, Hihakim

yawn   chinniak

year   ahidag, a'ahidag
   last year   ha'akid

yeast   jewajidakuD

yell   hihnk
   yell at   hihnko'id

yellow   oam, o'am, s-

yes   heu'u

yesterday   tako

yet, but   eDa; oi wa

yet, not yet   (pi) koi

yield something, to   dagito

yoke   yehwa

you, your   ahpi (ap, m-)

you plural, your   ahpim (am,
   em)

young, new   wechij

youth   aljeg

yucca   howi, uhmug

Yuman   Yuhmi

Z

zigzag   jujul, juhu'ujul, s-
   to be zigzag   jujulk,
      juhu'ujulk, s-

APPENDICES
APPENDIX I.
THE ALPHABET OF O'ODHAM

Papagos and Pimas have chosen the letters for their sounds through reading and writing tests.

a	ahli	'child'
b	babad	'frog'
ch	chuhwi	'jackrabbit'
d	dahk	'nose'
e	esh	'chin'
g	gohki	'footprint'
h	huawi	'muledeer'
i	ispul	'spur'
j	je'e	'mother'
k	keihina	'folkdance'
l	lahbis	'pencil'
m	muhwal	'fly'
n	nahk	'ear'
o	ola	'toka puck'
p	pistohl	'pistol'
s	sihl	'saddle'
sh	shobbiaD	'doll'
t	toka	'field hockey'
u	u'uwhig	'bird'
w	wonami	'hat'
'	a'an	'feather'
D	juDumi	'bear'

The letters of O'odham sound the same as the letters of English, except that an English letter may have a number of different sounds but an O'odham letter has only one sound. Where an English letter has several different sounds, the sound which that letter also has in Spanish is the sound of the letter in O'odham.

The letter a has several sounds in English but the sound that it has both in English water and Spanish agua is the sound it has in O'odham wa'igi. The O'odham letter e has the sound of unstressed e as in nickel and O'odham hetasp, but there is no like sound in Spanish. Notice the sound each of the five vowels has in:

	English	Spanish	O'odham
a	water	agua	wa'igi
e	nickel		hetasp
i	police	charifo	chi-lihhi
o	short	corto	shopol
u	mule	mula	muhla

A vowel may be short or long in duration. There is a short o in ton 'to shine', but a long o in tohn 'knee'. The length is indicated by h, as in tohn. Each vowel occurs short or long:

a	ban	'coyote'	ah	pahn	'bread'
e	hegam	'those'	eh	hehgam	'jealous'
i	chini	'mouth'	ih	chihchini	'mouths'
o	ton	'to shine'	oh	tohn	'knee'
u	chuhug	'night'	uh	chuhhug	'meat'

Note that when h occurs before a vowel as in chuhug, it is h sound and not length, Two instances occur, hihhim 'moves' and hehhem 'laughs, in which hh is a consonant cluster. Other sequences of vowel and consonant are always two separate sounds as in waw 'rock', rhyming with English cow.

Sequences of vowels are always two separate sounds such as ia in mia 'near', ai in waik 'three', au in haupal, 'red tailed hawk', ua in chuagia 'net bag', etc.

Technically there are long and short vowels in unstressed positions but the short vowels, with the exception of i following b, p, g, k, m, n, w, or a vowel, are deleted or reduced to schewa, ə a neutral transition sound, and therefore not written, allowing long vowels to be written as normal vowels, with the exception of long ih.

The short vowel i is voiceless (whispered) after b, p, g, k, m, n, w, or a vowel when final as in nowi 'arm' or amai 'there', or before a voiceless consonant as in chegito 'to think'. Final i is voiced in NEGATIVE pi 'not' and PRONOUNS ahni 'I' and ahpi 'you'. There are also isolated instances of voiceless u in some dialects:

ikus	'cloth'
wahkus	'mat'
hikuchk	'to cut'

All of the vowels are voiceless if final or before voiceless consonants in words or syllables consisting of consonant plus vowel plus (h or ') plus vowel as in:

mia	'near'
cheho	'cave'
mo'o	'head'
s-toha kawiyu	'white horse'

When a short vowel is followed by a voiced consonant which does not precede a long (unreduced) vowel it has full vowel quality and reappears in writing. The reduced vowel that reappears is <u>i</u> following <u>ch</u>, <u>j</u>, <u>l</u> or <u>s:</u>

huhch + j→huhchij	'his claw'
aj + j→ajij	'its narrow'
hahl + g→hahlig	'being squash'
wehs + j→wehsij	'all of'

The reduced vowel is <u>a</u> following any consonant other than <u>ch</u>, <u>j</u>, <u>l</u>, or <u>s:</u>

him + d→himad	'will be going'
nahk + j→nahkaj	'his ear'

The neutral transition sound occurs following word final consonants as in tonə and between consonants which are not made at the same point of articulation, sən, kət, dəm, bəw,ləd, etc. In addition it occurs between voiceless and voiced, or between stop and continuant consonants made at the same point of articulation təd, pəb, bəm, tən, etc. The transition sound is voiced before a voiced consonant and voiceless elsewhere.

This leaves the following types of phonetic consonant clusters with no intervening transition sound:

1. voiced continuant plus glottal, (mh, n', wh, l' etc.)
2. consonants made at the same point of articulation in which stop does not precede continuant, and voiceless does not precede voiced (dd, pp, mm, '', ll, mb, nt, ng, dt, gk, etc.)

The consonants are all voiceless (whispered) when final or before a voiceless vowel or consonant, much like the <u>d</u> in breadth or the g̲ in length. Thus the following are voiceless;

m in kahm
w in nowi
g̲ in chegito

An n̲ before e̲, i̲, or u̲ sounds like Spanish ñ̲ as in ne'i ' song', ahni̲ ' I ', nuhwi ' buzzard '. Entries given in quotes are Spanish loan words in which n̲ is not pronounced ñ̲: ' nuhmlo ' ' number ', ' ni̲ ' ' neither '.

For D̲, l̲, and sh̲ the tongue is curled back to the roof of the mouth as for English r̲ as in juDumi̲ ' bear ', ahli̲ ' child ', sha'i ' trash '.

There are two glottals in O'odham, stop ' and continuant h̲. The apostrophe ' stands for glottal stop, a catch in the throat like a boy imitating a machine or like the sound between syllables in Ohoh!, as in mo'o ' head '. In O'odham writing, initial glottal stop is not written. Thus words that begin with a vowel actually begin with glottal stop, as ahli̲ 'child'.

The sounds of h̲ and w̲ are deleted initially in certain O'odham words just as they are in certain English words. In English I saw him can be pronounced I saw im, deleting h̲, and I will go can be pronounced I'll go, deleting w̲. In O'odham hahawa ' afterwards ' loses its first sound after a consonant or i̲ so that am hahawa is pronounced am ahawa. In the same circumstance wo̲ 'will ' loses its first sound so that am wo is pronounced am o. The following words lose their first sound following a consonant or i̲:

hahawa	'afterwards'
wa hekaj	'immediately'
wa	'previously mentioned'
wabsh	'just'
wabshaba	'but'
wa'i	'only'
wo	'will'
wuD	'to be'

For the consonants ch̲, j̲, and sh̲ the lips are unrounded and relaxed in O'odham in contrast to English.

In other respects the consonants of O'odham are pronounced the same as in English.

The writing of any language, however, represents the sounds of that language and no other. Even sounds which are written the same because they are similar in two languages still have differences. So while some O'odham words look like English or Spanish words they must be pronounced in O'odham.

STRESS AND TONE

Stress or accent occurs on the first vowel of O'odham words, and is therefore not written. Many short words like ha, e, wabsh, etc., are unstressed particles. In compound words like hoas-ha'a 'dish' stress occurs on the first vowel of each part but strongest on the second part of the word. Late Spanish loan words with non-initial stress are treated like compounds with stress on both parts: papa-lohdi ' windmill ', kos-nihlo 'cook'. When these are reduplicated both parts are affected as in koks-ninilo.

In a word or phrase, tone is high from the first stress to the last stress and low elsewhere:

hegai cheoj   'that man'   Nt wo dagito 'I'll leave it'

Since stress and tone are not written, the non- O'odham reader must learn certain features of grammatical structure in order to use the proper stress and tone.

HISTORIC CHANGES WITHIN O'ODHAM

Certain sequences of sound in early O'odham undergo a change of pronounciation according to dialect. In the southeast bilabials are omitted from certain words:

wabsh	wash	'just'
wabshaba	washaba	'but'

u'uwhig	u'uhig	'bird'
wawhia	wahia	'well'

Also h replaces the voiceless stop consonants of certain words with assimilation of the following vowel:

ahpim	ahham	'you all'
uhpam	uhhum	'back home'
chuhkug	chuhhug	'flesh'
ehkeg	ehheg	'to be shaded'

In the north and west sequences of vowels oa, ea, and eo are changed whether contiguous or interrupted by glottal (h or '). In these areas oa is pronounced ua:

doakag	duakag	'soul'
s-toha	s-tuha	'white'
ko'a	ku'a	'eating'

Also e is pronounced i between a palatal consonant (ch, j, n) and a low vowel (a, o):

neok	niok	'talking'
cheho	chiho	'cave'

ne'oki	ni'oki	'word'
chehani	chihani	'commanding'

Other than after a palatal consonant e is pronounced o if before o, u if before a:

wehoh	wohoh	'true'
mea	mua	'kill'
me'a	mu'a	'killing'

The plurals of these words retain the original vowels of O'odham in all dialects since the vowels are in separate syllables and separated by full consonants: dodakag, s-tohta, neneok, chehcho, etc.

HISTORIC CHANGES THROUGH BORROWING

Several changes have been made in O'odham as a result of the incorporation of loan words from Spanish. First, some consonants became two consonants. The sounds of t were t before a or o, and ch elsewhere, acting like the t in "native" in contrast to "nature", but loan words upset this balance so that now both t and ch must be written. The same is true of d which now must be written d and j. The sounds of n were n before a or o and ñ elsewhere, but ñ is now written ni where it would otherwise be ambiguous.

The sounds of s were s before i, and ş (sh) elsewhere, but now both s and sh must be written. The sounds of l were likewise l before i and d elsewhere, but now both l and d must be written. The sound d is written D.

The consonant y did not exist in O'odham, and is written now only in loan words.

APPENDIX II.

USE OF THE DICTIONARY

Like any language, Papago has thousands of word forms which it would be impractical to list as separate dictionary entries. The most essential of these are given following a basic form in the dictionary section. Others are made from these forms plus affixes given in Appendix III.

Meaning entries are given with no quotes while translations are given with single quotes:

<u>wo'o, wohp, wo'owop</u>   to lie
wo'o, wohp, wo'owop 'is lying, are lying, are lying scattered'

Words that have more than one form are listed under their basic singular form, followed by plural and/or distributive forms. Plural is formed by reduplication or doubling of the first sound or sounds in the following word classes:

NOUN STEM:

ban, bahban	'coyote, coyotes'
cheoj, checheoj	'man, men'

VERB STEM:

him, hihim	'it's moving, they're moving'
cheposid, chechposid	'branding it, branding them'

Initial w, and in some words noninitial w, reduplicates as p:

wako, wapko	'gourd, gourds'
gewkdag, gewpkdag	'power, powers'

Distributive f o r m , indicating different locations for actions, features, or things, is shown by insertion of ' or h, if not already present, plus normal reduplication (not that given for w):

Topographical NOUN STEM

```
do'ag, dohda'ag          'mountain, mountains'
siwulog, si'isiwulog     'twister, twisters'
tohk, to'otonk           'dike, dikes'
nawoj, naipiju, nan'aipiju 'friend, friends, many friends'
```

ADJECTIVE STEM:

```
chew, che'echew  'long (single thing, separate things)
shopol, sho'oshpol  'short (single thing, separate things)
```

VERB STEM:

```
chikpan, chichkpan  'working in one place, different places'
wo'o, wohp, wo'owop  'is lying, are lying, are lying scattered'
```

PREPOSITION STEM:

```
dahm, da'adam 'over (in one place, in different places)'
wecho, wepcho, we'ewecho 'under (a thing, things, scattered
                                                    things'
```

NUMERAL STEM:

```
            gohk, go'ogok  'two, pairs'
            waik, wa'awaik  'three, triplets'
```

Nondistributive forms of PREPOSITION STEMS and certain VERB STEMS function as singular and plural:

```
        am dahm g kih 'over the house'
        am ha-dahm g kihki  'over the houses'
        am ha-da'adam g kihki  'over the scattered houses'

        Chikpan o. 'He's working, They're working'
        Chichkpan o.  'They're working in different places.'
```

Certain words have one form, either the reduplicated or nonreduplicated, for singular, plural, and distributive:

```
            chewagi 'cloud, clouds'
            kakaichu 'quail'
            neid 'seeing one or more things'
```

The plural and distributive forms of some VERB STEMS are suppletive or radically different from the singular:

```
        jiwia, dada  'arrive (singular, plural)'
        meD, wohpo 'is running, are running'
        kahch, wehch, we'ewech  'is lying, are lying, are
          lying scattered'
```

In this case the plural is alphabetically listed with cross reference to the singular:

dada	see jiwia
<u>wohpo</u>	see <u>meD</u>
<u>wehch</u>	see <u>kahch</u>

The most essential forms of the VERB STEM are given in parenthesis following the basic forms in the following order:

basic singular (noncontinuative, repetitive, imperative)
basic plural (noncontinuative, repetitive, imperative)
   meaning

The basic form is usually continuative, corresponding to the -ing form in English. All forms except noncontinuative are underlined (in which h<u>h</u> is consonant cluster.):

<u>him</u> (hih, <u>hihhim</u>, <u>hihm</u>), <u>hihim</u> (hihih, <u>hihhim</u>, <u>hihim</u>) 'to move'

More specifically the meanings are:

him	'is moving'
hih	'moved (singular)'
hihhim	'moves (singular, plural repetitive)'
hihm	'move! (singular)'
hihim	'are moving"
hihih	'moved (plural)'

If the basic form is noncontinuative it is not underlined:

jiwia (<u>jijiwhia</u>), dada (<u>daiw</u>) to arrive

If possible noncontinuative is shown by underlining part of continuative to conserve space:

<u>chik</u>pan, <u>chichk</u>pan to work

The noncontinuative forms are:

chikp	'worked (in one place)'
chichkp	'worked (in separate places)'

Forms which are identical to the basic form are not listed so the entry above indicates that there are repetitive and imperative forms identical to the basic as in:

Chum ani hekid chikpan.	'I always work.'
Chum ach hekid chikpan.	'We always work.'
Hahasko ach chichkpan.	'We work in different places!'
Oi g chikpan!	'You work!'
Oi g wo chikpan!	'You all work!'

Entries whose definition includes 'be' or 'have' have only continuative forms:

<u>ge'ej</u>, <u>ge'edeDaj</u> to be big

111

<u>mahkch</u>   to have given to

Words having alternate forms in different dialects are separated by diagonal line:

<u>uhpam/uhhum</u>   back to previous place

Synonyms are separated by semi-colon:

door   <u>etpa, e'etpa; kuhpaDag, kuhkpaDag; pualt, pupualt</u>

Papago Word entries requiring occurrence of some other part are followed by a key indicating the part. Words which consistently follow reflexive PERSON are indicated by e:

<u>waila, e</u>   to dance

Reflexive PERSON indicator ni-, t-, or e precedes the word:

ni-waila	'I dance'
t-waila	'we dance'
e waila	'you, he, she, they dance'

Words which consistently follow VERB PHRASE QUALIFIER are indicated by hab:

<u>mahs, mams, hab</u>   to be like

Some form of the QUALIFIER precedes the word in the CLAUSE:

hab mahs; bo mahs	'is like'
has mahs	'what it's like'

Words which consistently follow AFFIRMATIVE s- or NEGATIVE pi are indicated by s-:

kehgaj, kehegaj, s-   to be beautiful

words which follow AFFIRMATIVE or NEGATIVE and chu or ta are given as subentries of the main word:

<u>ehbid, s-</u>   to be afraid of
<u>s-chu ehbid</u>   to be fearful
<u>s-ta ehbidam</u>   to be dangerous

Sources of loanwords are given in parenthesis following meanings with the abbreviations:

(Az.) Aztec
(Eng.) English
(Sp.) Spanish

The most complete entries of Papago words and loanword sources are given in the Papago-English section. Basic forms to use in locating these entries are given in the Eng-

112

lish-Papago section.

Since underlining differentiates Papago VERB STEM forms, the Papago entries are underlined in both vocabulary sections unless the form is noncontinuative :

<u>kaiha</u>m   to listen to
<u>kakaichu</u>   quail
ko'ito   to eat up

eat up, to   ko'ito
listen to, to   <u>kaiha</u>m
quail   <u>kakaichu</u>

APPENDIX III.
GRAMMAR

This is a sketch of the rules of sentence composition of Papago. It is written in generative form following Chomski,[1] with modifications to facilitate understanding for the normal reader. Since it is a sketch it is only partially generative.

Although evidence of paragraph and discourse structure may be observed in this sketch, only the structure of the sentence is in view, with its main part, the clause.

1. SENTENCE

The basic SENTENCE consists of INTERJECTION plus CLAUSE plus modifying SENTENCE, of which only the clause is obligatory. Names of structures are given in capital letters. With branches indicating parts, and obligatory part underlined, sentence structure is as follows:

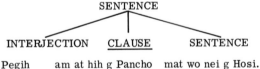

	SENTENCE	
INTERJECTION	CLAUSE	SENTENCE
Pegih	am at hih g Pancho	mat wo nei g Hosi.
'Well	Pancho went there	to see Jose.'

1.1. INTERJECTION

Interjections are:

ah 'oh'	dahpi 'unknown'	dohwai 'ready'
hah 'what'	heu'u 'yes'	hiji 'out of the way'
ih 'oh'	kaij 'take heed'	kia 'wait'
neh 'look'	pegih 'well, agreed'	pia'a 'no'
	shah 'get along animal'	

---

[1] Chomski, Noam, SYNTACTIC STRUCTURES, Janua Linguarium, Mouton & Co., (1957)

Combinations occur such as: <u>ah heu'u</u> 'oh yes', <u>kaij neh</u> 'behold', etc.

2. CLAUSE

The CLAUSE consists of INITIATOR plus <u>VERB PHRASE</u> plus NOUN PHRASE plus NOUN PHRASE plus RELATIONAL PHRASE plus TIME PHRASE plus ATTRIBUTIVE PHRASE. Note again that the underlined part is obligatory.

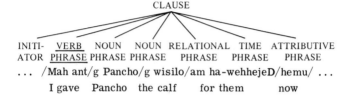

```
                          CLAUSE
INITI-   VERB   NOUN   NOUN RELATIONAL TIME  ATTRIBUTIVE
ATOR   PHRASE PHRASE PHRASE   PHRASE  PHRASE   PHRASE
...  /Mah ant/g Pancho/g wisilo/am ha-wehhejeD/hemu/ ...
      I gave   Pancho  the calf   for them      now
```

At each stage in the description, the reader may find it helpful to assemble the parts given with those given previously. For example, CLAUSE is given as a part of SENTENCE and then later the parts of CLAUSE are given, the parts would be assembled as follows:

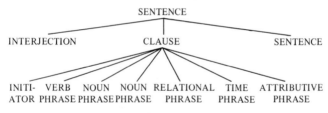

```
                        SENTENCE
INTERJECTION            CLAUSE            SENTENCE

INITI-  VERB   NOUN   NOUN RELATIONAL TIME  ATTRIBUTIVE
ATOR  PHRASE PHRASE PHRASE   PHRASE  PHRASE   PHRASE
```

Each phrase type consists of smaller parts and is named for its main part. The main part of the VERB PHRASE is VERB; that of NOUN PHRASE is NOUN, etc. Each phrase type begins with optional NEGATIVE <u>pi</u> plus optional QUAL-IFIER which is described after the description of various phrase types.

A single NOUN PHRASE under CLAUSE is object. Two NOUN PHRASES are indirect object plus object. The subject NOUN PHRASE is a part of the VERB PHRASE.

2.1. INITIATOR

INITIATOR is attached to AUXILIARY, replacing its vowel. It is subordinating or nonsubordinating. Note that the kinds of a given structure are given in small letters rather than in capitals like the structure names.

Subordinating INITIATOR <u>ma</u> initiates first clause of modifying SENTENCE:

> Am at hih g Pancho mat wo nei g Hosi.
> ' Pancho went there to see Jose. '
>
> hegai o'odham mat wo chikpanad
> 'the person that works'

Nonsubordinating INITIATOR is <u>ku</u> 'and', <u>na</u> 'is ? was ? will? etc. , <u>na'a</u> 'maybe':

Kut wo chikp g Hosi.	'And Jose will work. '
Nat wo chikp g Hosi?	'Will Jose work?'
Na'as wo chikp g Hosi.	'Maybe Jose will work. '

2.2. VERB PHRASE

The VERB PHRASE consists of NEGATIVE plus QUALIFIER, plus DEGREE plus POINT plus AFFIRMATIVE plus <u>VERB</u> plus <u>AUXILIARY</u> plus NOUN PHRASE. VERB and AUXILIARY are obligatory. The NOUN PHRASE under VERB PHRASE is subject of the SENTENCE.

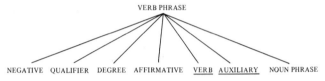

NEGATIVE QUALIFIER DEGREE AFFIRMATIVE <u>VERB</u> <u>AUXILIARY</u> NOUN PHRASE

DEGREE is: sha'i 'sort of, a bit'
            si   'really'
            sha'i si 'quite a bit'

POINT is i, indicating a certain point in time or space.

AFFIRMATIVE <u>s-</u> is attached to the word   immediately following it and is deleted (removed) if immediately following NEGATIVE <u>pi.</u>

2.2.1. VERB

The VERB is a word consisting of <u>VERB STEM</u> plus STATIVE plus ASPECT plus CONJUNCTION. Parts of a word are given with connecting plus signs (+).

VERB

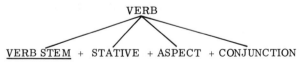

<u>VERB STEM</u> + STATIVE + ASPECT + CONJUNCTION

ASPECT is imperative or nonimperative, future if imperative, future or nonfuture otherwise, repetitive or nonrepetitive, continuative if repetitive or if following STATIVE, continuative or noncontinuative otherwise. ASPECT is indicated by shortening, reduplicating or doubling of sounds, or suffixing of a basic form. The following forms are given when each form is different:

basic (noncontinuative, repetitive, imperative)
him (hih, hihhim, hihm) to move or walk

with the meanings:

him	'is walking'	Him o g Pancho. 'Pancho is walking.'
hih	'walk, walked'	Hih at g Pancho. 'Pancho walked.'
hihhim	'walks'	Hihhim o g Pancho. 'Pancho walks.'
hihm	'walk!'	Oi g hihm! 'Go!'

Where possible the shortened noncontinuative is shown by underlining part of the basic form rather than being given in parentheses:

chikpan   to work

The forms indicated are:

chikpan 'is working' Chikpan o g Pancho. 'Pancho is working.'
chikp 'work, worked' Chikp at g Pancho. 'Pancho worked.'

If noncontinuative, repetitive, or imperative form is identical to the basic form it is not listed. Since there are no forms given in parenthesis following the entry chikpan, SENTENCES calling for repetitive or imperative use the same form:

'Chikpan o g Pancho wehs tashkaj. 'Pancho works every day.'
Oi g chikpan. 'Now work!'

Continuative future ASPECT indicator d and continuative nonfuture ASPECT indicator him are suffixed to basic and repetitive forms:

T wo himad g Pancho.   'Pancho will keep going.'
T wo hihhimad g Pancho. 'Pancho will go repeatedly.'
T wo chikpanad g Pancho. 'Pancho will keep working.'
T wo chikpanad g Pancho wehs tashkaj.
'Pancho will work every day.'
Oi g chikpanad.   'Keep working!'
Chikpanahim o g Pancho. 'Pancho was working.'

STATIVE indicator is zero preceding present ASPECT, k otherwise:

eniga_ 'has something'
enigakahim 'had something'
wo enigakad 'will have something'

VERB STEM is stative preceding <u>STATIVE</u> indicator, nonstative otherwise. Continuative ASPECT indicator <u>d</u> may be deleted (left out) following <u>STATIVE</u>:

wo enigakad ⟶ wo enigak

An arrow is used as above to indicate that the utterance following it is derived (formed) from the utterance preceding it.

Nonstative VERB STEM is intransitive if it occurs with one noun phrase:

Hih at g Pancho. 'Pancho went.'

Nonstative VERB STEM is transitive if it occurs with two noun phrases:

Bei at g Pancho g wisilo. 'Pancho got the calf.'

Nonstative VERB STEM is dative if it occurs with three noun phrases:

Mah at g Pancho g Hosi g wisilo. 'Pancho gave Jose the calf.'

Many VERB STEMS have different singular and plural forms. Usually the singular and plural are related, the plural being formed by reduplicating or doubling the first sounds of a word:

him, hihim 'to move along'

Sometimes the forms are suppletive or unrelated:

bei, ui 'to get something'

Intransitive VERB STEMS agree with the subject NOUN PHRASE in number:

Him o g cheoj. 'The man is walking.'
Hihim o g chechoj. 'The men are walking.'

Transitive and dative VERB STEMS agree with the object NOUN PHRASE in number:

Bei at g Pancho g wisilo. 'Pancho got the calf.'
Ha at ui g Pancho g wipsilo. 'Pancho got the calves.'

The VERB STEM is singular with mass (uncountable) NOUN STEMS such as shuhdagi:

MeD o g shuhdagi. 'The water is running.'
Wa'i at g Pancho g shuhdagi. 'Pancho got the water.'

The VERB STEM is plural with aggregate NOUN STEMS, referring to things usually considered in pairs or groups:

Ui at g Pancho g shuhshk. 'Pancho got the shoes.'
Ui at g Pancho g lial. 'Pancho got the money.'

Stative VERB STEM is equasional or possessive preceding two noun phrases, essive or stance preceding one noun phrase.

Equasional VERB STEM wuD occurs with second noun phrase displacing it from other VERB parts:

K wuD wakial g Pancho.   'And Pancho is a cowboy.'
K wuD wakialkahim g Pancho. 'And Pancho was a cowboy.'
Kut wuD wo wakialkad g Pancho.'And Pancho will be a cowboy.'

Stative possessive VERB STEM is eniga 'to have something', shoiga 'to have an animal'.

Eniga o g Pancho g jeweD. 'Pancho has land.'
Shoiga o g Pancho g wisilo. 'Pancho has a calf.'

Essive VERB STEM is ha'ichug, g, or zero 'to be somewhere', occurring with continuative ASPECT indicators:

ha'ichug 'is somewhere'
ha'ichugkahim 'was somewhere'
wo ha'ichugkad 'will be somewhere'

If the VERB STEM is ha'ichug:

Nat am wo ha'ichugkad g o'odham amai?
'Will the people be there?'

If essive VERB STEM is g the NOUN PHRASE is moved to precede it and the NOUN is attached to it:

Nat wo s-o'odhamagkad amai? 'Will the people be there?'

If essive VERB STEM is zero the RELATIONAL PHRASE is moved to precede it but is not attached:

Nat amai wo _kad g o'odham? 'Will the people be there?'

Stance VERB STEM is daha 'to be sitting', kih 'to be living at', kehk 'to be standing', wo'o 'to be lying', kahch 'to be lying (inanimate)', etc. :

wo'o   'is lying'
wo'okahim 'was lying'
wo wo'okad 'will be lying'

2.2.2. AUXILIARY

The AUXILIARY consists of ASPECT plus MOOD plus FUTURE:

119

AUXILIARY

ASPECT + MOOD + FUTURE

Auxiliary ASPECT is merely an agreement indicator without meaning. It is t if following noncontinuative TENSE or preceding FUTURE, and zero otherwise (except that t does not occur preceding dubitative s, and must occur preceding conditional p).

MOOD is indicative zero, conditional p, dubitative s, evidential ki, imperative g, reportative sh, and others which are not given names here. Some MOOD indicators and rough translations are p 'if', s 'wonder if', ki 'evidently', g 'Do it!', hems 'might', p-hems 'perhaps', s-hems 'expected', huh i 'hope', s-huh 'how can', shp 'guess', etc. Zero MOOD indicates simple declarative or interrogative sentence.

A PERSON indicator agreeing with the PRONOUN of the subject NOUN PHRASE is placed in the AUXILIARY preceding its ASPECT agreement indicator.

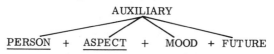

AUXILIARY

PERSON + ASPECT + MOOD + FUTURE

PERSON is imperative if ASPECT is imperative, nonimperative otherwise. PERSON and PRONOUN agree as follows:

imperative			
PERSON	PRONOUN	PERSON	PRONOUN
ni	ahpi 'you'	wo	ahpim 'you all'
nonimperative			
ani	ahni 'I'	ach	ahchim 'we'
ap	ahpi	am	ahpim
a	ihda 'this'	a	ihdam 'these, they'
	hegai 'that'		hegam 'those, they'

The PERSON indicator a becomes o if AUXILIARY ASPECT agreement indicator is zero and MOOD is zero or ki:

Chikpan ani ahni.	'I'm working.'
Chikpan ap ahpi.	'You're working.'
Chikpan o hegai.	'That one's working.'
Chikpan oki hegai.	'That one's evidently working.'
Chikpan ach ahchim.	'We're working.'

Chikpan am ahpim.	'You all are working.'
Chikpan o hegam.	'They are working.'

Preceding AUXILIARY ASPECT agreement indicator t, the PERSON indicator ani becomes an and ach becomes at:

Chikp ant ahni.	'I worked.'
Chikp apt ahpi.	'You worked.'
Chikp at hegai.	'That one worked.'
*Chikp att ahchim.	'We worked.'
Chikp amt ahpim.	'You all worked.'
Chikp at hegam.	'They worked.'

*The plural chichkp is used if the participants are working in separate places.

AUXILIARY normally follows the first word of the CLAUSE. If VERB is not the first word, AUXILIARY is moved to second position in CLAUSE.

The AUXILIARY may follow NEGATIVE:

Pi o chikpan hegai.	'That one isn't working.'
Pi ant i gei ahni.	'I didn't fall.'

The AUXILIARY may follow INITIATOR, which is attached to it replacing its vowel:

Nat pi i gei hegai?	'Didn't he fall?'
Na'as pi i gei hegai.	'Maybe he didn't fall.'
Na'anis pi i gei ahni.	'Maybe I didn't fall.'
Kupt pi i gei ahpi.	'And you didn't fall.'

The INITIATOR ku may be deleted:

Kunt pi i gei ahni. -- Nt pi i gei ahni. 'And I didn't fall.'

FUTURE indicator is wo. If the AUXILIARY contains FUTURE, the AUXILIARY move previously given is obligatory:

Pi ant wo i gei ahni.	'I will not fall.'
Kunt wo i gei ahni.	'And I will fall.'

Imperative PERSON indicators ni and wo partially overlap imperative MOOD indicator g in function. Therefore if AUXILIARY follows VERB, g is deleted and the AUXILIARY attached to VERB:

Chikpanani ahpi!	'You work!'
Chikpano ahpim!	'You all work!'

If AUXILIARY precedes VERB imperative singular PERSON ni is deleted:

Am g wabsh si chikpan ahpi! 'You just work hard!'

Both FUTURE wo and imperative plural PERSON wo are moved to immediately precede DEGREE:

Nt wabsh wo si chikpanad.   'I'll just be working hard.'
Am g wabsh wo si chikpanad.'You all just keep working hard!'

2.3. NOUN PHRASE

NOUN PHRASE consists of NEGATIVE plus QUALIFIER plus PRONOUN plus NOUN plus REFLEXIVE plus modifying SENTENCE:

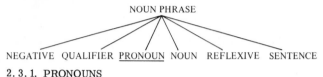

NEGATIVE QUALIFIER PRONOUN NOUN   REFLEXIVE   SENTENCE

2.3.1. PRONOUNS

The PRONOUNS are:

ahni	'I'	ahchim	'we'
ahpi	'you'	ahpim	'you all'
ihda	'this, he, she'	ihdam	'these, they'
hegai	'that, he, she'	hegam	'those, they'

PRONOUN is emphatic or nonemphatic. Nonemphatic PRONOUN is g if third person, zero otherwise.

2.3.2. PERSON INDICATOR

For each NOUN PHRASE except one following a NOUN PHRASE, a PERSON indicator is placed before the nucleus of the preceding structure. For the NOUN PHRASE following AUXILIARY in the VERB PHRASE the PERSON indicators have been shown.

For any other NOUN PHRASE, the PERSON indicators are slightly different. They agree with the PRONOUN as follows:

PERSON	PRONOUN	PERSON	PRONOUN
ni	ahni 'me'	t-	ahchim 'us'
m-	ahpi 'you'	em-	ahpim 'you all'
zero	ihda 'this, him, her' hegai 'that, him, her'	ha	ihdam/hegam 'them'

PERSON indicating object of transitive VERB STEM:

Ni-nei at g Pancho ahni.   'Pancho saw me.'
M-nei at g Pancho ahpi.   'Pancho saw you.'

Nei at g Pancho hegai.	'Pancho saw him. '
T-nei at g Pancho ahchim.	'Pancho saw us. '
Em-nei at g Pancho ahpim.	'Pancho saw you all. '
Ha at nei g Pancho hegam.	'Pancho saw them.'

PERSON indicating indirect object of dative VERB STEM:

Ni-mah at g Pancho ahni g wisilo.	'Pancho gave me the calf
M-mah at g Pancho ahpi g wisilo.	'Pancho gave you " ". '
Mah at g Pancho hegai g wisilo.	'Pancho gave him " " '
T-mah at g Pancho ahchim g wisilo.	'Pancho gave us " " . '
Em-mah at g Pancho ahpim g wisilo.	'Pancho gave you all
Ha at mah g Pancho hegam g wisilo.	'Pancho gave them ".

PERSON is ha or zero if NOUN STEM is mass (referring to uncountable things):

| T wo ha ih g Pancho g ka-whih. | 'Pancho will drink some coffee! |
| T wo ih g Pancho g ka-whih. | 'Pancho will drink coffee. ' |

PERSON is zero if NOUN STEM is aggregate (referring to things which are handled together):

| T wo ui g Pancho g shuhshk. | 'Pancho will get the shoes. ' |
| T wo ui g Pancho g lial. | 'Pancho will get the money. ' |

PERSON is reflexive if NOUN PHRASE included REFLEXIVE. REFLEXIVE is hejel, hehe'ejel 'self' or a'ai 'each other', and is moved to precede VERB PHRASE. Reflexive PERSON ni- with ahni, t- with ahchim, e otherwise:

Object of VERB:

Hejel ani ni-neid ahni.	'I see myself. '
Hejel ap e neid ahpi.	'You see yourself. '
Hejel o e neid hegai.	'He sees himself. '
Hehe'ejel ach t-neid ahchim.	'We see ourselves. '
Hehe'ejel am e neid ahpim.	'You all see yourselves. '
Hehe'ejel o e neid hegam.	'They see themselves. '
A'ai ach t-neid ahchim.	'You-all see each other. '
A'ai am e neid ahpim.	'You-all see each other. '
A'ai o e neid hegam.	'They see each other. '

Possessor:

Bei ant g hejel ni-wisiloga ahni.	'I got my own calf. '
Bei apt g hejel e-wisiloga ahpi.	'You got your own calf. '
Bei at g hejel e-wisiloga hegai.	'He got his own calf. '
Bei att g hejel t-wisiloga ahchim.	'We got our own calf'

Bei amt g hejel e-wisiloga ahpim. 'You all got your own calf.'

Bei at g hejel e-wisiloga hegam. 'They got their own calf.'

Object of PREPOSITION:

> Bei ant g wisilo am hejel ni-wehhejeD ahni.
> 'I got the calf for myself.'

> Bei apt g wisilo am hejel e-wehhejeD ahpi.
> 'You got the calf for yourself,'

> Bei at g wisilo am hejel e-wehhejeD hegai.
> 'He got the calf for himself.'

> Bei att g wisilo am hejel t-wehhejeD ahchim.
> 'We got the calf for ourselves.'

> Bei amt g wisilo am hejel e-wehhejeD ahpim.
> 'You all got the calf for yourselves.'

> Bei at g wisilo am hejel e-wehhejeD hegam.
> 'They got the calf for themselves.'

2.3.3. NUMERAL

NUMERAL consists of any number of MILLINUMERAL:

NUMERAL

MILLINUMERAL MILLINUMERAL MILLINUMERAL
etc.

MILLINUMERAL consists of MULTIPLE plus NUMERAL STEM plus CENTINUMERAL:

MILLINUMERAL

MULTIPLE NUMERAL STEM CENTINUMERAL

CENTINUMERAL consists of MULTIPLE plus NUMERAL STEM plus DECINUMERAL:

CENTINUMERAL

MULTIPLE NUMERAL STEM DECINUMERAL:

DECINUMERAL consists of MULTIPLE plus NUMERAL STEM:

DECINUMERAL

MULTIPLE NUMERAL STEM

NUMERAL STEM is:

_____	'zero'
hemako	'one'
gohk	'two'

124

waik	'three'
gi'ik	'four'
hetasp	'five'
chuhdp	'six'
wewa'ak	'seven'
gigi'ik	'eight'
humukt	'nine'

MULTIPLE is:

> o west-mahm gamai 'ten' if under DECINUMERAL
>
> siant 'hundred' if under CENTINUMERAL
>
> mihl 'thousand' if under MILLINUMERAL odd numbered from the right
>
> mi-yohn 'million' if under MILLINUMERAL even numbered from the right

(In prehispanic O'odham, NUMERAL consisted of any number of DECINUMERAL. The additional structure represented by the rules above was imposed on O'odham with the borrowing of higher MULTIPLES from Spanish: siant from 'ciento'; mihl from 'mil'; mi-yohn from 'millión'.)

The following rules operate in the order given on the output;

1. MULTIPLE is deleted if there is not an immediately preceding structure with NUMERAL STEM:

> o west-mahm gamai hemako ⟶ hemako '1'
>
> mihl gohk siant ⟶ gohk siant   '200'

2. o is attached to preceding NUMERAL STEM, replacing any vowel and causing shortening of long vowel of gohk:

> hemako o west-mahm gamai gohk
>
> ⟶hemako west-mahm gamai gohk '12'
>
> gohk o west-mahm gamai gohk
>
> ⟶goko west-mahm gamai gohk '22'

3. hemako is deleted if not following gamai:

> hemako west-mahm gamai hemako
>
> ⟶west-mahm gamai hemako '11'
>
> hemako siant ⟶siant '100'
>
> hemako mihl ⟶ mihl '1000'
>
> hemako mi-yohn ⟶ mi-yohn '1,000,000'

4. gamai is deleted if not preceding NUMERAL STEM:

> goko west-mahm gamai⟶ goko west-mahm '20'

5. west-mahm may be deleted if preceding gamai:

> goko west-mahm gamai gohk
> ⟶goko gamai gohk '22'

6. gamai may be deleted if between NUMERAL STEMS:

> goko gamai gohk ⟶ goko gohk '22'

A NUMERAL consisting of three occurrences of MILLI-NUMERAL and gohk 'two' as NUMERAL STEM in each case is:

> gohk siant goko (west-mahm gamai) gohk mi-yohn gohk
> siant goko (west-mahm gamai) gohk mihl gohk siant goko
> (west-mahm gamai) gohk '222,222,222'.

The parenthetical parts represent optional deletions of rules 4 and 5.

2.3.4. NOUN

NOUN consists of NOUN STEM plus added parts to be shown later. NOUN STEM is alienable or inalienable with regard to possession. Inalienable NOUN refers to inherently possessed things such as body parts , states and emotions, relatives , and man made items. Mo'o'head', tatchuidag 'desire', hohnig 'wife', kih 'house', etc., are inalienable NOUNS. JeweD 'land', wisilo 'calf', etc. are alienable NOUNS.

When possessed, alienable NOUN occurs with stative VERB STEM shoiga if animal, eniga otherwise:

> Shoiga o g Pancho g wisilo.   'Pancho has a calf.'
> Eniga o g Pancho g jeweD.   'Pancho has land.'

Inalienable NOUN usually occurs with nonstative VERB STEM eDagid:

> EDagid o g Pancho g kih.   'Pancho owns a house.'

A modifying SENTENCE with possessive VERB STEM may be reduced to POSSESSIVE plus GENITIVE suffix j plus NOUN PHRASE. POSSESSIVE and GENITIVE are suffixed to NOUN STEM as part of NOUN.

The POSSESSIVE suffix is ga with alienable NOUN:

hegai wisilo(mo shoi) ga g Pancho --hegai wisilogaj g Pancho
  'that calf that Pancho has'   'that calf of Pancho's '

hegai jeweD(mo eni)ga g Pancho --hegai jeweDgaj g Pancho
  'that land that Pancho has'   'that land of Pancho's '

The POSSESSIVE suffix is zero with inalienable NOUN:

hegai kih (mo eDagid) g Pancho -- hegai kihj g Pancho
  'that house that Pancho has'   'that house of Pancho's'

The PERSON rule (2.3.2) places the same indicators for possessor NOUN PHRASE as for object NOUN PHRASE, but if any indication of possession is placed before the NOUN STEM, the GENITIVE j is deleted:

ni-kih ahni	'my house'
m-kih ahpi	'your house'
kihj hegai	'his house'
t-kih ahchim	'our house'
em-kih ahpim	'your house'
ha-kih hegam	'their house'

Emphatic PRONOUN may be moved to precede the main part of the structure of which it is a part, resulting in deletion of GENITIVE j and shortening of third person singular PRONOUN hegai 'that' to heg and ihda 'this' to id:

kihj hegai o'odham ⟶ heg kih o'odham
'house of that man'   'that man's house'

kihj ihda o'odham ⟶ id kih o'odham
'house of this man'   'this man's house'

Since any NOUN PHRASE may have a modifying SENTENCE with possessive VERB STEM, an unlimited series is possible:

hegai wisilo mo shoiga g ahli mo eniga g Pancho...
'that calf that the child has that Pancho has...'

The modifying SENTENCE may be reduced:

⟶ hegai wisilo mo shoiga g ahligaj g Pancho
   'that calf that the child of Pancho has'

⟶ hegai wisilogaj g ahligaj g Pancho
   'that calf of the child of Pancho'

Possessive NOUN PHRASE may be embedded (inserted) preceding NOUN:

⟶ hegai wisilogaj g Pancho ahliga
   'that calf of Pancho's child'

⟶ hegai Pancho ahliga wisiloga
   'Pancho's child's calf'

The object NOUN PHRASE may be embedded in the reduced possessive VERB STEM. NEGATIVE ADJUNCT ha precedes the embedded NOUN PHRASE if following NEGATIVE, POSITIVE ge precedes the embedded NOUN PHRASE otherwise:

(Eni)ga o g Pancho g jeweD. ⟶ Ge o jeweDga g Pancho.
  'Pancho has land.'

(EDagid) o g Pancho g kih. ⟶ Ge o kih g Pancho.
                   'Pancho has a house'

Pi o (eni)ga g Pancho g jeweD. ⟶ Pi o ha jeweDga g Pancho.
                'Pancho doesn't have any land.'

    Pi o (eDagid) g Pancho g kih. ⟶ Pi o ha kih g Pancho.
                 'Pancho doesn't have any house.'

2.4. RELATIONAL PHRASE

RELATIONAL PHRASE consists of NEGATIVE plus QUAL-
IFIER plus <u>PRORELATIONAL</u> plus DEGREE plus ADVERB
plus RELATIONAL plus modifying SENTENCE:

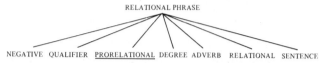

RELATIONAL PHRASE

NEGATIVE QUALIFIER <u>PRORELATIONAL</u> DEGREE ADVERB RELATIONAL SENTENCE

PRORELATIONAL consists of LOCATIONAL plus REMOTE:

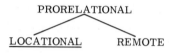

PRORELATIONAL

<u>LOCATIONAL</u>   REMOTE

REMOTE is huh 'way off, over there, over here'.

LOCATIONAL is a word consisting of DISTANCE plus
DIRECTION plus EMPHATIC:

LOCATIONAL

<u>DISTANCE</u>   <u>DIRECTION</u>   EMPHATIC

DISTANCE indicates relative distance of an object from the
observer:

Observer	Object
i ⋀ 'here'	
a ⋀ 'there'	
ga⋀ 'over there'	
gah ⋀ 'way over there'	
gaD ⋀ 'out of sight'	

DIRECTION indicates the way an object is facing relative
to the observer:

128

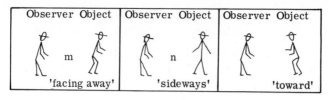

	Observer Object	Observer Object	Observer Object
	m	n	
	'facing away'	'sideways'	'toward'

DISTANCE and DIRECTION combine as follows:

DISTANCE \ DIRECTION	m 'facing away'	n 'facing sideways'	'facing toward'	'out of sight'
i 'here'	im	in	ia	
a 'there'	am	an	ab	
ga 'over there'	gam	gan	ga	gaD
gah 'way over there'	gahm	gahn	gahsh	

EMPHATIC is lengthened vowel plus a with 'here', ai otherwise:

DISTANCE \ DIRECTION	m 'facing away'	n 'facing sideways'	'facing toward'	'out of sight'
i 'here'	ihma	ihna	iia	
a 'there'	amai	anai	abai	
ga 'over there'	gamai	ganai	ga'abai	gaDai
gah 'way over there'	gahmai	gahnai	gahshaj	

DIRECTION refers to one of three different dimensions. Besides that described above, it may refer to level of an object with respect to the observer, or to position of an object with respect to the observer or another object. With reference to level, n̲ means 'above', m̲ 'below'. With reference to position, n̲ means 'on the outline of', m̲ 'behind', other 'in front of/on the front of'.

With time VERB STEM j̲u̲h̲k̲ (j̲u̲j̲j̲u̲), ga refers to approach of the sun, i̲m̲ or g̲a̲m̲ to it's retreat, d̲a̲h̲m̲ to overhead position:

ga huh i juhk	'being morning'
ga huh si i juhk	'being late morning'
im huh i juhk	'being early afternoon'
gam huh i juhk	'being afternoon'
gam huh si i juhk	'being late afternoon'

dahm juhk	'being noon'
dahm jujju	'being repeated noons'

With time NOUN STEM mi-nuhto 'minute', ohla 'hour', tash 'day', domig 'week', mashad 'month', ahidag 'year', gaD refers to past, gam to future:

gaD huh i gi'ik tash ch-eD	'in the fourth day previous'
gaD huh i gi'ik tash wehgaj	'before the fourth day previous'
gam huh i gi'ik tash ch-eD	'in the fourth day hence'
gam huh i gi'ik tash wehgaj	'after the fourth day hence'

ADVERBS are hab ha'ab 'one side'; mehk. me'emek 'far'; ta'i, tahta'i 'backward'; uhpam 'back to'.

RELATIONAL consists of PREPOSITION plus NOUN PHRASE

RELATIONAL

PREPOSITION   NOUN PHRASE

PREPOSITION consists of one PREPOSITION STEM or two: If there are two PREPOSITION STEMS the second one must be amjeD, a'amjeD 'from', and the first one some other PREPOSITION STEM:

aigo, a'ai	'on the other side, each way'
bahsho, babsho	'along, in front of'
ba'ich, bab'aich	'beyond, in front of'
dahm, da'adam	'above'
eDa, e'eDa	'in'
gahi, gahghai	'across'
miabij, mimiabij	'near to'
oidk, o'oidk	'through'
oidam, o'oidam	'during'
oij, o'oij	'after, following'
shahgid, sha'ashagid	'among'
tahgio, ta'atagio	'in the way of, direction of'
wecho, wepcho, we'ewecho	'under'
wehgaj, we'ewegaj	'behind, around'
wehm, we'ewem	'with living thing'
wehnadk, we'ewenadk	'with nonliving thing'
wui, wu'uwui	'to'

AmjeD may be reduced to jeD following a PREPOSITION STEM as in wechojeD 'from under', following ADVERB as in mehkjeD 'from far', following REMOTE as in ga huhjeD 'from way off there', following QUALIFIER as in hebaijeD 'from somewhere', following NEGATIVE as in pi'ajeD 'from nowhere'.

Certain PREPOSITION STEMS do not occur before amjeD. Among these are: ab 'on the near side of', am on the far side of', an 'on the outline of', wehhejeD, we'ewejeD 'for'.

The PERSON rule (2.3.2.) places the same indicators before PREPOSITION as before VERB and NOUN:

am ni-wui ahni	'there to me'
am m-wui ahpi	'there to you'
am wui hegai	'there to that one'
am t-wui ahchim	'there to us'
am em-wui ahpim	'there to you all'
am ha wui hegam	'there to them'

PRORELATIONAL may be moved to precede the VERB PHRASE:

Hih ant am wui g Chuk-shon →Am ant hih wui g Chuk-shon
'I went there to Tucson.'   'There I went to Tucson'

NOUN PHRASE may be moved to position preceding PREPOSITION STEM, with deletion of unemphatic PRONOUN:

Hih ant am wui g Chuk-shon.→ Hih ant am Chuk-shon wui.
'I went there to Tucson.'   'I went there to Tucson.'

Am ant hih wui g Chuk-shon.→Am ant hih Chukshon wui.
'There I went to Tucson.'   'There I went to Tucson.'

PREPOSITION, including NOUN PHRASE if it is attached, may be moved to precede VERB PHRASE:

Am ant hih wui g Chuk-shon.→Am ant wui hih g Chuk-shon.
'There I went to Tucson'   'There I went to Tucson.'

Am ant hih Chuk-shon wui.→Am ant Chuk-shon wui hih.
'There I went to Tucson'   'There to Tucson I went.'

Unpossessed NOUN is linked to PREPOSITION STEM with t preceding a, ch preceding e:

Chuk-shon t-ab	'at Tucson'
Chuk-shon t-amjeD	'from Tucson'
Chuk-shon ch-eD	'in Tucson'

2.5. TIME PHRASE

TIME PHRASE consists of NEGATIVE plus   QUALIFIER plus TEMPORAL plus TIME plus modifying SENTENCE:

TIME PHRASE

NEGATIVE QUALIFIER TEMPORAL TIME SENTENCE

If following TEMPORAL, TIME is:

chuhug	'last night'
ha'akid	'last year'
si'alim	'tomorrow'
tako	'yesterday'

TEMPORAL consists of LOCATIONAL plus REMOTE plus QUALIFIER hema plus POINT:

TEMPORAL

LOCATIONAL   REMOTE   QUALIFIER   POINT

LOCATIONAL here is gaD preceding REMOTE, D otherwise:

D hema _____	'another period away'
D hema chuhug	'night before last'
D hema ha'akid	'year before last'
D hema si'alim	'day after tomorrow'
D hema tako	'day before yesterday'
gaD huh hema i _____	'a further period away'
gaD huh hema i chuhug	'three nights ago'
gaD huh hema i ha'akid	'three years ago'
gaD huh hema i si'alim	'three days hence'

If not following TEMPORAL, TIME is:

eDa/wenog	'then'
hahawa	'afterward'
hemu	'now'
idani	'at this time, season'
oi	'soon'
si'alim	'tomorrow'
tako	'yesterday'
chuhug	'last night'
ha'akid	'last year'

References to other units of time or more remote time are made with time VERB STEM juhk (jujju) 'the sun being in position' or time NOUN STEMS mi-nuhto 'minute', ohla 'hour', tash 'day', domig 'week', mashad 'month', ahidag 'year'.

132

2.6. ATTRIBUTIVE PHRASE

ATTRIBUTIVE PHRASE consists of NEGATIVE plus QUAL-
IFIER plus <u>ATTRIBUTIVE</u>:

ATTRIBUTIVE PHRASE

NEGATIVE   QUALIFIER   ATTRIBUTIVE

ATTRIBUTIVE consists of AFFIRMATIVE plus <u>ATTRIB-</u>
<u>UTIVE STEM</u>:

ATTRIBUTIVE

AFFIRMATIVE   <u>ATTRIBUTIVE STEM</u>

ATTRIBUTIVE STEMS occurring with AFFIRMATIVE <u>s-</u> are

ap	'well'	jujul	'zigzag'
bahbagi	'slow'	kehg	'good'

STEMS without AFFIRMATIVE <u>s-</u> are :

chew	'long'	shawaD	'thick in diameter'
ge'e	'big'	shopol	'short'
huDa	'high'	sikol	'round'
shapol	'aspherical'		

2.7. QUALIFIER

QUALIFIER consists of COMPLIMENT plus <u>IDENTIFIER</u>:

QUALIFIER

COMPLIMENT   <u>IDENTIFIER</u> .

IDENTIFIER is different in different phrase types, but
definite or indefinite in each:

definite   indefinite

VERB PHRASE

hab	'thus'	has	'how'

ADVERB PHRASE

hab	'thus'	has	'how'
ha'as	'so much'	he'es	'how much'

NOUN PHRASE

hema	'a'	heDai	'which one'
ha'i	'some'	heDam	'which ones'

133

ha'ichu	'something'	haschu	'what thing'
ha'akia	'so many'	he'ekia	'how many'
hemako '1', gohk '2' etc.			
ha'akiachu 'such a number"		he'ekiachu	'what number'
ha'as	'so much	he'es	'how much'
ha'aschu	'such a size'	he'eschu	'what size'

RELATIONAL PHRASE

hebai	'somewhere'	hebai	'where'
hasko	'some direction'	hasko	'what direction'
ha'asko	'so far'	he'esko	'how far'
ha'akpa	'so many places'	he'ekpa	'how many places'

TIME PHRASE

hekid	'sometime'	hekid	'when'
ha'akio	'so many times'	he'ekio	'how many times'

IDENTIFIER in the QUALIFIER of NOUN PHRASE consists of IDENTIFIER STEM plus GENITIVE suffix. GENITIVE suffix 'of' is j with certain STEMS, zero otherwise:

hema	'one of'	heDai	'which one of'
ha'ij	'some of'	heDam	'which ones of'
ha'ichu	'class of'	haschu	'what class of'
ha'akiaj	'so many of'	he'ekiaj	'how many of'
ha'asij	'so much of'	he'esij	'how much of'

QUALIFIER or PHRASE with QUALIFIER is usually moved to focal position, before the VERB PHRASE in the clause, before the RELATIONAL in the RELATIONAL PHRASE:

> Kut bei g Pancho hema g wisilo.
> 'And Pancho got a calf. '

> ⟶ Kut hema bei g Pancho g wisilo.
> 'And Pancho got a calf. '

> Kut i wah g Pancho am eDa hema g kih.
> 'And Pancho entered a house. '

> ⟶ Kut i wah g Pancho am hema eDa g kih.
> 'And Pancho entered a house. '

COMPLIMENT is question or generic with indefinite IDENTIFIER, gesture otherwise.

Question COMPLIMENT i is placed before the VERB:

> K has i kaij g Pancho?
> 'And what does Pancho say?'

> Kut has masma hab wo i juh g Pancho?
> 'And how will Pancho do it?'

Kut he'es wo i ge'ejk g Pancho?
'And how big will Pancho be?'

Generic COMPLIMENT <u>wabsh chum</u> is placed before IDENTIFIER:

Kut wabsh chum has wo juh g Pancho.
'And Pancho will do anything.'

Kut wabsh chum hebai wo hih g Pancho.
'And Pancho will go anywhere.'

Kut wabsh chum he'ekia wo ha ui g Pancho g gogogs.
'And Pancho will take any number of dogs.'

When a QUALIFIER is present the number agreement stated in 2.2.1. is between VERB STEM and QUALIFIER:

Hema o ab him hegam chechoj.
'One of those men is coming.'

Ha'i o ab hihim hegam chechoj.
'Some of those men are coming.'

Hema ant ha bei hegam wipsilo.
'I got one of those calves.'

Ha'i ant ha ui hegam wipsilo.
'I got some of those calves.'

In 1. it was observed that a sentence can be embedded or inserted in another sentence as final part. One of the circumstances in which this can be done is when the two sentences have gesture compliments with the same features, for example if both are measure, the gesture compliments are deleted:

Ha'as (measure COMPLIMENT) o chewaj g Pancho.
'Pancho is so long.'

Ha'as (measure COMPLIMENT) o s-taDani g wo'ikuD.
'The bed is so wide.'

⟶Ha'as o chewaj g Pancho mo g wo'ikuD ha'as s-taDani.
'Pancho is as long as the bed is wide.'

Ha'akia (count COMPLIMENT) o wisiloga g Pancho.
'Pancho has so many (gestured) calves.'

Ha'akia (count COMPLIMENT) o kakawiyuga g Pancho.
'Pancho has so many (gestured) horses.'

⟶Ha'akia o wisiloga g Pancho mo ha'akia kakawiyuga.
'Pancho has as many calves as he has horses.'

If the gesture compliments are unequal in intensity, the QUALIFIER with the greater compliment is <u>ba'ich i</u>'more':

⟶Ba'ich o i chewaj g Pancho mo g wo'ikuD ha'as s-taDani.
'Pancho is longer than the bed is wide.'

3. COMPLEX STEMS

Complex STEMS consist of two or more parts in contrast to simple STEMS. Complex STEM, whether stative or non-stative, reflects the sum of transitive features of its parts. For example, <u>him</u> 'to move along' is a simple intransitive stem occurring in CLAUSES with no object NOUN PHRASE:

> Him o g Pancho. 'Pancho is moving along.'

However, it occurs with transitive SUFFIX chud to form transitive VERB STEM requiring an object NOUN PHRASE:

> Himchud o g Pancho g daikuD.
> 'Pancho is moving a chair along.'

Complex STEMS employ the following special NOUN STEMS indicating instrumentality, STEMS which do not occur as free forms in modern o'odham:

kei	'with the foot'
ki'i	'with the teeth'
ma'i	'with an object from the hand'
nu'i	'with the hand or unspecified'
shoni	'with an object in the hand'
wa	'with liquid'
wus	'with exhalation'
howi	'with inhalation'

The combination of parts of complex STEMS results in the substitution of certain sounds for others to form permissable sequences of sounds(a choice of alternate forms of the same sound until the intrusion of Spanish).

> <u>a</u> substitutes for <u>i</u> if following d, t, or n:

> neid + imk ⟶ neidamk
> kiht + imk ⟶ kihtamk

> <u>l</u> subtitutes for <u>D</u>, and <u>s</u> for <u>sh</u> if preceding <u>i</u>:

> meD + imk ⟶ melimk
> kohsh + imk ⟶ kohsimk

> <u>d</u> substitutes for <u>j</u> if preceding <u>a</u>:

> ge'ej + ahim ⟶ ge'edahim

The addition of certain suffixes is accompanied by shortening of long vowel in the STEM:

> juhki + shp ⟶ jukshp
> s-wehch + ma ⟶ s-wechma

In this section VERB STEMS are nonstative unless otherwise indicated. Stative VERB STEM retains the features of
included nonstative VERB STEM unless otherwise indicated.

3.1. Complex VERB STEM

VERB STEM consists of simple VERB STEM plus <u>ito</u> 'to
finish':

ba'ito	'to gobble up'
chegito	'to think'
dagito	'to leave something'
ehsto	'to hide'
gewito	'to beat'
hagito	'to burn up'
i'ito	'to drink up'
jukito	'to finish raining'
ko'ito	'to eat up'
mukito	'to finish dying'

VERB STEM consists of simple VERB STEM plus <u>chug</u> 'to
go about doing', <u>him</u> 'to go along doing'

<u>ahgachug</u>	'to go about saying'
<u>beichug</u>	'to go about getting'
<u>ahgahim</u>	'to go along saying'
<u>beihim</u>	'to go along getting'

VERB STEM consists of NOUN STEM or VERB STEM plus
<u>me</u>D, <u>o</u>p 'to go to do or get':

<u>chikpaname</u>D, <u>chikpano</u>p	'to go to do work'
<u>oname</u>D, <u>ono</u>p	'to go to get salt'
<u>chikpanidame</u>D, <u>chikpanido</u>p	'to go to do work for'
<u>neidame</u>D, <u>neido</u>p	'to go to see'

Following AFFIRMATIVE s-, VERB STEM consists of
simple, benefactive or motion VERB STEM plus <u>im</u>k 'to want
to do':

<u>s-chikpanam</u>k	'to want to work'
<u>s-chikpanidam</u>k	'to want to work for'
<u>s-chikpanidameli</u>mk	'to want to go to work for'

Transitive VERB STEM consists of simple transitive VERB
STEM or NOUN STEM plus <u>hun</u> 'to cause':

<u>bidhun</u>	'to cause to be dirty'
<u>gimaihun</u>	'to cause to boast'

| ho'ige'idahun | 'to cause to pray' |
| moihun | 'to cause to be soft' |

Transitive **VERB STEM** consists of simple **NOUN STEM** plus the following **SUFFIXES** as in the examples:

| chk | 'to push on with' |

| mo'ochk | 'to push on with the head' |
| honchk | 'to lay against' |

| chkwua, chshulig | 'to push along 'with' |

| mo'ochkwua, mo'ochshulig | 'to push along with the head' |
| honchwua, honchsulig | 'to push along with the body' |

| Dad | 'to put on' |

| enigaDad | 'to put clothes on' |
| uhshDad | 'to put arrow point on' |

| gid | 'to shake' |

| mo'ogid | 'to shake the head' |
| bahigid | 'to switch the tail' |

| ggan (ggash) | 'to pound' |

| mo'oggan (mo'oggash) | 'to bunt' |
| keiggan (keiggash) | 'to kick' |

| hain (haish) | 'to hit and destroy with' |

| mo'ohain(mo'ohaish) | 'to hit and destroy with head' |
| tonhain (tonhaish) | 'to hit and destroy with knee' |

| hin (hish) | 'to hit' |

| ma'ihin (ma'ihish) | 'to hit with a thrown object' |
| shonihin (shonihish) | 'to hit with a held object' |

| kon (kosh) | 'to deliver a glancing blow' |

| ma'ikon (ma'ikosh) | 'to glance with thrown object' |
| shonikon (shonikosh) | 'to glance with held object' |

| mad | 'to apply to' |

| onmad | 'to salt' |
| mihshmad | 'to preach to' |

| pig | 'to remove from' |

| maDpig | 'to remove fruit of' |
| wihpdopig | 'to castrate' |

| shch | 'to touch' |

mo'oshch	'to touch with the head'
nakshch	'to overhear'

shuD (<u>shush</u>)	'to crush'

ma'ishuD (<u>ma'ishush</u>)	'to crush with thrown object'
shonishuD (<u>shonishush</u>)	'to crush with held object'

<u>wia</u>	'to grind'

<u>kehiwia</u>	'to thresh with feet'
<u>shoniwia</u>	'to grind by hand'

Intransitive VERB STEM consists of body part NOUN STEM or stance VERB STEM plus wua (<u>wup</u>). When occurring with NOUN STEM the meaning is 'to bump or touch the part':

mo'owua (<u>mo'owup</u>),	mohmwua (<u>mohmwup</u>)	'to bump the head'
nakwua (<u>nakwup</u>),	nahnkwua (<u>nahnkwup</u>)	'to bump the ear'
tonwua (<u>tonwup</u>),	tohtonwua (<u>tohtonwup</u>)	'to kneel'

When occurring with stance VERB STEM the meaning is 'to assume the stance':

dahiwua (<u>dahiwup</u>),	daDaiwua (<u>daDhaiwup</u>)	'to sit down'
keķiwua (<u>keķiwup</u>),	gegokiwua (<u>gegokiwup</u>)	'to stand up'
wo'iwua (<u>wo'iwup</u>),	wohpiwua (<u>wohpiwup</u>)	'to lie down'

Intransitive VERB STEM consists of simple intransitive VERB STEM plus <u>idt</u>ahim 'to learn to':

<u>dahidt</u>ahim	'to learn to sit'
<u>da'idt</u>ahim	'to learn to fly'
<u>himidt</u>ahim	'to learn to walk'
<u>melidt</u>ahim	'to learn to run'

Stative VERB STEM consists of simple VERB STEM plus <u>dag</u> 'to be able to':

s-<u>dahidag</u>	'to be able to sit'
s-<u>himdag</u>	'to be able to go'
s-<u>meldag</u>	'to be able to run'

Stative intransitive VERB STEM consists of ADJECTIVE STEM plus '<u>e</u>, <u>k</u>, <u>j</u>, or zero, 'to be in the state of':

s-<u>ap'e</u>	'to be well'
<u>shopolk</u>	'to be short'
<u>ge'ej</u>	'to be big'
s-<u>toni</u>	'to be hot'

Nonstative intransitive **VERB STEM** consists of the stative **VERB STEM** above plus <u>t</u>ahim if following a vowel, <u>a</u>him otherwise (<u>ni</u> is a consonant):

<u>ap'etahim</u>	'to get well'
<u>shopolkahim</u>	'to get short'
<u>ge'edahim</u>	'to get big'
<u>tonihim</u>	'to get hot'

Transitive **VERB STEM** consists of the noncontinuative form of the **VERB STEM** above plus <u>chud</u> replacing <u>t</u>, <u>d</u> (i) following <u>ka</u>, <u>j</u>id otherwise:

<u>ap'echud</u>	'to correct'
<u>shopolkad</u> (shopolka<u>j</u>)	'to shorten'
<u>ge'edaj</u>id	'to enlarge'
<u>tonij</u>id	'to heat'

Passive **VERB STEM** consists of transitive **VERB STEM** plus jid 'to be done to':

<u>mu'aj</u>id	'to be killed'
behi<u>j</u>id	'to be taken'

Stative **VERB STEM** consists of NOUN STEM plus <u>Dag</u> 'to have on':

<u>enigaDag</u>	'to have clothes on'
<u>uhshDag</u>	'to have an arrowhead on'

Transitive **VERB STEM** consists of NOUN STEM plus <u>shp</u> 'to contact with' :

<u>bidshp</u>	'to plaster'
<u>gewshp</u>	'to snow on'
<u>jukshp</u>	'to rain on'
<u>ma'ishp</u>	'to cover'
<u>olshp</u>	'to hook'

Stative **VERB STEM** consists of transitive verb stem plus <u>i</u> 'to be in the state of being' :

<u>bidshpi</u>	'to be plastered'
<u>chekshani</u>	'to be lined'
<u>chelshani</u>	'to be roughened'
<u>haini</u>	'to be cracked'
<u>ma'ishpi</u>	'to be covered'
<u>olshpi</u>	'to be hooked'
<u>wul</u>	'to be tied'

Transitive VERB STEM consists of preceding VERB STEMS plus 'ok 'to reverse the action':

bidshpi'ok	'to unplaster'
ma'ishpi'ok	'to uncover'
olshpi'ok	'to unhook'
wul'ok	'to untie'

Stative VERB STEM consists of dative or transitive VERB STEM plus STATIVE k if noncontinuative plus ch 'to have in the state of':

bidshch	'to have it plastered'
chekshanch	'to have it lined'
ehstokch	'to have it hidden'
kuhpch	'to have it closed'
kuhpi'okch	'to have it open'
ma'ishch	'to have it covered'
ma'ishpi'okch	'to have it uncovered'
nahtokch	'to have it finished'

Stative VERB STEM consists of VERB STEM or complex NOUN STEM plus s 'to be in the state of':

ahgas	'to be told'
hims	'to be going(i.e. a road)'
iawuis	'to be spilled'
kihtas	'to be built'
kuhpi'okas	'to be open'
mahks	'to be given'
ma'ishpi'okas	'to be uncovered'
moihunas	'to be softened'
nahtois	'to be finished'

3. 2. Complex NOUN STEM

Complex NOUN STEM consists of transitive or dative VERB STEM plus a, i, ig, or zero 'action or result of action':

amichuda	'understanding'
gegosida	'feeding'
ho'ige'ida	'blessing'
kownalta	'appointment as chief'
nahda	'fire making, fire'
o'ohana	'drawing or writing'
behi, u'i	'gain, things taken'
muhki, ko'i	'death'

wa'igi	'procured liquid'
gegosig	'meal'
heki gehsig	'loss'
mahkig	'giving'
oimelig	'wandering'
hidoD	'cooking'

Complex NOUN STEM consists of the NOUN STEM above plus <u>Dag</u>, <u>lig</u>, or <u>g</u> 'quality, sphere, or domain of':

amichudaDag	'wisdom'
hemajimatalig	'gentleness'
ho'ige'idaDag/ho'ige'idalig	'blessings'
kownaltaDag/kownaltalig	'kingdom'
mahkigDag	'gift from'
muhkig, ko'iDag	'corpse'

<u>kuD</u> 'thing to accomplish an action with or in'

behikuD	'instrument to get something with'
gegosidakuD	'eating trough
nahdakuD	'fireplace'
o'ohanakuD	'writing instrument'
wa'igikuD	'water jug'

NOUN STEM consists of ADJECTIVE STEM plus <u>chu</u> 'the ___er one':

| ge'echu | 'the bigger one' |
| chumchu | 'the smaller one' |

3.3. ADVERB STEM

ADVERB STEM consists of NOUN STEM plus <u>ko</u> 'at, in':

jegko	'in the open'
s-apko	'on the right'
s-ohgigko	'on the left'
s-toniko	'in the heat'

3.4. ATTRIBUTIVE STEM

ATTRIBUTIVE STEM consists of ADJECTIVE STEM plus zero, <u>m</u>, or <u>ma</u> with intransitive VERB STEM as given below. ATTRIBUTIVE STEMS are given in their occurence with AFFIRMATIVE <u>s-</u>. Those with asterisk switch from zero to <u>m</u> or from <u>m</u> to <u>ma</u> with transitive VERB STEM. For plural (distributive) form see dictionary entry.

142

ATTRIBUTIVE STEM consisting of ADJECTIVE STEM:

chew	'long'
chum	'scarcely, ineffectively'
ge'e	'greatly'
shapol	'aspherically'
shawaD	'thickly in diameter'
*shopol	'shortly'
sikol	'roundly'
s-ap	'well'
*s-bahbagi	'slowly'
*s-jujul	'zigzaggedly'
s-kehg	'prettily'

ATTRIBUTIVE STEM consisting of ADJECTIVE STEM plus m̲:

gakolim	'crookedly'
giwulim	'constrictedly'
habalim	'flatly'
jumalim	'low'
komalim	'thinly'
shelinim	'straightly'
wechijim	'newly'
s-bagam	'angrily'
s-bihtagim	'dirtily'
s-gegokim	'steadfastly'
s-gewkam	'strongly'
s-hasigam	'difficultly'
s-haukam	'lightly, easily'
s-he'ekam	'sourly'
s-hehgigam	'happily'
s-hehogim	'coolly'
s-hehpagim	'painlessly'
s-hiwkam	'roughly'
s-hohtam	'quickly'
s-i'owim	'sweetly'
s-juhkam	'deeply'
s-kawkam	'difficultly'
*s-moikam	'softly'
s-muhaDagim	'greasily'
s-mu'ukam	'sharply (point)'
s-mu'umuhugam	'sharply (edge)'
s-pehegim	'easily'
s-olasim	'spherically'

s-taDanim	'widely'
s-ta'ikodagam	'inclining'
s-waDagim	'wetly'
s-wohom	'truely'
*s-wihnam	'tightly, difficultly'

ATTRIBUTIVE STEM consisting of ADJECTIVE STEM plus
ma require shortening of long vowel in the STEM:

ajma	'narrowly'
masma	'like'
siwma	'bitterly'
shelma	'erectly'
s-chukma	'darkly'
s-gakima	'dryly, thinly'
s-hukma	'warmly'
s-hepima	'coldly'
s-oamma	'yellowish'
s-tohama	'brightly'
s-tonima	'hotly'
s-wegima	'redish'
s-wechma	'heavily'

Following AFFIRMATIVE s-, ATTRIBUTIVE STEM consists of NOUN STEM plus m, or of chu or ta plus VERB
STEM plus m:

s-a'alim	'childlike'
s-chechojim	'manly'
s-chuhchpulim	'with corners'
s-u'uwim	'effeminately'
s-chu amichudam	'wisely'
s-chu ehbidam	'dangerously'
s-ta behim	'procurably'
s-ta eDam	'shamefully'
s-ta hohho'idam	'interestingly'

Stative VERB STEM consists of the preceding ATTRIBU-
TIVE STEM plus a:

s-a'alma	'to be childish'
s-chu amichudma	'to be wise'
s-ta behima	'to be procurable'

4. SENTENCE TRANSFORMATIONS

Certain kinds of SENTENCE structure occur only in certain contexts or with certain kinds of complex STEMS. These

structures can be most simply accounted for by operations on the whole SENTENCE called sentence transformations.

4. 1. Movement of other PHRASES to precede VERB PHRASE

A PHRASE in which there is question COMPLIMENT is moved to precede the VERB PHRASE. The normal order is seen in:

> Mua at g Pancho g wisilo ab e-kih-ab g wainomikaj.
> 'Pancho killed the calf at his house with a knife.'

If the subject NOUN PHRASE contains question COMPLI-MENT, as in heDai i, it is moved to precede the VERB PHRASE:

> Kut heDai i mua g wisilo?   'Who killed the calf?'

Other PHRASES containing question COMPLIMENT are so moved:

> Kut haschu i mua g Pancho? 'What did Pancho kill?'

>> Kut hebai i mua g Pancho g wisilo?
>> 'Where did Pancho kill the calf?'

>> Kut haschukaj i mua g Pancho g wisilo?
>> 'With what did Pancho kill the calf?'

>> Kut heDai haschu i mua?' Who killed what?'

A PHRASE which is in contrast to the parallel PHRASE in the previous SENTENCE is also moved to precede the VERB PHRASE. Such a contrast exists in response to question or in switch of reference. Response to the questions above (showing also move of AUXILIARY to second position) show the following order:

>> Pancho at mua g wisilo.
>> 'Pancho was the one that killed the calf.'

>> Wisilo at mua g Pancho.
>> 'The calf is what Pancho killed.'

>> E-kih-ab at mua g Pancho g wisilo.
>> 'At his house was where Pancho killed the calf.'

>> Wainomikaj at mua g Pancho g wisilo.
>> 'A knife is what Pancho killed the calf with.'

>> Pancho at g wisilo mua.
>> 'Pancho's the one, the calf is what he killed.'

When nonemphatic PRONOUN g occurs at the beginning of CLAUSE it is deleted. Move of PHRASE because of switch of reference is seen in the following:

>> Am at huh hih g Pancho. Kut g Hosi pi hih.
>> 'Pancho went over there. And Jose didn't go.'

Mua at g Pancho g wisilo. Kut g Hosi g kohji mua.
'Pancho killed the calf. And Jose killed the pig.'

If the PRONOUN or PRORELATIONAL is emphatic it is
moved instead of the main part of the phrase. When thus
moved the PRONOUNS hegai, ihda, and the emphatic PRO-
RELATIONALS amai, abai, etc. are reduced to heg, id, am,
ab, etc., but retain their stress.

Kut haschu i mua g Pancho? Heg at mua wisilo.
'And what did Pancho kill?''That calf he killed.'

Kut hebai i hih g Pancho? Am at hih Chuk-shon-wui.
'And where did Pancho go?''There he went to Tucson.'

Certain words have special forms when occurring at the
beginning of a CLAUSE. When the form is a single syllable
it is attached to the AUXILIARY.

hab ⟶ Ba
Am g hab cheh'i! 'Say it!'
Bag cheh'i!'Say it!'

has i ⟶ Shah
K has i kaij? 'And what does he say?'
Shah'o kaij? 'What does he say?'

haschu i ⟶ Shahchu
K haschu i neid g Pancho? 'And what does Pancho see?'
Shahchu o neid g Pancho? 'What does Pancho see?'

hasko i ⟶ Shahko
K hasko i him g Pancho? 'And which way did Pancho go?'
Shahko o him g Pancho?'Which way did Pancho go?'

hebai i ⟶ Bah
K hebai i kih g Pancho?'And where does Pancho live?'
Bah'o kih g Pancho? 'Where does Pancho live?'

heDai i ⟶ Doh
K heDai ab i him? 'And who's coming?'
Doh'o ab him? 'Who's coming?'

wuD ⟶ D
K wuD Pancho. 'And it's Pancho.'
Do Pancho. 'It's Pancho.'

4.2. Deletion of parts in redundant reference

Parts having redundant reference in previous CLAUSES or
SENTENCES may be deleted, except for QUALIFIER. Deleted
parts are given in parentheses below:

Kut heDai i mua g wisilo ?   Pancho (at mua g wisilo).
'Who killed the calf?'   'Pancho (killed the calf). '

Kut haschu i mua g Pancho ? Wisilo (at mua g Pancho).
'What did Pancho kill?'   'The Calf (Pancho killed)'

Kut has i e juh g Pancho?   Mua at g wisilo (g Pancho).
'What did Pancho do?'   'He killed the calf (Pancho). '

Mua at g wisilo.   (Kut)heDai i (mua g wisilo).
'He killed the calf. '   'Who (killed the calf) ? '

Kupt hebai wo hih?   Pi (ant) hebai (wo hih).
'Where are you going?'   '(I'm going) nowhere. '

Kupt hebai wo hih?   Am (ant wo hih) Chuk-shon-
'Where are you going?'   '(I'm going) to Tucson.' wui.

Kupt hebai wo hih?   Pi ani mahch (manis hebai wo hih).
'Where are you going ?' 'I don't know (where I'm going). '

Napt am wo hih Chuk-shon-wui? Heu'u (nt am wo hih ...).
'Are you going to Tucson?'   'Yes, (I'm going to Tucson)'

Kup has i kaij?   Pi (ani) has (kaij).
'What do you say?'   '(I say) nothing. '

K haschu ahg ch s-waDagi? (S-waDagi o) heg hekaj mo si juhk.
'Why is it wet?'   '(It's wet) because it's raining hard.'

4. 3. SENTENCE CONJOINING

As a part of the VERB, CONJUNCTION agrees with ASPECT,
ch if continuative, k otherwise. CLAUSES with the same
subject are conjoined with CONJUNCTION. There are two
types of conjoining. In the first, a modifying SENTENCE is
reduced by deleting INITIATOR and AUXILIARY:

> Heg at wo i gei mat heDai wo i meh.
>
> → Heg   at wo i gei, heDai i meDk.
>   'He will fall who runs. '
>
> Heg at wo i gei mat heDai wo i meDad.
>
> → Heg at wo i gei, heDai i meDadch.
>   'He will fall who will be running. '
>
> Heg at wo i gei mat hebai wo i meh.
>
> →Heg at wo i gei, hebai i meDk.
>   'He will fall where he runs. '
>
> Heg at wo i gei mat hekid wo i meh.
>
> →Heg at wo i gei, hekid i meDk.
>   'He will fall when he runs. '

In the second type of conjoining, CLAUSES of separate
SENTENCES with the same subject NOUN PHRASE are conjoined in one SENTENCE. CONJUNCTION of each CLAUSE
in a sequence is moved to precede the following CLAUSE:

> T wo i meh g Pancho. Tki wo i gei g Pancho.
> 'Pancho will run. Pancho will evidently fall. '

→ T wo i meh g Pancho k atki wo i gei.
'Pancho will run and evidently will fall. '

MeD o g Pancho. Chikpan oki g Pancho.
'Pancho is running. Pancho is evidently working. '

→ MeD o g Pancho ch oki chikpan.
'Pancho is running and evidently is working. '

If AUXILIARY is identical to that of the preceding CLAUSE
it may be deleted:

T wo i meh g Pancho. T wo i gei g Pancho.

→ T wo i meh Pancho k wo i gei.
'Pancbo will run and fall. '

4. 4. Instrumental phrase and reason SENTENCE formation

Instrumental phrase and reason clause are formed by
reduction of a clause with instrumental verb stem hekaj.

Mua ant g wisilo.   Hekaj ant hegai wainomi.
'I killed the calf. '   'I used that knife. '

Auxiliary is deleted:

Mua ant g wisilo hekaj hegai wainomi.
'I killed the calf using that knife. '

QUALIFIER or emphatic PRONOUN may be moved to precede hekaj:

Mua ant g wisilo hekaj hema g wainomi.

→ Mua ant g wisilo hema hekaj g wainomi.
'I killed the calf with a knife. "

Mua ant g wisilo hekaj hegai wainomi.

→ Mua ant g wisilo heg hekaj wainomi.
'I killed the calf with that knife. '

Unemphatic PRONOUN plus NOUN replace first syllable of
hekaj:

Mua ant g wisilo hekaj g wainomi.

→ Mua ant g wisilo g wainomikaj.
'I killed the calf with the knife. '

A reason SENTENCE is formed from a NOUN PHRASE
with modifying SENTENCE but no NOUN:

Pi ant wo hih hekaj hegai mat wo juh

→ Pi ant wo hih heg hekaj mat wo juh.
'I'm not going because it will rain. '

A reason SENTENCE may be reduced to a questioned
negative:

148

Pi ant wo hih heg hekaj mat wo juh.
'I won't go because it'll rain.'

⟶ Pi ant wo hih nat pi wo juh.
'I won't go for won't it rain?'

A double NEGATIVE may be produced in this way:

Pi ant wo hih heg hekaj mat pi wo juh.
'I won't go because it won't rain.'

⟶ Pi ant wo hih nat pi pi wo juh.
'I won't go for won't it not rain?'

NEGATIVE plus NEGATIVE may be reduced to POSITIVE ge:

⟶ Pi ant wo hih nat ge wo juh.
'I won't go for will it rain?'

NEGATIVE ADJUNCT ha is not deleted when double negative is reduced:

Pi ant wo hih nani pi pi ha wisiloga.
'I won't go for don't I have no calf?'

⟶ Pi ant wo hih nani ge ha wisiloga.
'I won't go for do I have any calf?'

4.5. Incorporation of object NOUN in factorial VERB STEM

Factorial VERB STEM is nahto or t 'to complete or make.'
IF the stem is t, the object NOUN is incorporated in the STEM

Pancho at hema nahto kih.
'Pancho made a house.'

⟶ Pancho at hema kiht.
'Pancho made a house.'

Pancho at ha'i ha nahto g kihki.
'Pancho made some houses.'

⟶ Pancho at ha'i kihkit.
'Pancho made some houses.'

4.6. Formation of benefactive VERB STEM

A RELATIONAL PHRASE with benefactive PREPOSITIONAL STEM wehhejeD may be moved to follow the VERB PHRASE, and the PREPOSITIONAL STEM reduced to benefactive SUF - FIX of VERB STEM. PERSON indicator is moved according to rule given previously. The benefactive SUFFIX is chud replacing t or following chud, jelid or id otherwise:

Hema ani kiht am ha-wehhejeD hegam.
'I'm making a house for them.'

⟶ Hema ani ha kihchud hegam.
'I'm making them a house.'

Hema ani ap'echud g kih am ha-wehhejeD hegam.
'I'm fixing a house for them.'

→ Hema ani ha ap'echuda<u>chud</u> hegam g kih.
'I'm fixing them a house.'

Chikpan ani am <u>m</u>-<u>wehhejeD</u> ahpi.
'I'm working for you.'

→ <u>M</u>-chikpan<u>id</u> ani ahpi.
'I'm working for you.'

Hema ani ha mahk hegam g kih am <u>m</u>-<u>wehhejeD</u> ahpi.
'I'm giving them a house for you.'

→ Hema ani ha <u>m</u>-mahk<u>jelid</u> ahpi hegam g kih.
'I'm giving you them a house.'

4. 7. Reduction of modifying SENTENCE

A modifying SENTENCE following NOUN may be reduced
by deletion of AUXILIARY and moved to precede the NOUN.
If the VERB STEM is formed from ADJECTIVE STEM, the
SUFFIX <u>'e</u>, <u>k</u>, or <u>j</u>, is also deleted:

o'odham (mo) s-ap('e) →s-ap o'odham
'man that's righteous'   'righteous man'

o'odham (mo) shopol(k) → shopol o'odham
'man that's short'   'short man'

o'odham (mo) ge'e(j) → ge'e o'odham
'man that's big'   'big man'

Otherwise modifying NOUN is formed of the generic future
VERB (VERB STEM plus continuative future ASPECT <u>d</u>) plus
m:

o'odham (mat wo)chikpanad → chikpandam o'odham
'a man that works'   'a working man'

NOUN PHRASE object of modifying SENTENCE is moved
to precede VERB PHRASE:

o'odham(mat wo)behed g toki → toki behedam o'odham
'a man that picks cotton'   'a cotton picking man'

o'odham(mat wo)enigak g haiwani
' a man that owns cattle'

→ haiwani enigakam o'odham
'cattle owning man'

NOUN may be deleted following its modifier:

ge'e o'odham → ge'e
'big man'   'big one'

chikpandam o'odham → chikpandam
'working man'   'worker'

haiwani enigakam o'odham → haiwani enigakam
'cattle owning man'   'cattle owner'

5. Conclusion of grammar sketch

Since this is a grammar sketch, it fails to provide all the structures and rules for composing all kinds of sentences. It does, however, seek to provide the reader with the most essential information for understanding and composing sentences. The sketch assumes two types of rules of composition accounting for the production of basic sentences and for revisions in basic sentences for various purposes. It is possible that some of the rules given in section 3. should be given in sentence transformations, allowing some simplification of the basic sentence generating rules. It is also possible that some of the rules given in section 4. are historic rather than presently active rules, necessitating a more complex set of basic sentence generating rules. Let the reader take his choice. A definitive grammar of the language has yet to be written.

APPENDIX IV.
TECHNICAL TERMS
A. Sociological

The relationship terms are related to the extended family in which a man's sons and occasionally daughters and their families build their homes and live around his home. So while I call my brother or sister ni-wehnag, I also call my cousin ni-wehnag, as they are all my constant companions. If my brother or sister is older than I he is ni-sihs, but if he is younger he is ni-shehpij. This senior-junior relationship is passed on to our children, so the child of my senior ni-sihs is the sihs of my child whether he is older or younger. Their children in turn have the same senior-junior relationship, etc. Thus seniority among cousins depends on seniority of previous generations rather than on the age of the cousins themselves. These three terms are important for understanding the extensions and seniority expressed by other relationship terms.

My parents are ni-jehj and I call my father's sihs and shehpij by different terms and my mother's sihs and shehpij by different terms, including not only their brothers and sisters but cousins as well.

I call my father ni-ohg and he calls me ni-alidag. I call his male sihs ni-kehli and his female sihs ni-oksi, and they both call me ni-chuhchuD. I call his male shehpij ni-hakit and his female shehpij ni-wowoit, and they both call me ni-hakimaD.

I call my mother ni-je'e and she calls me ni-maD. I call her male sihs ni-je'es and her female sihs ni-dahd, and they both also call me ni-maD. I call her male shehpij ni-tatal and her female shehpij ni-jisk, and they both call me ni-ma'i.

I call my father's father ni-wosk, his male wehnag ni-wosk or ni-wosk kehli, and his female wehnag ni-wosk-oks.

They call me ni-wosmaD.

I call my father's mother ni-kahk, her male wehnag ni-kahk-kehli, and her female wehnag ni-kahk or ni-kahk-oks. They all call me ni-ka'amaD.

I call my mother's father ni-bahb, his male wehnag ni-bahb or ni-bahb-kehli, his female wehnag ni-bahb-oks They all call me ni-ba'amaD.

I call my mother's mother ni-hu'ul, her male wehnag ni-hu'ul kehli, her female wehnag ni-hu'ul or ni-hu'ul oks. They all call me ni-mohs.

I call any great-grandparent ni-wihkol and he or she calls me ni-wihshaD. (In the ChukuD Kuk dialect these are reversed.)

I call any great-great-grandparent or child ni-sikul. Seniority is expressed by calling the aged sikul by the junior term ni-shehpij and the young by the senior term ni-sihs, reflecting the responsibility of the young for the aged. These terms mark the limits of relationship, mo am sikol bijim g ihmigi 'where relationship turns back '.

Marriage creates other relationships. My wife is ni-hohnig and I am her kun, but informally I call her ni-oksga and she calls me ni-kehliga. And although we call our child by different terms ni-alidag and ni-maD, we also can refer to ' our child ' t-ahliga.

The terms for in-laws are made by extension through the child. My father's sihs who calls me ni-chuhchuD calls my mother ni-chuhchuD-je'e. My father's shehpij who calls me ni-hakimaD calls my mother ni-hakima-je'e. My mother's sihs who calls me ni-maD calls my father ni-maD-ohg. My mother's shehpij who calls me ni-ma'i calls my father ni-ma'i-ohg. These are sometimes now called by a borrowed term ni-kihe.

My father's father's side and generation who call me ni-wosmaD call my mother ni-wosma-je'e. My father's mother's side and generation who call me ni-ka'amaD call my mother ni-ka'ama-je'e. My mother's father's side and generation who call me <u>ni-ba'amaD</u> call my father <u>ni-ba'amaD-ohg</u>. My mother's mother's side and generation who call me <u>ni-mohs</u> call my father <u>ni-mohs-ohg</u>. Each of these reciprocate with exactly the same term so that my mother also calls one of my father's father's side and generation <u>ni-wosma-je'e</u>, etc.

I would call my stepfather <u>ni-hakit,</u> and he would call me <u>ni-hakimaD</u>. I would call my stepmother <u>ni-jisk,</u> and she would call me <u>ni-ma'i</u>.

Buzzard and Coyote Moieties

We were long ago divided into Buzzard and Coyote moieties. The Buzzard people are divided into Mahmgam who call their father <u>Mahm</u>, and Wahwgam who call their father <u>Wahw</u>. The Coyote people are divided into Apapagam who call their father <u>Apapa</u>, and Apkigam who call their father <u>Apkih</u>. Everyone is in the group of his father. Each group had to be represented in ceremonies at the four directions indicating the perfect number. There was great rivalry and some still tease one another about their group. There is another group added later called Ogolgam who call their father <u>Ogol</u>.

RELATIONSHIP CHART

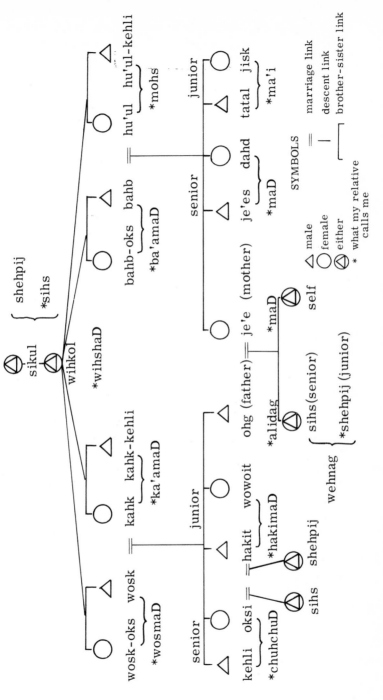

155

PAPAGO CLASSIFICATION OF PEOPLE

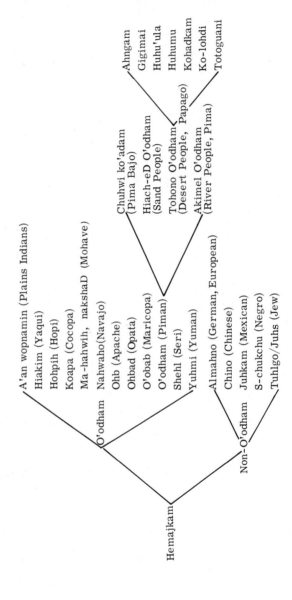

B. Medical

afterbirth	koshagi, kokshagi
ankle	chekwo, chechkwo
anus	at, a'at
anal hair	atpo
arm, hand	nowi, nohnhowi
armpit	hek, hehek
hair of	hekpo
back	oh, o'o
small of back	komi, kohkomi
upper back	gegkio, gegegkio
backbone	eDa wa'ug
bladder	hi'ush, hihi'ush
blood	eh'eD
blood vessels	eDhaidag, e'eDhaidag
body	hon, hohon/honshpaDag
hair of	wopo
bone, beak	oh'o
brain, nerve	oaga, o'aga
buttock	a'atapuD
calf	uhksh, u'uksh
chin	esh, e'esh
beard	eshpo
cheek	kahm, kahkam
chest	bahsho, babsho
hair of	bashpo
clavicle	ownagi, o'ownagi
crotch	kaishagi, kakaishagi
discharge, nasal	shosha
ear	nahk, nahnk
hair of	nakpo
elbow	sihsh, sisish
eye	wuhi, wuhpui
eyebrow	hehewo
eyelash	wuipo
eyelid	wuhi elidag
face	wuhiosha, wuhpiosha
fat	gihgi
foot	taD, tahtaD
finger	chum nowi, chu'uchum nohnhowi
flesh	chuhkug/chuhhug
forehead	koa, koka
hair of	koapo
groin	hiwchu, hihiwchu

157

gums	a'ada
hand, arm	nowi, nohnhowi
head	mo'o, mohm
back of	kusho, kuksho
hair of	mo'o
side of	mo'o huDa
top of	mo'o dahm
heart	ihbdag, i'ibdag
heel	chehm, chehchem
hip	çhuhl, chuhchul
intestine	hihih
jaw	tahtko
joint	shohba, shoshoba
kidney	o'olopa
knee	tohn, tohton
leg	kahio, kakio
liver	nem
lung	hahawuk
mouth	chini, chihchini
lips'	chini eldag
mustache	chiniwo
nail, hoof	huhch, huhuch
navel	hik, hihik
hair of	hikpo
neck	kuswo, kukswo
hair of	kushpo
nipples	wipih
nose	dahk, dahdk
hair of	dakpo
nostril	shoshkdag
palate	ha'apaga
palm	matk
penis	wiha, wihpia
pubic hair	wiapo
rib	hoho'onma
shoulder	kotwa, koktwa
skin	eldag, e'eldag
skull	koshwa, kokshwa
stomach	wohk, wohpk
tendon	tatai
testicle	wihpdo
thigh	um, u'um
toe	machpot, mamachpot
tooth	tahtami
tongue	nehni

throat - inside	ba'itk, bab'aitk
outside	ba'ichu, bab'aichu
vaginal orifice	muhs, muhms
pubic hair	muspo
vertebra	hon-eD oh'o
cervicle	kuswo oh'o
waist, midriff	huDa

ADDITIONAL ANIMAL PARTS

beak	oh'o
down	wihgi
feather, wing	a'an
horns, antlers	a'ag
stinger	uhsh, u'ush
tail	bahi, bahbhai
topknot of bird	sihwdag, sisiwdag

ANIMAL PRODUCTS

eggs	nonha
leather	hogi
milk	wihb
cheese	gihsho

BODILY FUNCTIONS

Ingestive and Digestive

To eat something	ko'a (huh, huhgi)
Eat this!	Oi g huhgi!
to eat (feed self)	e gegosid
Eat!	Oi g e gegusid!
to feed	gegosid
to serve someone	bi'i (bih, bihd)
to swallow	ba'a (bah, bah'i)
Swallow!	Oi g bah'i!
to eat up	ko'ito
to drink	ih'e
Drink this!	Oi g ih'e!
to make drink	i'ichud
to give a drink	wasibid
Give me a drink!	I g ni-wasibid!
to have gas	koDog

159

Pulmonary

to breathe	ihbhe
to sigh	ihbheiwua
to breathe convulsively	ihbhuni/ihbtog
to cough	i'ihog
Cough!	Oi g i'ihog!
to cause to cough	i'ihogchud
to clear the throat	e i'oshan
to sneeze	bischk
to cause to sneeze	bischkchud
to blow the nose	shohwua
to hiccup	henihop

Bodily States

to be chilled	heumk, heukk
to be hungry	bihugimk, bihugk
hunger	bihugimdag
to be thirsty	tonomdag
fever	tonjig, s-
pain, to be painful	ko'ok, s-
to get tired	gewko
fatigue	gewkogig
to tremble	gigiwuk
to be obese	gihg, s-
to be thin	gaki, s-
to get old	
male	kehlit, kekelt
female	okst, o'okit

Bodily Discharges and Excretive Functions

to belch	haDwuag
sweat	wahuDdag
to be sweaty	wahuDdag, s-
to sweat	wahuD, s-
tears	oh'og
nasal discharge	shosha
to blow the nose	shohwua
urine	hi'i
to urinate	hi'a, (hia, hia'i)
to go to urinate	hi'ameD
Urinate in this!	Hi'ini id eDa!
feces	biht

to defecate	biht
to go to defecate	bihtameD
Defecate in this!	Higtani id eDa!
to be constipated	bihim
to pass gas	uwio
to wash	wakon
Wash yourself!	E g wakon!
Wash your hands	Am g ha wapkon g e nohnowi.

C. Fauna and Flora

| 1. Animal life | Ha'ichu doakam |

1.1 Domestic	Shoiga, shoshoiga
camel	ka-miio, kaka-mimio
cat	mihstol, mimistol
cattle	haiwani
cow	haiwani, hahaiwani
bull	tohlo, totolo
calf	wisilo, wipsilo
ox	woiwis, wopoiwis
steer	nowiyu, nonowiyu
dog	gogs, gogogs
donkey	wuhlo, wuplo
goat	siwat, siswat
horse	kawiyu, kakawiyu
stallion	kalioni, kakalioni
mule	muhla, mumla
pig	kohji, kokji
sheep	kahwal, kakawal

1.2 Wild	Ha'ichu s-doajkam/Mischini
antelope, pronghorn	kuhwid, kukuwid
badger	kahw, kakaw
bat	nanakumal
bear	juDumi, jujDumi
beast	nehbig
beaver	kohwih
bobcat	gewho, gegewho
cottontail	tohbi, totobi

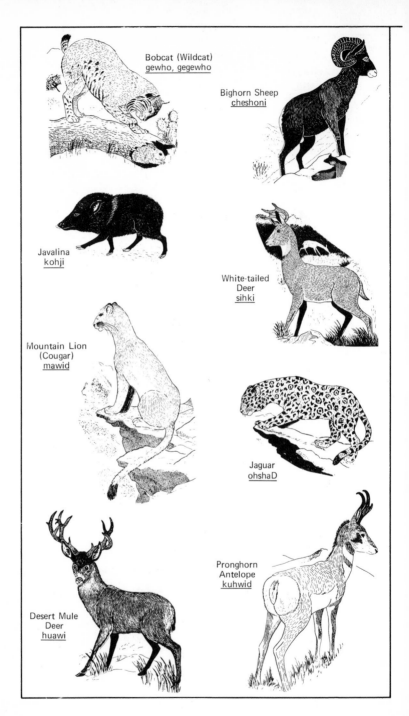

Bobcat (Wildcat)
gewho, gegewho

Bighorn Sheep
cheshoni

Javalina
kohji

White-tailed
Deer
sihki

Mountain Lion
(Cougar)
mawid

Jaguar
ohshaD

Desert Mule
Deer
huawi

Pronghorn
Antelope
kuhwid

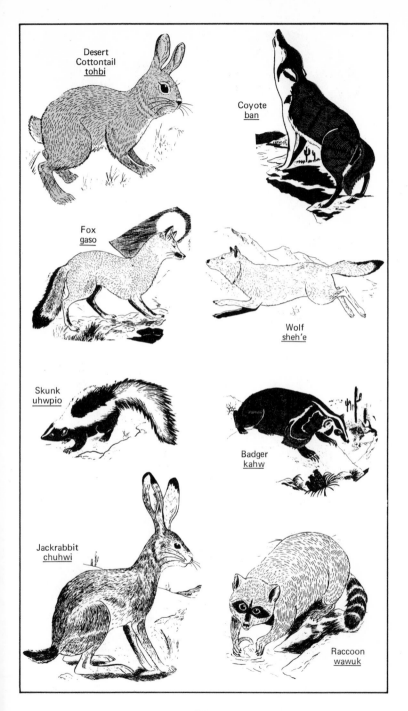

Desert Cottontail
tohbi

Coyote
ban

Fox
gaso

Wolf
sheh'e

Skunk
uhwpio

Badger
kahw

Jackrabbit
chuhwi

Raccoon
wawuk

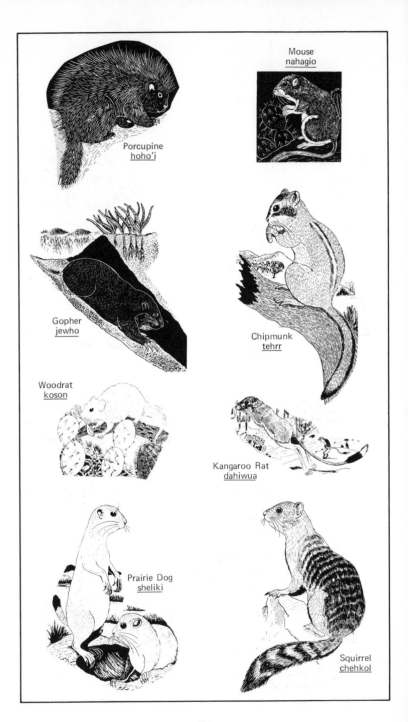

Mouse
nahagio

Porcupine
hoho'i

Gopher
jewho

Chipmunk
tehrr

Woodrat
koson

Kangaroo Rat
dahiwua

Prairie Dog
sheliki

Squirrel
chehkol

coyote	ban, bahban
deer, mule	huawi/huai
whitetail	sihki
elephant	al-whahndi
fox	gaso, gagso
gopher	jewho, jejewho
ground squirrel	chuawi
jackrabbit	chuhwi
jaguar, leopard	ohshaD, o'oshaD
javelina	kohji, kokji
kangaroo rat	dahiwúa, dahDhaiwua
lion	mawid, maipid
monkey	gogs o'odham, chango (Sp. chango)
mountain sheep	cheshoni, chechshoni
mouse	nahagio, nanhagio
porcupine	hoho'i
prairiedog	sheliki, shesheliki
racoon	wawuk, wawpuk
rat	wosho, wopsho
skunk	uhwpio, u'uwpio
squirrel	chehkol, chechekol
wolf	sheh'e, shesh'e
woodrat	koson, kokson
*chipmunk	tehrr/chehrr

1.3 Birds   U'u whig

blackbird	shashani
buzzard, red headed	nuhwi, nunuwi
black headed	nuwipa
cactus wren	hokkaD, hohokaD
cardinal	sipuk
chicken	chuchul
crane, goose, heron	kohkoD
crow	hawani, hahawani
curved-bill thrasher	kul-wichigam
duck	pahdo, papdo
eagle, bald or golden	ba'ag
buzzard hawk	al ba'ag
red-tailed	haupal, hahupal

---

*In tehrr/chehrr 'chipmunk, the trilled rr is onomatopoetic, not included in the regular sound system.

Western Red-Tailed
Hawk
haupal

Western Meadowlark
tosiw

Killdeer
chiwi-chuhch

Burrowing Owl
kokowha

Elf Owl
kuhkul

goldfinch	oam u'uhig
hairy woodpecker	hikiwij, hihikiwij
hawk	tobaw, totbaw
chicken hawk	wisag, wipsag
night hawk	nehpoD, nenepoD
hummingbird, small	wipismal
large	gihsoki
killdeer	chiwi-chuhch
mocking bird	shuhg, shushug
mourning dove	hohhi/hohhoi
mudhen	wakaig, wapkia'ig
owl	chukuD, chuhchkuD
burrowing	kokowha
elf	kuhkul
peacock	ahDho, a'aDho
pigeon	paplo
quail	kakaichu
roadrunner	taDai, tatDai
swallow	gigitwal
western meadowlark	tosiw
whippoorwill	kohlo'ogam
whitewinged dove	okokoi
unidentified birds	ba'i chuklim, bichpoD hehwasjel, huchgam, komalk mo'okam, kuDat, kuhigam, o'oDopiwa, wachumukdam, wawasjel

1. 4 Reptiles Ha'ichu BanimeDdam

1. 4. 1 Lizzards Huhu'ujuD

black lizzard	hujuD, huhu'ujuD
gila monster	chiadag, chichiadag
horned toad	chemamagi, chechemamagi
sand lizzard	watksh ; oDkol, o'oDkol
whiptail lizzard	wajelho, wapjelho/wahn ohg
unidentified	jusukal

1. 4. 2 Turtles Komkch'eD, kokomkch'eD

1. 4. 3 Frog family

frog	babad
toad	mo'ochwig, mom'ochwig
tadpole	mo'okwaD, mom'okwaD

1.4.4	Snakes	WahammaD
	blue racer	chuk wamaD
	bullsnake, gopher	sho'owa
	garter	wamaD
	gopher snake	sho'owa
	king snake	jewakag, jejewakag
	prehistoric snake	kohds
	rattlesnake	ko'owi, kohko'owi
	red racer	wegi wamaD
	sonoran coral	s-wawpani
	striped snake	s-o'owi wamaD
1.4.5	Fish and Worms	Waptopi
	fish	shuhdagi watopi
	worms	jeweD watopi
	thousand legged worm	kommo'ol
	centipede	maihogi, mamaihogi
1.5	Spiders	TotkihtuD
	black widow	hiwchu-wegi, hihiwchu wepegi
	mule leader	muhla wanimeDdam
	tarantula	hiani
1.6.	Scorpion	nakshel, nanakshel
1.7	Insects	Mumuwal
1.7.1	Ants	Totoni
	black	chuchk totoni
	fire ants	wepegi totoni
	harvester	kuadagi, kukadagi
	little	a'al totoni
	orange	kuchul, ku'ukchul u'umam
1.7.2	Other	
	bee, bumble bee	pa-nahl
	butterfly	hohokimal
	cicadia	kohntpul, kokontpul
	cowkiller	uhimal
	cricket	chukugshuaD , chuchkug shuaD
	firefly	taiwig, tataiwig
	flea	chehpsh
	fly	muhwal, mumuwal

Walking Stick
gakimchul

Centepede
maihogi

Cicadia
kohntpul

Butterfly
hohokimal

Praying Mantis
gakimchul

Fly
muhwal

Bee
pa-nahl

Mosquito
wahmug

fly, slender	mukchwidam
gnat	chukmug
grasshopper	shoh'o, shosh'o
green fruit beetle	ma-yahdi/wainomi kohlasham
louse, body	hiopch
louse, head	ah'ach
mosquito	wahmug
stink bug	bitokoi, bibtokoi
tick	mahmsh
walking stick	gakimchul
wasp	wihpsh
wasp, black cane	hu'udagi, huhu'udagi

2 Plant life — Ha'ichu wushanig

2.1 Trees — Uhs, u'us

catclaw	uhpaD, u'upaD
cottonwood	auppa, a'uppa
ironwood	ho'idkam, hoho'idkam
mesquite	kui, kukui
mulberry	gowhi
oak	
edible acorn	wi-yohdi
inedible acorn	toha
mountain	bitoi
white oak	ka'al
tamarisk	onk kui
palo verde	
dark	ko'okmaDk
crucifixion thorn	ahgowi
light	kuk chehedagi
small	ohbgam
unidentified	kalistp
pine	huk
thorny fruit (hackleberry)	kohm
willow	che'ul
desert willow	ahn

2.2 Brush and grass — Sha'i

algae	mamtoD
bean, red	bahwui
bitterweed	siwstaD, siw u'us, tatshshagi

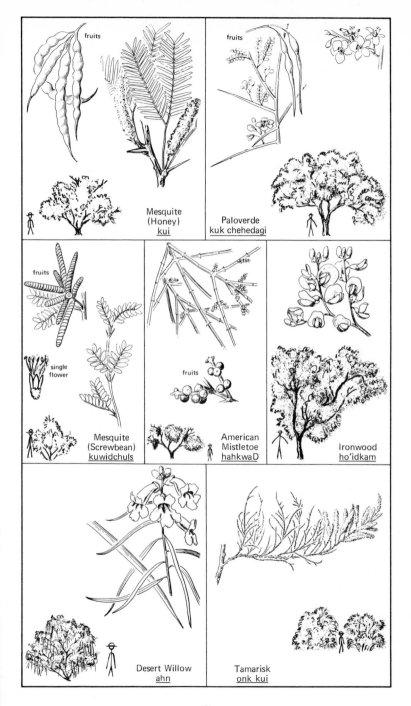

fruits

Mesquite
(Honey)
kui

fruits

Paloverde
kuk chehedagi

fruits

single
flower

Mesquite
(Screwbean)
kuwidchuls

fruits

American
Mistletoe
hahkwaD

Ironwood
ho'idkam

Desert Willow
ahn

Tamarisk
onk kui

171

bouvardia	wipismal jehj
brittle bush	tohawis
buffalo gourd	aDaw
canaigre	hiwidchuls/siwidchuls
castor bean	mahmsh
cattail	uDawhag
century plant	a'ut
cocklebur	waiwel
daisy	ban chinishani
desert tobacco	wiw
devilsclaw	ihug
evening primrose	wipih si'idam
fairy dusters	chuhwi wuipo
four o'clock	tash mahhag
gold poppy	hohhi e'es
gourd	wako
grass	sha'i, washai
bear grass	moho
six week grama	chuchk muDagkam
unidentified:	ba'imuDkam, gi'in, ka'akwoDk, noD, ohki, taDkam, wepegi
greasewood	shegoi
greens	ihwagi
careless weed	ihwagi
unidentified:	chuhugia, hawani tahtaD, jual, kahshwaD, ko'okmagi shahD, ku'ukpalk, opon
larkspur	chuchul i'ispul/kuksho wuhplim
locoweed, jimson	kotDobi
marigold, desert	gihkoda
mariposa lily	hahdkos
milkweed	wihbam
mistletoe	hahkwaD
morning glory	bihbhiag
ocotilla	melhog
owl clover	chuhwi taDpo
papagolily	hahd
potato, wild	shahD
puncture vine/bullhead	jeweD ho'idag
scarlet bugler	hewel e'es/wupiostakuD
side oats	dadpk washai
sunflower, desert gold	hihwai, hihiwai

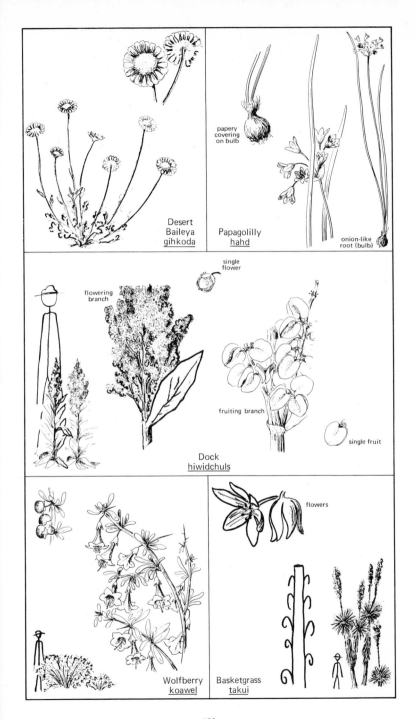

Desert
Baileya
gihkoda

papery
covering
on bulb

Papagolilly
hahd

onion-like
root (bulb)

single
flower

flowering
branch

fruiting branch

single fruit

Dock
hiwidchuls

Wolfberry
koawel

flowers

Basketgrass
takui

173

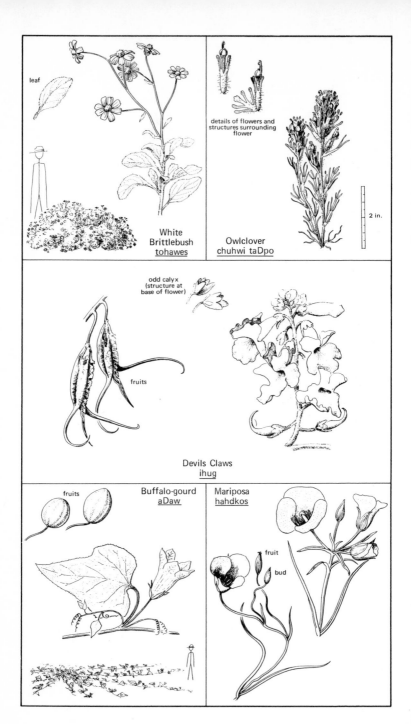

leaf

White
Brittlebush
tohawes

details of flowers and
structures surrounding
flower

Owlclover
chuhwi taDpo

2 in.

odd calyx
(structure at
base of flower)

fruits

Devils Claws
ihug

fruits

Buffalo-gourd
aDaw

Mariposa
hahdkos

fruit

bud

tansy mustard	dahpk
tumbleweed	siw toDshagi
wolfberry	koawel
yucca, banana	howi
elata(for baskets)	takui
narrowleaf (rope)	a'ulhai
(for mats)	uhmug
unidentified flowers:	gewio, haDam tatk, hihkimul
	ihbda, ban ihbda, kopondakuD,
	shuh'uwaD
unidentified bushes:	ihkol, ihkowi, kokmagi u'us,
	mostois, onkoi, owgam, tohtk

2.3 Cactus   Ho'i

barrel cactus	jiawul
cholla, cane	cheolim
christmas	wipnoi
teddybear	haDshadkam
tree	hanam
walking stick	naw
hedgehog	ihswig
night blooming cereus	ho'ok wah'o
organpipe	chuhchuis
prickly pear	gisoki, ihbhai
saguaro	hahshani
senita	chehmi
strawberry cactus	bahban ha-ihswig
staghorn	kokaw

2.4 Crops   E'es

barley	si-wahyo
beans	muhni
cane	kahnia
chickpeas	kalwash
corn	huhni
cotton	tokih
grape	uhDwis
fig	suhna
lentil	lanjeki
lettuce	li-juhwa
lima beans	hawol
muskmelon	miloni/milini
onion	siwol

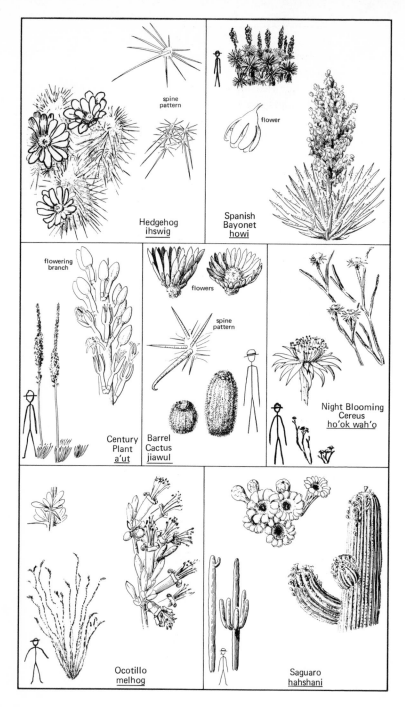

spine pattern

Hedgehog
ihswig

Spanish
Bayonet
howi

flower

flowering
branch

flowers

spine pattern

Century
Plant
a'ut

Barrel
Cactus
jiawul

Night Blooming
Cereus
ho'ok wah'o

Ocotillo
melhog

Saguaro
hahshani

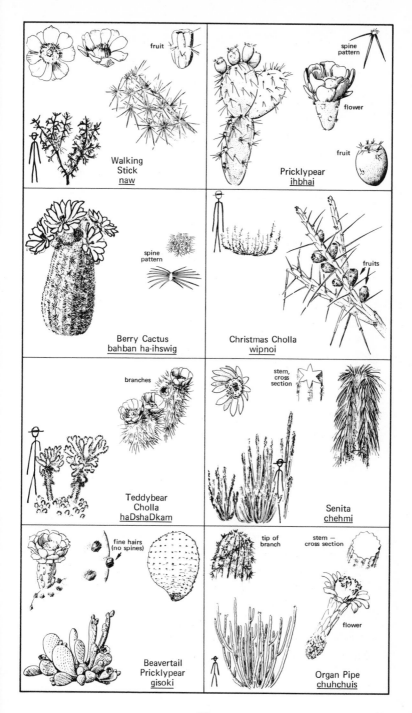

fruit

Walking
Stick
naw

spine
pattern

flower

fruit

Pricklypear
ihbhai

spine
pattern

fruits

Berry Cactus
bahban ha-ihswig

Christmas Cholla
wipnoi

branches

stem,
cross
section

Teddybear
Cholla
haDshaDkam

Senita
chehmi

fine hairs
(no spines)

tip of
branch

stem —
cross section

flower

Beavertail
Pricklypear
gisoki

Organ Pipe
chuhchuis

177

peas	wihol
pomegranate	gal-nahyo
potato	bahbas
soapweed	utko jehj
squash, pumpkin	hahl
irregular shaped	shapij
sunflower	hihwai, hihiwai
watermelon	miloni/gepi
wheat	pilkani

2.5 Plant Parts   Ha'ichu wuhshanig chu'idag

bark	eldag
beans	wihogdag
mesquite	wihog
branches	mamhaDag
fiber of stalk	shahwaidag
flowers	heosig
fruit	bahidag
leaves	hahhag
resin, pitch	ushabi
root	tatk
sap	waDagi
seed	kai
stalk	wa'ug
tassle	muDadag
thorn	ho'i
trunk	shon
vein	e'eDhaidag

D. Calendar

THE YEAR

The O'odham yearly cycle consists of Toniabkam 'The Hot Season' and S-hehpich'eDkam 'The Cold Season '.

Where occasion demands reference to Spring it has been referred to as Huhkalig 'The Warm-up Season' and Fall as Wi'ihanig 'Things Left after Frost'.

THE MONTHS

The word mashad 'moon' also designates the month. The lunar months, variously rendered by different dialects of Papago and Pima are now roughly equated with the calendar months.

HAHSHANI BAK MASHAD

The year begins with the Saguaro Fruit Month, June, when people go to their camps for Saguaro harvest.

JUKIABIG MASHAD

Next is the Rainy Month, July, when Saguaro harvest ends and people go to their fields for planting.

SHOPOL ESHABIG MASHAD

Then comes Short Planting Month, August, when late crops are sown and the summer rains end.

WASHAI GAK MASHAD

By September the sun has baked the desert soil dry again for Dry Grass Month.

WI'IHANIG MASHAD

In old times when people moved from their summer fields to their mountain well villages, it was very important to know what food plants survive the frost. Surviving Month is about October.

KEHG S-HEHPIJIG MASHAD

Relief from summer heat is welcomed in the Fair Cold Month, November. Hunting is best as cold weather approaches.

EDA WA'UGAD MASHAD

As the back-bone, eDa wa'ug, divides the body, the Backbone Month, December, marks the mid-year. This is also called Ge'e S-hehpijig Mashad, Severe Cold.

GI'IHODAG MASHAD

Then comes the Lean Month, January, when big game animals begin to lose their reserve of flesh, (gi'iho).

UHWALIG MASHAD

Next is the Odor Month, February, mating time for deer, so timed that their young will arrive for the summer's abundance.

KOHMAGI MASHAD

In late February and early March comes the Gray Month, the bleak time before the burst of Spring.

CHEHDAGI MASHAD

The first blush of Spring ushers in the Green Month, late March, when leaves begin to appear.

OAM MASHAD

After leaves come flowers decking the desert with rich colors for the Orange Month, April.

KO'OK MASHAD

Finally before summer's abundance comes the Painful Month, May, when game and food are scarce and hunger a close companion. Since the introduction of winter wheat, it is also called, Hihkugiabig Mashad, 'Grain Cutting Month'.

THE WEEK

The Week, as a measure of time was introduced from Spanish and is referred to as domig (Spanish domingo).

The days of the week are all from Spanish.

domig	Sunday	(Sp. domingo)
luhnas	Monday	(Sp. lunes)
mahltis	Tuesday	(Sp. martes)
mialklos	Wednesday	(Sp. miércoles)
huiwis	Thursday	(Sp. jueves)
wialos	Friday	(Sp. viernes)
shahwai	Saturday	(Sp. sábado)

In some dialects Tuesday, Wednesday and Thursday are gohk tash (second day), waik tash (third day), and gi'ik tash (fourth day), respectively.

TIME OF DAY

Day is tash, which also means 'sun' or 'time'. Night is chuhug. The morning before sunrise is called si'alig which also means East. The evening is called huDunk which also means West and refers to the going down of the sun.

CUSTOMARY TIME

sisi'alimad	in the mornings
huhuDukad	in the evenings
chuchkad	nightly
dahm jujju	at noon
wehs tash-ab	every day

Celestial bodies are referred to as sitting in position juhk (jujju), the proper locationals specifying what position. Reference is to the sun as a measure of time of day unless some other body is referred to.

In the morning the sun is approaching, so the time is given as:

ga huh i juhk	morning
ga huh si i juhk	late morning

In the afternoon the sun is retreating so the time is given as:

gam huh i juhk	afternoon
gam huh si i juhk	late afternoon

The time of morning or afternoon is indication more exactly by pointing to the position of the sun for that time.

At noon the sun is overhead and the time indicated as:

dahm juhk   noon

The hours were introduced from Spanish using the word ohla, (Sp. hora) hour, and minuhto (Sp. minuto) minute.

hemako ohla ch-eD	'at one o'clock'
gohk eDa hugkam ohla ch-eD	'at half past two'
west-mahm minuhto mat wo e ai g waik ohla	'ten minutes to three'
gamai hetasp minuhto gam huh ba'ich g gi'ik ohla	'15 minutes past four.'

APPENDIX V.
DIALECTS AND
RELATED LANGUAGES

A. Dialects

The dialect areas of Papago are shown on the following map. All dialects of Papago except one are located on four reservations. The Ak Chin (Aki Chini) and Gila Bend (Sihl Mek / Ta'ik) reservations are Huhhu'ula dialect. The San Xavier (Wahk) reservation is Totoguani. One dialect, the S-ohbmakam or Hiach-eD O'odham, is not shown since it is scattered from Ajo south and west. The Kohadk dialect is Pima. Village names are given in standardized spelling with a key to traditional spelling, translation, and non-Indian name, following the map.

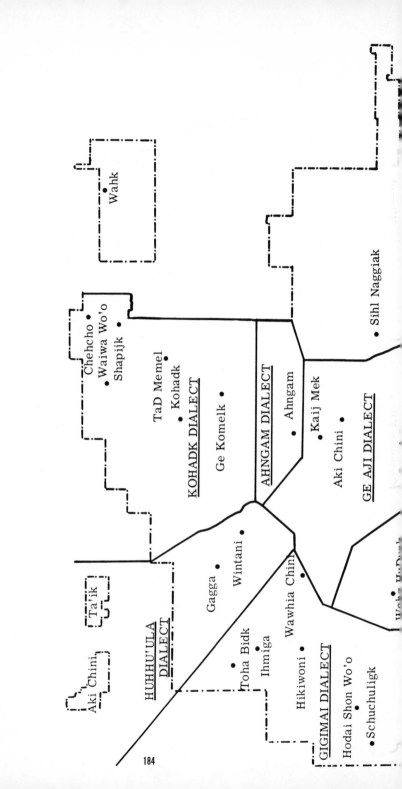

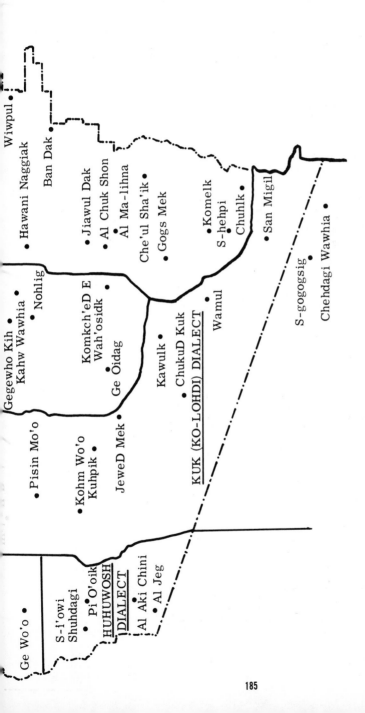

Dialect areas of Papago

Papago Villages

Indian Name	Translation	Non-Indian Name
Ahngam (Anegam)	Willows	
Aki Chini (Ak Chin)	Arroyo Mouth	San Serafin
Al Chuk shon (Ali Chukson)	Little Black Base	Little Tucson
Al Jeg (Ali Chuk)	Little Pass	Meneger's Dam
Ban Dak (Pan Tak)	Coyote Sitting	Coyote Village
Chehcho (Chuichu)	Caves	
ChukuD Kuk (Chukut Kuk)	Owl Hooting	Tecolote
Chuhlk (Choulic)	Corner	
Gagga (Kaka)	Clearing	
Ge Komelk (Gu Komelik)	Big Flat	
Ge Oidag (Gu Oidak)	Big Field	Big Field
Ge Wo'o (Gu Vo)	Big Pond	Kerwo
Gogs Mek	Burnt Dog	Topawa
Hawani Naggiak (Havan Nakya)	Crow Hanging	Crow Hang
Hikiwoni (Hickiwan)	Jagged Cut	
Hodai Shon Wo'o (Hotason Vo)	Rock Base Pond	Charco 27
Jewak (Quijotoa)	Rotted Place	Covered Wells
Jiawul Dak (Chiawuli Tak)	Barrel Cactus Sitting	Fresnal Village
Kahw Wawhia (Ko Vaya)	Badger Well	
Kaij Mek	Burnt Seed	Santa Rosa
Kawulk (Cowlic)	Hill	
Kohadk (Kohatk)	Dried & Burnt	
Kohm Wo'o (Kom Vo)	Kohm Tree Pond	Santa Cruz
Komelk (Komelik)	Flat	
Komkch'eD e Wah'osidk	Turtle Wedged	Sells (Indian Oasis)
Nohlig (Nolic)	The Bend	
Pih O'oik (Pia Oik)	Homely	
Pisin Mo'o (Pisinemo)	Bison Head	
Schuchk (Schuchk)	Black	Santa Rosa Ranch
Schuchuligk (Schuchuli)	Many Chickens	Gunsight
Shapijk (Shopishk)	Standing Out	White Horse Pass
S-hehpi Oidag (Supi Oidak)	Cold Field	Cold Field
Sihl Mek (Sil Merk)	Burnt Saddle	Gila Bend

Sihl Naggiak (Sil Nakya)	Saddle Hanging	Saddle Hang
TaD Memel (Tat Momoli)	Foot Runner	Jackrabbit
Ta'ik (Tahi)	Eastern	Gila Bend
Toha Bidk (Stoa Pitk)	White Clay	
Waiwa Wo'o (Vaiwa Vo)	Cocklebur Pond	Cocklebur
Wamul (Vamori)	Watery	
Wawhia Chini (Vaya Chin)	Well Mouth	
Wintani (Ventana)	Window	Ventana
Wiwpul (Viopuli)	Wild Tobacco	San Pedro
Wohg HuDunk	Road Dip	San Simon

B. Related Languages

The languages related to Papago in the Sonoran branch of the Uto-Aztecan language family are shown on the following map.

The diagram below shows more exactly the linguistic relationships within the Sonoran branch as well as in the whole Uto-Aztecan language family. Papago and Pima together form one of the four language groups within the Piman (or Tepiman) subbranch, the others being Pima Bajo (lower Pima), Northern Tepehuan, and Southern Tepehuan. This subbranch, together with Yaqui-Mayo, Cora-Huichol, and Tarahumara form the Sonoran branch. Sonoran and Shoshonean together form the Non-Aztec side of the family, which with Aztec forms the Uto-Aztecan language family.

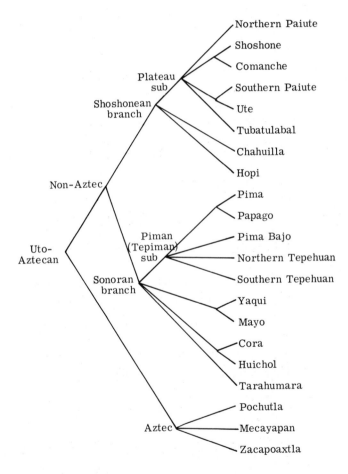

BIBLIOGRAPHY

Arizona Highways   Photographs and Illustrations
       Vol. XXXIV #3 1958
       Vol. XXXVII #7 1961
       Vol. XLVI #1 1961

Bach, Emmon,   An Introduction to Transformational
       Grammars, New York: Holt, Rinehart and
       Winston Inc. , 1965 (205 pages)

Bascom, Burton William Jr. ,   Proto-Tepiman, Doctoral
       Dissertation: unpublished, 1965 (188 pages)

Chomski, Noam,   Syntactic Structures, The Hague,
       Netherlands: Mouton and Company, 1967, (115 pages)

                     Aspects of the Theory of Syntax,
       Cambridge, Massachusetts; The M. I. T. Press,
       1965, (252 pages)

Dodge, Natt N. ,   Flowers of the Southwest Deserts
       (illustrated by Jeanne R. Janish), Globe, Arizona:
       McGrew Printing and Lithographing Co. , The
       National Park Service, 1951, Popular Series No. 4
       (112 pages)

Dolores, Juan,   "Papago Verb Stems", Publications in
       American Archeology and Ethnology, University of
       California, Vol. 10, No. 5, 1913, (pp. 241-263)

                     "Papago Nominal Stems", op. cit., Vol.
       20, No. 1, 1923, (pp. 19-31)

Fodor, Jerry A. and Katz, Jerrold J. ,   Readings in the
       Philosophy of Language, Englewood Cliffs, New
       Jersey, Prentice-Hall, Inc. , (612 pages)

Hale, Kenneth L.   A Papago Grammar, Indiana Doctoral
       Dissertation, International Journal of American
       Linguistics, Vol. 31, No. 4, 1965

       and Casagrande, Joseph B. , Semantic Relationships
       in Papago Folk-definitions, University of Illinois,
       dittoed

       and Voeglin, C. F. and F. M.   Typological and
       Comparative Grammar of Uto-Aztecan: I (Phon-
       ology), 1962, (144 pages)

Mason, J. Alden   The Language of the Papago of Arizona,
        University of Pennsylvania Museum Monographs,
        1950,   (84 pages)

Mathiot, Madeleine,   "Noun Classes and Folk Taxonomy",
        American Anthropologist: Vol. 64,   No. 2,   1962
        (pp 340-350)

Olin, George,   Mammals of the Southwest Deserts
        (Illustrated by Jerry Cannon),   Sante Fe, New
        Mexico: National Park Service,   1951,   Popular
        Series,   No. 8,   (112 pages)

Parker, Kittie F.,   Arizona Ranch, Farm and Garden
        Weeds   (illustrated by Lucratia Braeziale Hamilton),
        Tucson, Arizona: University of Arizona Press,
        Circular 265,   1958,   (288 pages)

Peterson, Robert Tory,   A Field Guide to Western Birds,
        Cambridge, Massachusetts : The Riverside Press,
        1941,   (366 pages)

Saxton, Dean   "Papago Phonemes"   International Journal of
        American Linguistics, Vol. 29,   No. 1,   1963, (pp. 29-35)

Scott, S. H.   T The Observer's book of Cacti and Other
        Succulents,   London, England : Frederick Warne
        and Co. Ltd.,   1958,   (159 pages)

Smith, Gusse Thomas,   Birds of the Southwestern Desert
        (illustrated by Harriet Morton Holmes),   Scottsdale
        Arizona : Doubleshoe Publishers, 1941,   (68 pages)

Underhill, Ruth Murray,   Social Organization of the Papago
        Indians,   New York,   Columbia University Press, 1939
        (280 pages)

        People of the Crimson Evening (illustrated by Velino
        Herrera), United States Indian Service , 1951
        (127 pages)

        The Papago Indians of Arizona and Their Relatives
        the Pima (illustrated by Velino Herrera) Bureau of
        Indian Affairs: Haskell Press Sherman pamphlet
        No. 3,   (68 pages)

Werner, Jane,   Walt Disney's Living Desert, A True-Life
        Adventure,   New York: Simon and Shuster;   1954
        (124 pages)